BOOKS BY

ROY F. NICHOLS

WITH

JEANNETTE P. NICHOLS

BLUEPRINTS FOR LEVIATHAN: AMERICAN STYLE

ROY F. NICHOLS

BLUEPRINTS FOR LEVIATHAN: AMERICAN STYLE

ATHENEUM

NEW YORK

1963

Copyright © 1963 by Roy F. Nichols
All rights reserved
Library of Congress card catalog number 62–17286
Published simultaneously in Canada by McClelland & Stewart Ltd.
Manufactured in the United States of America by H. Wolff, New York
Designed by Harry Ford
First Edition

TO

EDWIN B. WILLIAMS
JONATHAN E. RHOADS
LOREN C. EISELEY
DAVID R. GODDARD

FRATRES IN UNIVERSITATE ET AMICI IN CII

FOREWORD

THOMAS HOBBES, hardheaded political philosopher of the seventeenth century, ascribed to mankind a somewhat paradoxical "love of Liberty, and Dominion over others," which involved society in an eternal political dilemma. For whereas many desire to be free, and large numbers desire to be safe, the wish for freedom and safety are not universals; there are always those who seem comfortable under dominance, while others like to live dangerously. These variations complicate the art of politics.

In order to insure a mastery of this complex art and the preservation of society, Hobbes believed that men had introduced "restraint upon themselves" by living in commonwealths, thereby "getting themselves out from that miserable condition of Warre, which is necessarily consequent . . . to the naturall Passions of men, when there is no visible Power to keep them in awe and tye them by fear of punishment to the performance of their Covenants, and observation of [the] Laws of Nature." [1]

Such a commonwealth was denominated by Hobbes "a great Leviathan, created by Art, an Artificiall Man, though of greater stature and strength than the Naturall, for whose protection and defence it was intended." This Leviathan Hobbes described as one of those "Automata" or "Engines that move themselves by springs and wheeles as doth a watch" and therefore could be said to have "an artificiall life." [2] He implied that this Leviathan possessed the attributes both of an organism and a mechanism. As a mechanism the "engine" could be reduced to blueprints and thereby revealed to the world. As an organism, Leviathan, like the great "beast" in the Scriptures, is capable of growth and adjustment to circumstances and possesses a species of cognition governed by something resembling a nervous system.

According to the fanciful theory formulated by John Locke—to employ the thinking of another seventeenth-century political philosopher—naked savages, some time in the millennia before history, made a social contract whereby they surrendered some of their absolute liberty to a power or, in Hobbes's term, to a Leviathan of their own creation. They accepted this control in order to enjoy the peace and safety that they believed they would secure when they freed themselves from anarchy. Therefore they agreed to submit to certain rules of safety that they were to make and that agents of their choice were to enforce. In some way, probably not embraced in seventeenth-century fancy, "governments were instituted among men," to use Jefferson's words. Some of them were based on force, others on the consent of the governed. Thus two principles have long been functioning —force and consent.

For centuries these governments operated in western Europe, particularly in the British Isles, in such fashion as to form the matrix of American political institutions. In Great Britain the functioning of history, that daughter of time, placed the emphasis upon self-government, and for this the British developed a peculiar talent. To accomplish one of the major purposes of such control— the substitution of order for capricious force—ingenious men invented a series of devices or recorded rules, a Leviathan designed to achieve this object and thereby to obviate the need for compulsion by the force of despotism. The Anglo-American community in a sense became a laboratory wherein political artificers invented mechanisms to insure their liberty. Yet they never banished the possibility of the application of force, and examples of its use dot the pages of the chronicles.

One of the most significant of the achievements of those operating this laboratory was the construction of that constitutional mechanism that Hobbes called a Leviathan. He wrote at a time when, because of the discovery of America, citizens operating the British system were busy readjusting it and creating a new Leviathan beyond the seas. The "art" that was their chief instrument was the political use of the pen to make unnecessary any resort to the sword. Probably no society has ever achieved greater faith in self-government and the efficacy of the written word to implement it than has the Anglo-American.

The Leviathans previously existing in fact had been accidental, pragmatically and haphazardly achieved, largely unstructured. With America came the concept of one specifically contrived. Man's capacity for political invention was challenged by the extraordinarily difficult, often frightening experience of creating a body politic in a region so distant, so strange, so perilous and so vast. In America there had to be constant ingenious contrivance if the feeble outposts were to survive.

The process of self-government in this growing society was therefore marked by a succession of inventions to fit the needs constantly arising in an ever-changing body politic. The history of the United States is in large part the account of how American ingenuity has been called upon time after time to create designs to enable the citizens to meet problems that at one point or another seemed to threaten destruction. During the growth of the American polity these have been incorporated in a succession of charters, compacts, resolves, associations, declarations, articles, constitutions, ordinances and statutes. No move of significance in the developing republic has been made without a written manifestation of purpose and authority.

Though creation and use of these inventions has made some of the brighter pages of human history, they have not been panaceas of universal application. Force has been resorted to with unhappy frequency. This Anglo-

American society has striven with great diligence and appreciable success to substitute the rule of law for the rule of force, to substitute thinking and maneuvering for fighting; but even within it the outbreak of violence and civil war has been a phenomenon of unfortunate recurrence. Despite faith in and constant resort to thought and politics, the Leviathan has on occasion been threatened by force and a century ago was for four troubled years disjointed and in part dismantled by a "condition of Warre . . . consequent . . . to the . . . Passions of men" that frantic recourse to the pen was not able to prevent. The nature of the conflict can be better understood if it is considered as part of an ancient pattern rather than as an isolated incident, as a part of a long contest rather than as a struggle merely of moment in the mid-nineteenth-century United States. This conflict was in significant part quelled by political and legislative skill.

The ingenuity that has been characteristic of the American phase of the art of politics was art designed to enable society to organize itself so that it could through representatives of its own choice create and administer law. The focus of American history has generally been upon the process of securing the administrative power, the control of the executive, but often—and particularly in more recent times—the control and operation of the lawmaking power has been of greater importance. As man's faith in contracts, laws, charters and constitutions has increased, the power to draft and enact them has become greater.

The American Leviathan has been the product of hard, adroit thinking. As an "engine," it requires constant attention and frequent overhauling. Its operators must be men capable of complex intellectual activity, able to adjust the mechanism, to change the specifications as time changes and to be ingenious in supplying new parts. In the midst of the calamity of 1861-1865, the American people had to face a dilemma. "Must a government, of necessity, be too strong for the liberties of its own people, or too weak to maintain its own existence?" [3] In this language of characteristic cogency Lincoln formulated the problem. The control of the lawmaking function was perhaps the basic issue at stake in the contest, and the war was to be fought by lawmakers with their weapons of draftsmanship as well as by armies in the field—with the quill as well as with the sword. One of the tactical instruments in the operation was the use of legislation, proclamations and other political utterances and tactics, something like the pieces in a game of chess.

This book is an effort to explain the problems connected with the invention, the construction and the adjustment of Leviathan, particularly those that have been associated with the legislative process in self-government, rather than the usual historical concern over the executive. American society has produced a succession of ingeniously minded political inventors and engineers who had unusual success in solving by their intellectual talent the problems involved in creating and maintaining the republic. Only once was their ingenuity found wanting. These men of mind and psychological skill achieved an unusual ingenuity, which there is perhaps some reason to believe their descendants have now in less generous measure. Periodically, particularly in times of stress, it is well to review the nature and history of the art of producing constitutional documents and laws, of choosing gifted lawmakers and to gain renewed inspiration from a knowledge of the nation's proficiency in its practice. It is well to keep in mind the essential fact that in the art of government the pen can be mightier than the sword, that in the mind of man rather than in his arm may be found his salvation.

ACKNOWLEDGMENTS

I RECORD my thanks to various editors of historical and other periodicals who originally published certain of my words, some of which are here put to this other use. They preside, or have presided, over the editorial sanctums of: *The American Heritage, The Proceedings of the American Philosophical Society, The American Quarterly, The Cambridge Journal, The Louisiana Historical Quarterly, The Mississippi Valley Historical Review, Nebraska History, The Pennsylvania Magazine of History and Biography* and *The Journal of Southern History*.

I am particularly indebted to Mrs. Barbara Rex, and to Professor Charles Boewe of the University of Pennsylvania, for expert advice. The staff of the University Library has been a staff indeed. Those skilled ladies who preside at the reference desk, Mrs. Flora D. Colton, Mrs. Edith B. Hampel and Mrs. Marjorie H. Milde, had good reason to dread the sound of my voice over the phone, but never once did they fail to make a cheerful and effective response. I never asked them whether the sea was boiling hot or whether pigs had wings, but had I done so, I am sure they would have called back in a few minutes with the correct answer. In the circulation and inter-library loan divisions, Mrs. Delphine Richardson and Messrs. Jesse C. Mills and Bernard J. Ford assembled everything under the sun, not only from all over the Library but also from various parts of the world. Mr. Eberhard Geiger helped me in translation. In College Hall and Bennett Hall, Mrs. Ruth Hamilton Lin, Mrs. Ann Shirley and Mr. William H. Scott made it possible for me to have something other people could read, no matter how much I changed the drafts.

My colleague, Professor Lynn M. Case, kindly shared with me his command of the material in the French Foreign Office Archives to my great advantage.

I cannot say too much in praise of Mr. Hiram Haydn, Mr. Herman Ziegner, Miss Lillian Brahms, and the other members of the Atheneum staff whom I never saw, for the consideration with which they treated an author's idiosyncrasies. The one who deserves the most thanks has endured them for forty-three years.

ROY F. NICHOLS

University of Pennsylvania
Christmas Day, 1962

CONTENTS

CONTENTS

BLUEPRINTS FOR LEVIATHAN: AMERICAN STYLE

===

CHAPTER ONE

THE NEED FOR LEVIATHAN

HAMILTON FISH, urbane, polished patrician, was an anomalous figure in the curious group which General U. S. Grant so secretively selected to serve in his cabinet when he became President of the United States. But despite the incongruity of his position, Fish found satisfaction in sitting in the chair of his old friend William H. Seward, whom he succeeded as Secretary of State. For eight years he presided over the State Department in its temporary location, the Orphan Asylum at 14th and S Streets. On March 30, 1870, an associate brought him an unusual document to sign—the proclamation declaring the Fifteenth Amendment of the Constitution of the United States to be duly ratified and in effect. It probably did not occur to the Secretary as he dipped his pen that he was also proclaiming the completion of the American Leviathan.

The Secretary's signature that March day in a sense finished another phase of a process which had been going on for at least eight centuries in Anglo-American experience. The generations following one another in this society had found many times that the efficient assignment of the power to govern had taxed their political capacities. In this they were in no way peculiar, for the human race has always found it so. Among some peoples this problem has been solved by despotism. Other societies have never solved it at all and as a result suffer from constant turmoil and instability. In the Anglo-American world stability has been purchased at the expense of much blood, treasure and energy, physical and intellectual, and, at that, it has been neither as continuous nor as untroubled as is sometimes carelessly assumed. The struggle for political balance has constantly demonstrated how easily stable government may be disrupted and its equilibrium destroyed.

During the eight centuries between the Norman Conquest of 1066 and the American conflict of 1861-1865, a myriad ingenious men and women sought an orderly system of self-government that would free their society from the perils of social war, from the destruction of life and happiness—they sought to invent a Hobbesian Leviathan. They came to believe that some such effective mechanism could be specified in a series of written agreements, definitions of responsibility for order reduced to covenants and social contracts; these would in a sense be the blueprints for the desired "engine."

The circumstances that were dominant in England in the period of the Norman invasion had a determining influence in setting this pattern. The Norman conquerors were confronted with the problem of governing the English population, hitherto independent, with only a skeleton force of French supporters. This meant that some form of "cooperation" had to be insured with the "conquered." The Normans were legally minded, and they attempted by devices found in their feudal customs and to some extent inherited from Roman law to secure some enforceable agreement. The device they adopted was the charter or contract defining political and other privileges and compensating responsibilities that the Norman King offered to his new "lieges."

In the centuries following the Conquest, the Normans, through their chancellors, undertook to develop a system of keeping the peace by defining and recording the "good customs" of the realm in a series of documents beginning with the Constitution, or Charter of

Liberties, of Henry I in 1101 and including such notable examples as the Constitutions of Clarendon (1164), Magna Charta (1215), and the Provisions of Oxford (1258), to cite but a few.

The labors of these practical governors were stimulated by the fact that they were living in a society plagued by well-established confusion that made their politics frequently desperate. They had to cope with periodic outbreaks of civil commotion and bloodshed, wherein the governing power might be overthrown and rulers slain. The Norman Conqueror and his immediate successors sought to contrive a system of administering a conquered people by depending heavily on a military contingent of feudal barons living in fortresses and maintaining armed bands of retainers. But this system encouraged conflict as well as submission. To be sure, these feudal barons considered the king as their liege lord, but their military strength often led them to act independently of him and not only to aid him but also upon occasion to challenge his authority. It was to the baronial interest to see to it that the king did not become too strong. Therefore the kings had to try to develop devices that would curb the barons. They were skillful in invoking the cooperation of lesser men, often from the Anglo-Saxon population, in forms of local self-government, at the king's command reduced to writing; this device aided the monarch in providing inexpensive administration of the realm and at the same time prevented too much baronial independence or insubordination.

Even the shrewdness of the Norman kings and their advisers, and the documents they drafted, could not quell the elemental passions of the warrior barons nor conflicts arising from a divided people. Drives for power, jealousies, rivalries, fears and suspicions, greed for lands and retainers worked to cause these barons and lesser landlords to take up arms easily to fight for new perquisites or old privileges. These periodic outbreaks gave evidence that a pattern of occasional civil war was a disquieting feature of government. It was becoming apparent that about once in each century a new, almost predictable, outbreak of violence would occur. Between 1100 and 1688 six English monarchs were slain and one fled the realm. Such a habit made the invention of some sort of a Leviathan necessary if such disorders were to be eliminated or controlled.

The church played a significant role in the construction of the Leviathan that was slowly taking shape. The archbishops and bishops were not only spiritual lords but wealthy feudal lords as well, often with military resources and usually with money. They could aid the king or they could seek to check him. Then, too, their power and functions were complicated by their relationship to the papacy and its international or supranational implications. Finally there was their religious power over the bodies and souls of such a large portion of the inhabitants, their power to invoke excommunication and the interdict, a power which would make kings fear. The Church was a mighty organization within, at the same time that it was above, the earthly kingdom.

Some of the most active and ingenious designers of this Leviathan were found among the churchmen, and they supplied it with a moral and religious definition. These priests served as the scribes and registrars because they could write, a talent they shared with few, and hardly ever with kings and military lords. But more important was the fact that they were frequently ministers of state and chancellors. A long series of clerics labored with the English kings, from Lanfranc, Anselm and Langton to Morton, Wolsey and Cranmer. These men had been notably and notoriously influential in government and the English people had long been conditioned to ecclesiastical participation in polity. There was a religious tone to law, and the divine sanction was customarily invoked in statements of legal obligation. A Leviathan of sorts therefore was created by uneasy agreement between the crown and the barons temporal and spiritual. Nevertheless civil war was still possible, and the intermittent Wars of the Roses of the fifteenth century produced a species of anarchy.

But a new interest was rising to power, for a basic socioeconomic change had been taking place in Britain that produced a second type of document, a second set of specifications for Leviathan. In the twelfth and thirteenth centuries came the rise of towns, cities and trade. As men's imaginations, their knowledge, their wants, all expanded in the years clustering around the twelfth century and onwards, men traveled more, traded more, and began to seek and establish closer association. Towns and cities grew, not merely as defense posts but as places of trade, and there emerged a substantial citizenry possessed of money rather than titles. Certain events, such as the crusades, increased the power and influence of the townsmen, because in order to finance ventures to the Holy Land, many of the feudal lords had to get money and were willing to exchange municipal privilege for it, granting charters and liberties that gave municipalities and their inhabitants new power and recognition.

Charters that contained political specifications were likewise granted to trading companies. Such corporations as the Merchants of the Staple, the Merchant Adventurers and later the Muscovy Company had specified in their charters the right to establish trading compounds in foreign lands, and in these compounds their agents and servants conducted self-government under prescribed rules. Edward I (1272-1307) recognized this interest as having a function in government and skillfully used it in pursuing his successful ambitions at home and abroad. Parliament at the same time was enlarged to include elected representatives of the

new middle class. There were now two houses—Lords
and Commons. Together they made laws and voted
taxes.

The fourteenth century brought other signs of social
change that were to effect Leviathan. Much, perhaps too
much, has been ascribed to the Black Death of the
mid-century; but there is no doubt that the great loss
of life and the attendant fear and misery had a tremendous influence upon society. The plague decimated
labor; it also destroyed a large section of the clergy. In
many places clerical forces were now totally inadequate
to carry on ecclesiastical control, and the way was open
for new ideas.

Shortly after the Black Death, as time goes, John
Wycliffe began new religious teaching and Wat Tyler
led a peasants' revolt. These two developments are
early indications of a new pattern of checking authority
that was to have tremendous influence upon the internal peace of the realm. Wycliffe's teachings had political as well as religious significance. His questioning of
the ways of religious authority attracted to himself a
following that demanded in effect a new political dis-
pensation. Though many of his followers, the Lollards,
were humble folk, men and women of the middle class
were also included. Together with Wat Tyler and his
band, they represented the idea of protest and revolt
on the part of the underprivileged, an early manifestation of populism, of the class struggle.

It is well, however, not to confuse a feudal proclivity
for marauding and fighting with popular discontent in
the modern sense of proletarian unrest. The violence
that is a characteristic of feudalism is perhaps more akin
to modern gangsterism and springs not only from lack
of economic and social opportunity but also, possibly,
from the fact that fighting and restless roving are often more fun than hard work.

It was not until the sixteenth century that certain

of the implications of these movements from the masses became manifest. On the whole there seems to be little evidence of any rise of popular influence. For this was the Tudor age, the point in English history at which the power and majesty of the monarchy achieved its height. The Tudors were making much common cause with the wealthy middle class and with the leaders in Parliament who desired peace and order so that their own prestige, wealth, and power might flourish under assured stability. What had happened was that a Leviathan had been achieved, a workable "engine" of government.

During these centuries following the Norman Conquest, English rulers and subjects had learned to accept certain limitations set by a growing body of law derived primarily from immemorial usages that by acceptance over the years had acquired a character of permanence and inviolability. In effect, these usages had become rights that administrators, judges and legislators were bound to respect and that had been carefully described in documents. These charters, laws and judicial decisions set limitations on the power of government that were to become accepted descriptions of the nature of the government itself. The English experience was particularly remarkable for the fact that the power of government was limited in the interest of the individual by a scattered series of documents and understandings.

In such a variety of ways Englishmen had been practicing the art of designing governmental operation to promote stability. Charters, constitutions, covenants, contracts, statutes—these written instruments had been drafted to meet specific situations or to serve given institutions. Parliament was the source of law, the king executed it and the courts defined it. Men were gaining significant skill in the work of lawmaking, of administration and of chancery. In these early centuries their work was largely fragmentary and governed by the expediency of the immediate. But larger horizons were opening up. The sum total of such documents and their judicial interpretations in the expanding system of courts had been developing into a great common law or unwritten constitution. Scholars of the law had been laboriously codifying and expounding it. As early as the twelfth century a *Treatise on the Laws and Customs of England* had been compiled by someone and ascribed to Ranulf de Glanvil, an Angevin jurist. This was followed by the treatise known as Bracton's *Concerning the Laws and Customs of England,* which was a product of the great thirteenth century and which set a pattern of a concept of law. Compilers of Year Books reporting court decisions followed, and these in turn led to other compilations and abridgements. In the sixteenth century Sir Anthony Fitzherbert in *La Grande Abridgement* attempted to systematize the corpus of English law. But it was Sir Edward Coke who placed the capstone on the edifice; at the beginning of the seventeenth century he laboriously compiled the four volumes of his *Institutes.* Here was one of the beginnings of the idea of a British constitution based on the common law. It is significant that this apparatus was at hand when the discovery and settlement of the New World placed before the ingenious the challenge of the possibility of a new Leviathan constructed not by chance but according to well-thought-out specifications and formulated as a system designed to insure permanent order.

CHAPTER TWO

DRAWING LEVIATHAN'S ENGLISH PATTERN

IN THE ancient English university town of Cambridge at the opening of the sixteenth century was an inconspicuous place of public entertainment known as the White Horse Inn. This hostelry stood back from the High Street, not far from Queens' College and separated from King's by the narrow filth of Plute's Lane. It had the advantage for certain purposes of being off the beaten track. Those wishing to enter unobserved might, particularly in the dark of night, approach it from the rear along the Backs, where flowed the silent Cam, and slip in by a side door. To a number of alert Cambridge students who were discussing new and forbidden ideas in 1521, the White Horse Inn was a convenient gathering place for clandestine meetings.[1]

For ten years there had been increasing intellectual curiosity at the university about the new concepts that were destined to change much in English life. The Dutch teacher Erasmus, who had been in residence at Queens' for three fruitful years, had opened the minds of many who heard his lectures on the meaning of the New Testament. These followers of Erasmus undertook to read the Bible with new understanding and inspiration. Recently the more revolutionary ideas preached by Luther had come out of Germany, and his writings had become a center of discussion. Since the German preachments attacked the government and practices of the Church, Henry VIII, who as King of England essayed to be also Defender of the Faith, refused to tolerate such heresies. Significant documents, such as Luther's works, therefore, had been burned at St. Paul's in London in May, 1521, and not long after, during the Easter Term, at Cambridge. Cambridge scholars were forbidden to read Luther's books.

But ideas were not easily killed in Cambridge. A vigorous group among the scholars and students were East Anglians, who had come across the fens and broads from Norfolk and Suffolk, bringing with them a sturdy atmosphere of independence and turbulence. Some had come from the cathedral city of Norwich. The capital of Norfolk was encircled by a low range of hills in the valley of the Wensom, where the river Yare joins its kindred stream. Even as late as the thirteenth century the city still stood at the head of a great estuary to which vessels put in from the German ocean. It was a natural landing place for Dutch and German traders and in earlier days had been the favorite approach of Teutonic invaders.

Dominated by its magnificent cathedral and protected by its castle, Norwich had lived a feverish, frequently disturbed existence. For East Anglia, stretching out into the German ocean and separated from the rest of the realm by marshes and fenlands, was a corner far removed from most of England. The inhabitants of this region had been conditioned by their danger and their isolation into a headstrong and truculent people. Indeed, its lords had made it even more remote by building across the narrow isthmus of firm, dry land connecting it with England a great rampart called the Devil's Dyke.

Religious and political activity were pronounced in East Anglia—it was said that there was a church in Norwich for every week in the year. Outside the city, in a hollow beneath the hill on which St. Leonard's Priory stood, was the spot known as the Lollard's Pit, where religious reformers had been martyred by fire.

It was at Norwich, too, that Wat Tyler had raised his standard of revolt. The students from this enterprising and vital society who came across the fenland to Cambridge were not men to give up ideas merely because of royal fiat.

Norfolk men from Corpus, from Trinity Hall, and from Gonville's College picked their way silently in the dark through "detestable and filthy" Plute's Lane to enter the White Horse Inn by the hidden door. Here in "Little Germany," as it was called, under the chairmanship of a Norfolk cleric Robert Barnes, prior of the community of Augustan friars at Cambridge, they discussed the new religious concepts. The Norfolk men were prepared for these ideas, since some of them had already received an indoctrination from German merchants, agents and ship captains who put into Great Yarmouth and came on to Norwich.

The instrument for their new explorations into theology—and it proved the science of government as well —was the reconsideration of the great document, the Bible. This ancient scripture, hitherto hidden in its original tongues or in Latin and therefore unknown to the mass of the English people, was now to be printed in English and for the first time made available to all who could read or could hear it read. Tyndale at Oxford was busy with a translation, and the scholars at Cambridge had great concern for distributing the new printings.

These fellows of the Cambridge colleges were restudying the Scriptures and were talking about and teaching what they were discovering in the newly interpreted words of the Gospels. The more they studied, the more they realized how far the Church had departed from the writings. There must be reform, they concluded, well knowing that the whole force of hierarchy, government and social inertia would be against them. One of the youths who left the White Horse charged with the burning impress of new ideas to return to Norwich was known affectionately as "Little Bilney." In his home county Bilney sought to distribute the New Testament in English and went among the people sharing his revolutionary thoughts. His superior, Bishop Nix, could tolerate no such activity, and in 1531 brave Bilney was burned to death in the Lollard's Pit. The flames that destroyed Bilney's body, however, lighted another torch that was to flare so all could see.

Once again the spirit of religious zeal for reform was abroad—heresy, some called it—like that which had last been stirred by the Lollards in the fourteenth and fifteenth centuries. The White Horse Inn gatherings had counterparts elsewhere; the spirit of Lollardism driven underground began to respond, and other fires were set. All told, these primarily religious influences were to open a new epoch in political behavior.

The sixteenth century was to be a period of deep-seated religious reorientation. Ideas of individualism and independence, Biblical Christianity, and religious nationalism combined to produce a far-flung revolt against the power and practices of Roman Catholicism. These ideas joined forces with English Lollardism, English humanism, and English nationalism to present a situation that the English government could manipulate. Henry VIII was a monarch of capacity and ambition, a true nationalist who sought to increase England's power and his own, but he suffered a series of frustrations, most notably in his foreign policy, in his financial policies and in his desire to secure a male heir. Frustrations in a Tudor were bound to produce some form of vigorous compensating action, and Henry's was spectacular. He would reorganize England. He would seize control of the church, confiscate its wealth, and at the same time he would create a new aristocracy. But it is not possible to disturb the patterns of religious thought and observance, no matter if only superficially and for political reasons, without causing infinite repercussions.[2]

The significant fact is that a new age of political literacy was beginning in the sixteenth century and that it too had its source in religion. The era of the Protestant Reformation was at hand, and for this new wave of thinking there was a huge literary base. In the first place there was the great constitution, the Bible, and much of the enthusiasm was defined in terms of its meaning. In a sense the argument often involved the constitutional implications of its injunctions. And so close and interlocking were the ecclesiastical and the political interests that in the sixteenth and seventeenth centuries it was almost impossible to distinguish between them. Religious controversy was to be inevitably political controversy. More than ever must there be recourse to writing or to the drafting of what were in reality constitutional blueprints.

In this era society was to participate in its own governance on a grander scale than men had heretofore dreamed. The power of those governing was to be limited and directed by public opinion to a degree hitherto unknown. The will of a haphazard variety of citizens of high and low degree was to be expressed and recorded by mechanisms that were constantly to be adjusted, augmented, and redesigned, that were ever to be the object of restudy and experiment, particularly by those who sought devices that might more accurately capture and record the popular will. The right of humble individuals, who had no claim to distinction, to express opinions about those in power and to have a voice not only in shaping their policies but also in determining whether they were to continue to exercise power, was not an altogether new concept in the world, but it had hardly been tried out in any large population. Experiments were now to begin on a grand scale.

This democratic ideal burst forth in England with some force in the sixteenth century and was re-

emphasized at a time and under conditions that would
permit experiment in the America just discovered. The
active, inquiring scholars from East Anglia gathered
around their table in the Cambridge Inn represented
an attitude that was to become more frequently discernible in England in the sixteenth century and to
which American democracy was to owe much of its
essential quality.

What these men were investigating, clothed as it was
in religious terms, was a new concept of the relation
of the individual to society—a concept that would shortly
involve the question of the nature and power of government and the source of its authority. New political
patterns based upon novel types of thought and action
were in the making. The extent to which new institutional concepts and behavior patterns could be experimented with was enlarged, yet at the same time it was
limited by the characteristics of English politics. It
was eventually realized that the full force of these ideas
and attitudes could be developed only in an environment in which institutions were less crystallized than in
England. America was to prove a convenient laboratory. In both the old and the new society, a new literature and a new documentation was to be created; new
specifications were to be supplied for Leviathan.

During Roman Catholic Queen Mary's brief reign
(1553-1558) many who were in exile for their heresies
gained experience in new and independent forms of
church organization and government. One group had
established a congregation at the Weissfrauenkirche in
Frankfurt, another at Strasbourg. In Zurich a third
group of leaders had lived in Pastor Bullinger's manse
under the shadow of the Grossmünster. At Geneva
others had heard Calvin preach at the great cathedral
or had listened to their own ministers, notably John
Knox, at the Temple de l'Auditoire close by. They
had corresponded, visited, counseled, engaged in contro-

versy, and some had written propaganda books that had a furtive circulation in England. They had openly questioned royal authority and justified popular resistance to tyranny. John Ponet, erstwhile Bishop of Winchester, published *A Short Treatise of Politike Power;* Christopher Goodman wrote *How Superior Powers Oght To Be Obeyd,* which seconded and re-enforced Ponet's argument; and John Knox blew his *First Blast of the Trumpet against the Monstrous Regiment of Women.*[3] The more radical of the exiles worked out a new church organization, in which pastors and elders were to have much importance in the general governance of the English Church and presumably much more freedom of action in ordering the form of worship. Preaching was to supersede liturgy in importance. The exiles were eagerly awaiting the day when they might return to admonish a new sovereign and to advise how best to put their ideas into effect; they expected the chief seats in a new hierarchy which would "Genevate" the Church of England.

No sooner had word of Mary's death reached the Protestant cities on the Continent than the exiles hurried back to England hoping to receive from Elizabeth the authority to set up their new order. Their plan—a basic constitutional change—was to diminish the royal power and the authority of the bishops in matters ecclesiastical. But Elizabeth was her father's daughter; she was of no mind to tolerate such radical changes. She was, indeed, in a difficult position. Her father's excesses, her brother's minority reign, her sister's religious and matrimonial alliance with Rome and Spain had all weakened popular confidence in the throne. The monarchy was shaky. Elizabeth knew that vigorous religious reorganization, such as the exiles had in mind, would stir up strife that she could ill afford. Hence, she realized, she must act with caution. She herself had slight interest in religion, but she well understood that she had to maintain her own place and strengthen her power in religious matters. She realized also that placing the parishes in charge of independent priests and elders would take from her hands valuable instruments of government and would create a situation that might be difficult, if not impossible, for her and her bishops to control.

As soon as Elizabeth was proclaimed Queen in November, 1558, a battle of propaganda began. The restored Roman bishops of Mary's reign had anticipated what was coming and had sought to organize against the event. At Mary's funeral one of her prelates had warned the throng that "The Wolves be coming out of Geneva —and have sent their books before, full of pestilent doctrines, blasphemy and heresy, to infect the people." The Roman bishops and their priests continued earnest in their preaching. Other priests, who wished for the Anglican liturgy, urged a middle way, while the returning exiles and the emerging underground forces sought a new order. Nor was preaching confined to the churches. Religious enthusiasts without parishes or pulpits—"gospellers," as they were called—were exhorting wherever they could gain a circle of listeners. Elizabeth, fully realizing the danger of such action, decided that Parliament, not the pulpit, was to be the forum. In December, by royal proclamation, she forbade preaching; religious services were to be solely liturgical for the time being. Forthwith she summoned Parliament; there must be lawmaking and the drafting of statutes.[4]

Like her father, Elizabeth was clever in understanding the uses of Parliament. When that body met, she discovered that there was in the Commons a strong exile group ardently interested in the effort to Genevate the Church. On the other hand, she found a Catholic party in the House of Lords, where Mary's bishops attended in force. Elizabeth moved skillfully to secure the repeal of the return to Rome, which Mary had obtained after so much difficulty. English nationalism wanted no Romish control. The Queen would have been content merely to restore things as her father had left them, but, pushed by the exiles, she had to accept the provisions of a new law that acknowledged her as Supreme Governor of the Church (not its Supreme Head) and an Act of Uniformity prescribing a new Anglican prayer book. A bill that would have enabled Elizabeth to restore those bishops and priests who had been deprived of their positions during Mary's day failed, probably by reason of the Catholic influence in the House of Lords.

Despite this compromise, Elizabeth did gain the ecclesiastical power her father had had, but she was cautious in using it. She contented herself with sending commissioners throughout England to administer an oath, which could not be taken by Mary's Catholic leaders although most of the lesser clergy accepted it. Elizabeth now could begin to appoint her bishops. Once again the word was caution, and men of moderate views willing to cooperate with the Queen received the most important positions.

The moderate policy of the Crown and of Parliament was a grievous disappointment to many. Those sharing the ideas of the exiles refused to be content and began a course of action that was to have repercussions decidedly political in character. Controversy over policy, over basic institutional patterns, was going to permeate the realm; a new stream of documentation began to flow.

This flood was loosed because a great divisive issue was now before the English people, an issue of more general appeal than any other since the Norman invasion. This issue was charged with all kinds of emotional power, involving questions of intimate personal concern not only in this world, but in the next as well. Could government compose this issue by law, administrative practice, or new adjustments to Leviathan? Government had tried several experiments since the issue was presented, but to date none had worked for very long. There are certain popular attitudes that do not yield readily to government fiat.

Because it was evident that the Puritan interest in Parliament would usually be helpless against the Queen's command, the Puritans realized that they would have to operate independently of Parliament. They therefore proceeded to organize to reform religion within the parishes, despite the Queen's displeasure and without benefit of political sanction. On a realm-wide basis they used techniques of planning, promotion, propaganda and organization that look surprisingly like modern political methods. In effect they were unconsciously creating a political organization for ostensibly nonpolitical purposes and were developing habits of behavior that their descendants were to find useful in America.

This tendency to organize and, in effect, to form parties had begun on the Continent. Among the English exiles, particularly in Frankfurt, there had been an Episcopal faction and a reform faction. Although the reformers had been defeated in Frankfurt and some of them had gone to Geneva, those at Zurich and Strasbourg took vital interest in their differences of opinion and at times attempted either to arbitrate or to direct them. When they returned to England at Elizabeth's succession, the exiles did not forget what they had learned.

Some of these men were still living in 1572 when the Puritans began to organize, and one of them, Anthony Gilby, became a leader in the Puritan campaign. He with John Field, Thomas Wilcox, and several others met in London during the session of Parliament to frame and promote legislation and to organize support for it. These men urged a presbyterian form of church government, in which clergymen and elders would manage the parishes and send delegates to synods that would in turn rule the Church. Their principal item of propaganda was a pamphlet, *An Admonition to the Parliament,* which obtained wide circulation and stimulated replies in similar form from the Anglican hierarchy. This central committee organized correspondence and encouraged the formation of synods or classes, which some of the enthusiasts had already experimented with along Genevan lines. For their temerity some, including Field, went to jail. But Field continued to act as a kind of national secretary of the party and to direct propaganda even from behind the walls of Newgate Prison. These men accomplished nothing in Parliament at the time, but their efforts in some localities bore fruit.

For ten years they labored manfully, and by 1583 they were ready for a new trial of strength. In that year, shortly after the Puritan-Presbyterians were able to hold their first general conference at Cambridge, their talents were stimulated by a new move on the part of the Queen. In 1583 Elizabeth appointed John Whitgift, sometime Master of Trinity and Vice-Chancellor of Cambridge, as Archbishop of Canterbury. He had been the principal author of counterpropaganda in the preceding decade, and he now undertook to enforce conformity to the Anglican system of worship and doctrine. This once more aroused the political genius of the Puritan-Presbyterian group. Field again took over the office of corresponding and organizing secretary. His purpose now was to organize resistance to Canterbury's subscription test for religious uniformity, which all pastors were urged to refuse to sign. A great stream of petitions began to pour in upon Canterbury and Elizabeth's Puritan-minded Council. Lawyers attacked Whitgift's proceedings, and the common-law courts were not loath to use every quibble to hamper the operation of his ecclesiastical court. In addition to all this, a modified English version of the Geneva prayer book was prepared and printed.

In 1584 and during a meeting of Parliament in 1585

several convocations of Puritan-Presbyterian members met. They established a lobby in London, and during Parliamentary sessions they met nightly with their parliamentary members. William the Silent had recently been assassinated in the Netherlands, and hatred of the Roman Catholics was at a new high. The Queen's safety was feared for and the Puritan members of Elizabeth's Council were particularly solicitous. This concern led the Council to persuade the Archbishop to accept a compromise that would forestall the displacement of many Puritan divines in their parishes. The Puritans themselves quickened their own efforts.

In 1585 these efforts took on the aspect of a political campaign to elect a friendly Parliament. Puritan leaders prepared propaganda statistics to show how many parishes were vacant or occupied by the unlearned and the unfit. They began working on a legislative program for the new Parliament, and they were also thinking along the lines of what would in another time have been the party platform. A general conference, not unlike a party convention, was held at Cambridge in July.

When the new Parliament assembled in 1586, the results of these efforts were apparent. There was a larger and more clearly defined Puritan group, which sat together in the House of Commons, caucused and dined together and acted in unison. Again this group had the aid of a Popish plot, for it was during this Parliament that Mary Queen of Scots was executed. With the Scottish problem apparently solved, Peter Wentworth and his associates sought to secure legislation authorizing a Presbyterian reorganization. This the Queen forbade. In ten pertinent questions Wentworth raised the matter of the privileges of the House of Commons. For this he was sent to the Tower, though the ostensible reason was the organization of a Puritan lobby in synod form.

The Puritans again failed to accomplish anything in the way of law, but their leaders did complete the Book of Discipline, which was finally approved at a synod held at St. John's College, Cambridge, in September, 1589, during the Stourbridge Fair. This "Disciplina Ecclesiae," the Puritan Discipline, was in effect a statement of principles for political as well as ecclesiastical action, a blueprint for Leviathan. It outlined a theocratic system of pastors and elders, ruling according to the laws of God. Despite the almost unlimited power given to the pastors and officers elected by the congregation, it was stipulated that "in all the greater affairs of the Church, as in excommunicating of any and in choosing and deposing of Church members, nothing may be concluded without the knowledge and consent of the Church [congregation]." In this statement lies one of the germs of American democracy.

While those who sought to reorganize the Church and to curb the power of the Queen and bishops accomplished little that can be found in the statutes of the realm, they gained an influential place in government and society. They had protected themselves from any very active government prosecution. The Queen's punitive measures were reserved almost exclusively for such secessionists as the Brownists, Separatists and the more radical sectarians who defied the Church and left it. Such persons were placed under the ban and were liable to banishment or execution. Under this threat some fled to Holland at various times and in their congregational meetings at Amsterdam and Leyden developed ideas of political independence and self-government that were to be potent in America.

The Puritan-Presbyterian group ceased to be very active politically in the closing years of Elizabeth's reign. But some who had been engaged in the more political aspects of the movement, organization, propaganda and lobbying did not forget their craft and were ready to act again in the days of the Stuarts. They had circulated ideas about limiting central authority and enlarging popular government; they had become familiar with and had spread a concept of a society of equal men who were mutually responsible, which they urged as an improvement upon the older concept of a stratified society with fixed status. They had stirred among the people a new interest in Parliament and had given to some of its members a sense of representing the people. This produced a theory stated at the University of Cambridge, where Scripture was invoked to demonstrate that episcopacy was not in the law of God and that civil government could not therefore rightfully establish such. Civil government was to create and protect a scriptural Church, but there its ecclesiastical authority ended.

This concept Richard Hooker in his *Ecclesiastical Polity* hastened to deny. In so doing, he descanted on the nature of political society in terms resembling a theory of social contract and condemned the Puritan claim to a right to disobey the commands of the state Church as a denial of political obligation. He denounced any right of forcible rebellion. The Puritans on their part, though they had no faith in human reason and would not admit any authority divorced from Scripture or that reason without scriptural obedience could get anywhere, nevertheless would neither rebel nor advocate the use of force. Instead, they bored from within and in as many parishes as possible modified the service and maintained exasperating independence of the bishops, leaving it to a few Congregational extremists, such as the Brownists, actually to defy the law.

Thus on the eve of the migration the predominant theory was obedience to royal authority, but the philosophy of scriptural inerrancy, which was maintained by Puritan divines, had in it the germs of appeal to higher authority, and Hooker's effort to refute it had brought the idea of social contract and human reason into the picture. Furthermore, it should be remembered that ministers who had been deprived of their parishes by Elizabeth and her bishops in some instances became tutors and teachers and communicated to a new generation ideas of individual worth and public responsibility that had their influence upon those from whom were to come the founders and directors of the New England across the sea.

Following this epoch, during the seventeenth century, or the first century of colonization, political developments in England again supplied a series of ideas and notable documents that were to be drawn upon literally in writing specifications for what was to be the American Leviathan. The Scottish Stuarts had understood little of the intricacies and the spirit of their English constitution. They undertook to establish the concept of their divine right as kings. When the Stuarts, James I and Charles I, had shown their incapacity to promote English prowess, when they had evoked anti-Catholic antipathies by the marriage of Charles to a French princess, when a rising cost of living had pinched many country gentlemen living on fixed incomes, when Charles endeavored to increase tax burdens arbitrarily in order to play expensive but ineffective international politics, and when his ecclesiastical politicians began their effort to put screws on nonconforming and semi-independent parishes, only one result was possible in England.[5]

Tactics that had been used by the barons in King John's day, by those who had curbed Edward II and Richard II, by Jack Cade and Wat Tyler, were withdrawn from the archives of tradition and put to use again. This time the quill was the first instrument, and such documents as the Petition of Right (1628), the Grand Remonstrance (1641) and the Agreement of the People (1647) laid down new political theory. In the name of the traditional rights and liberties of the English people, arbitrary power was denounced, definite checks upon royal behavior were formulated and the right of resistance against arbitrary government was claimed for the people. This reformation and elaboration of ancient custom was enforced by the sword. Charles I went to his death and a commonwealth was established. This violent break with tradition proved too radical, and in less than a dozen years the Stuarts were welcomed back again on the understanding that they had been educated in English constitutional tradition.

Charles II undoubtedly had been, but his brother James was less aware of reality. His greatest error was in raising the religious issue, for in the blindness of his faith in Catholicism he lost sight of the nature of his people and their dislike for Papists. Within three years he had fled to France. This time the British political leaders were going to leave nothing to chance —they had welcomed Charles II back with only the vaguest tacit understanding as to the relation of the King to the realm. Now in 1688 this relation was to be put in writing, framed into law—into law based upon reformulated political theory.

Between the writings of the Puritan Revolution of 1628-1649 and 1688 there had been further lucubration. The Roundheads had developed an intensely narrow didacticism, which was but a reflection of the attitude of many of their pastors and the communicants of their churches. In religious language so much of the letter, the literal interpretation of the Scriptures, was killing the spirit. The educated leaders were splitting hairs and wasting their time in bootless argument over meanings of texts, thereby neglecting their high calling of preaching Christianity. A reaction to this narrow and pedantic prostitution of religious leadership came from the great intellectual center of Puritanism in the University of Cambridge. The fellows in the colleges had been rereading Plato and drinking at the new-sprung fountain of Descartes. One Sunday in 1641 John Sherman rose in the Chapel at Trinity and preached a sermon, "A Greek in the Temple." God had not confined His revelation of Himself to the pages of Scripture. God was expressing Himself "in the vast and ample volume of the world." "As truths supernatural are not contradicted by reason, so neither surely is that contradicted by Scripture which is dictated by right reason." Nature and reason were instruments of God to show man the way of life.

Of greater fame was Benjamin Whichcote, student at Emmanuel and later Provost of King's, who for many years was the preacher in one of the parish churches of Cambridge; he became the Socrates of these Cambridge Platonists. They were to follow reason which was the Candle of the Lord. Religious faith was founded not so much upon documentary evidence as upon experience. God as universal love and holy affection could only be known by those who experienced love and affection toward their fellow men and developed thereby a happy union of souls with God. Like Plato, these men stressed morals, conduct. The mind of God was the home of truth and the seat of ideas. Of the ideas of God man's reason had an intuitive and certain perception, particularly of moral ideas. Thus reason was brought back into respectability and could be invoked as man's guide in his search for truth and the road of righteous conduct. In this fashion the Cambridge Platonists called the pedantic Puritans to account in the very seat of Puritanism within the courts of Emmanuel. Reason could discover God by learning the laws of nature which were God's revelation to man. So they challenged the infallibility of Scripture and of the Church and brought forth reason as a spark of divine light that produced an inward apprehension of duty and God. Away with cant, dialectics and the tyranny of the written words of ancient revelation! Man through reason might discover God continuously, and by union with Him in nature he might confound the Puritan concept of man as fundamentally wicked.

An Oxford man, John Locke, was delving into the politics of the day, and it fell to his task to justify in theory the overthrow of the Stuarts in 1688. He had associations with the Cambridge Platonists, and their doctrines did much for him. From them and from Richard Hooker he drew ideas, and forth came the fine flower of rational justification of revolution against tyrannical authority. Man had perceived that his original state of nature was intolerably chaotic, so by use of his reason he grasped the fact that he could introduce order. All men were created equal, reason told him, and were endowed with certain inalienable rights, among which were life, liberty and the power to hold and enjoy property. But these rights could not be enjoyed while man lived lawlessly in a state of nature. Therefore these equal, intelligent, rational individuals, each conscious of his capacity and his dignity, had united to form a social compact that established a government for the purpose of keeping order. The authority of this government and its ultimate sanction was the consent of the governed. But if the government disregarded the wishes and the rights of the governed, then the governed might overthrow their government.

Thus the individual, the rational individual who through reason learned these laws of the Creator, was in a position to maintain his rights and his dignity. This was the high point of individualism, of equalitarian participation in authority. It was during this transition in political theory from the dogma of the supremacy and unchallengeable permanency of constituted authority to the supremacy of the social compact that the colonists migrated to America.

Other influences had been working side by side with

this wondrously complex and pervasive religious trans-
formation to guide the pens of those planning the new
American experiments. These were less obvious, and
they affected—and were effected by—a smaller segment of society in any fashion of which they were conscious, but they were mighty in their implications. In
this seventeenth century the battle, which Sir Edward
Coke started as Chief Justice of the Court of Common
Pleas, was won. He did not win it; in fact, he lost his
ermine in fighting it; but it was won. He, following
Markham, Fortescue and Littleton, had maintained that
the common law was superior to the king and to the
ecclesiastical and equity courts and that even parliament
must mind its limiting principles. The Puritan Revolution cost one Stuart his head, and the Glorious Revolution lost another one his throne. The monarch thereafter would rule according to the common law, which
had been established as supreme. While the American
Leviathan was in process of construction, England was
finally dedicated to the rule of law, and the designers
paid heed.

Anglo-American political institutions were subject to
another mighty force, the new English nationalism. The
United Kingdom was no longer a unit in a great theocracy, the Universal Church of Rome. The ambitions
and capacities of the Tudors synchronized with the
growing ambitions and aspirations of the rising middle
class. They made part of the complex force of nationalism that played such an important part in the English
Reformation, this declaration of independence from
Rome. They were expressing by political action the
hopes of the English humanists who were promoting
an English culture by speaking and writing the English tongue and providing Will Shakespeare to arouse
men to new national feeling by mighty lines spoken
from the stage in the vernacular.

England's ambition to be a world power was likewise

stirring. Tudors and Stuarts were engaging in world politics for England's profit. English political philosophers were defining England's position in a world of new nations and were phrasing and codifying an embryo international law while the ambassadors were playing diplomatic chess in the European courts. England wished to share with her rivals in the new quest for empire stirred by the discovery of America. Rather belatedly the activity of her rivals awakened her to the need of gaining her share in American treasure. In these news fields of enterprise, English merchants, English soldiers, English statesmen and English religious leaders all saw opportunity, and they set themselves to plan, and in planning to write new specifications, this time for a Leviathan beyond the seas.

In the century and a half of religious and political discussion that stretched over the years from the evenings at the White Horse Inn down to the publication of John Locke's treatises, a series of tracts and other documents interpreting the Bible, man's nature and English experience had produced a collection of ideas that could be freely drawn upon by those who were to create the American Leviathan. Such was the political ideology of those setting out on the terrible sea voyages to shores so far away. These skills and ideas would contribute vitally to fashioning the new American "engine" of government.

CHAPTER THREE

DRAFTING AMERICAN
SPECIFICATIONS

THE discovery of the Western Hemisphere brought many new challenges to the political inventiveness of mankind. The fact that people were going to emigrate thither and establish new societies meant that the problem of government must be faced. In this political realm the English promoters and their colonists were the most original in their inventions and adaptations. They came to America with a tradition of political thought and action that proved of great practical use in dealing with wilderness conditions on the other shores of the Atlantic. The emigrants drew heavily upon this store of English experience.[1]

The actual beginnings were made by commercial venturers. The needs of the British Isles, lands none too productive on the periphery of Continental Europe, had bred generations of traders and adventurers who had become accustomed to long voyages and to conducting difficult enterprises among strange people. Their ventures included the establishment of commercial depots where managers had certain political responsibilities. It was from this enterprise that the first colonies emerged, and it was in them that the first designs of the American Leviathan were contrived.

When English enterprisers began to think of a political Leviathan for America, they found available certain experiences upon which they could draw. Experiments in the establishment of English practice in self-government outside the realm had been going on for three hundred years, starting in the thirteenth century when certain English merchants broke away from the domination of the foreign traders who were then supplying England and sought to direct an independent line of export. These merchants were interested in selling wool, tin and hides to the Low Countries across the Channel. Known as the Merchants of the Staple, they secured a concession through Edward I from the authorities of Antwerp to establish a staple, or warehouse and offices, and a group of English traders thus set up in business for themselves in Antwerp. They had the right of self-government under the supervision of the London Merchants of the Staple; they elected a mayor and governed themselves, politically as well as commercially, within their compound in Antwerp.

Early in the fifteenth century, after the Staple had moved to Calais, Henry IV granted a charter to the Merchant Adventurers, who were to operate in the north European countries. Under this charter the Adventurers elected their own governors and made laws for themselves. A half-century later Edward IV gave a charter to the merchants operating in the Low Countries, defining their procedure for electing a governor and a court of twelve justiciars, as well as setting forth their legislative powers. This charter also provided that their laws must be approved by the Crown.

In Elizabeth's reign such precedents were useful. Far-seeing merchants noted the advantages Spain was reaping from her interests in the New World and from her control of southern and eastern trade routes. Goaded by England's lack of capital, her merchants were moved to seek sources of gold and eastern commodities by operating to the northeast, and some even thought of the northwest as a route to the Orient.

So it was that in 1553 a group of London Merchants formed "The Mysterie and Companie of the Marchants Adventurers for the discoverie of regions, dominions, islands and places unknown." An expedition was sent to Russia, or Muscovy, to establish contact with the East. The venture was so promising that under the leadership of Sebastian Cabot, son of the famous discoverer, the first English joint-stock company to operate the Russian franchise was formed. On February 6, 1555, the charter forming the Muscovy Company passed the seals, giving the Company a monopoly of all franchises and prescribing a form of organization of great significance in the history of American democracy.

The fellowship—that is, the stockholders in the corporation—was required to meet periodically to choose a "court" to operate the company. This court was to be presided over by Cabot as governor during his lifetime and after his death was to be headed by two governors. With them were to be associated twenty-eight other persons elected annually—four consuls and twenty-four assistants. A quorum of the court was to consist of the governor, two consuls and twelve assistants, or if the governor was away, of three consuls and twelve assistants. The court of the Company was empowered to make orders for the governing of trade.

Although the Muscovy Company was granted the franchise to venture to America by the northwest, it did not take advantage of this portion of its liberties; but some of the stockholders who frequented Muscovy House caught the spirit of a new adventure. One of these, Sir Humphrey Gilbert, had had the idea of exploration and the establishment of American outposts as early as 1566, just at a time when French Protestants were trying to establish a settlement in Florida and the mariners Hawkins and Stukely were bringing back reports of Spanish and French activities in America. Gilbert's interest was for a time deflected by a governmental assignment to help extend control in Ireland by military force and colonization. It was in Ireland that he met the sea dog Martin Frobisher, who was anxious to explore American waters for a northwest passage.

When Gilbert returned to England in the 1570's he tried to interest his Muscovy associates and other private interests in Frobisher's scheme of exploration and in his own plans of colonization. Finding his Muscovy friends not at all interested in giving him support for an enterprise independent of their monopoly, he next sought to interest the government. Sir Henry Sidney, the Earl of Warwick, and Lord Burghley were enlisted to bring pressure upon the Muscovy Company on his behalf, and at length the Privy Council urged the Muscovy directors to cooperate. This was of no avail, however, until Michael Lock, the chief capitalist of the Company, was converted. With the blessing of the Muscovy Company, Gilbert set out to sell shares to finance his plan, but only the final heavy investment by Lock himself made the venture possible. Frobisher made three voyages and found enough ore in Greenland to cause the Queen to charter the Cathay Company and to contribute £1,000 toward what she hoped would be a mining town and a trade station on a new northwest route to the Far East.

While this enterprise was developing under Frobisher, Gilbert planned a colony more to the south, and in 1578 he received from the government a charter "for inhabiting and planting our people in America,"— perhaps the first of the blueprints for the American Leviathan. He was given authority to exercise jurisdiction over a region within two hundred leagues of wherever he fixed his capital. Gilbert labored on his colony for five years and made two voyages on its behalf. During the second voyage he landed on Newfoundland and actually began settlement, but it came to nought, since he was lost at sea returning to England in 1583. His half-brother, Sir Walter Raleigh, however, carried on and was given a patent in 1584 to settle much farther south in a region called Virginia. Raleigh sent settlers to what is now North Carolina, and on the island of Roanoke he sought to establish government by incorporating his settlers in the fashion of an English municipality as "The Governor and Assistants of the City of Raleigh in Virginia." His governor was to have twelve assistants, and they were to rule as an English municipal council.

Raleigh's ventures also failed, but several steps had been taken toward laying the foundation of American colonization. The Crown had granted charters or patents to individual enterprisers, decreeing that they could create societies in the form of trading posts designed to be governed as English municipalities and that they should have land at their disposal with which to encourage settlement and possible speculation.

Raleigh was soon followed by others of similar interest. These first planners for America were primarily concerned with commercial success. Those merchants, soldiers and gentlemen from London and the outports who projected the first ventures thought in terms of business organization and incorporated chartered companies. Their charters provided a form of management that was cumbersome. A committee of the promoters, in cooperation with Crown officers, was to invite adventurers to go to America to join in raising or procuring the products that were to be sent back to Europe. They would be given opportunity to share in the profits and thus increase their fortunes. The local management of such trading posts was to be in the hands of a council chosen by the London promoters who were to operate under instruction from London.

When this plan was put into operation in 1607 in Virginia, two truths shortly became all too apparent. The first was that the three thousand miles of the Atlantic Ocean made the colony too distant for efficient management from London. It took at least four, and more often six, months for an exchange of correspondence, and in that time conditions usually had changed and the directives were outdated on arrival. The second truth was the very plain one that a committee—particularly one operating in a new venture, in a sickly climate, with debilitated and discouraged men—is not an effective governing body.

The result was first of all no profits for the promoters and secondly disputes in London over methods of operation. After seventeen years of experimentation and dispute between Crown and promoters, a pattern of political operation was achieved. The company soon abandoned the committee form of government, and after trying a manager or governor in whom was vested wide powers, they decided on an epoch-making experiment. Partly as an advertising inducement, they set up a miniature parliament in Virginia, a House of Burgesses. Each town or hundred or plantation was authorized to send two burgesses to the capital to levy taxes and make laws in cooperation with the Company's governor and his council. Five years later the political policies of the leaders of the company brought them afoul of King James I, with the result that the Crown took legal action to destroy the company and assume control of the colony. Thereafter the King appointed its governor. Thus a definite pattern had been achieved.

The government of royal governor, his council and the House of Burgesses quite apparently reflected the government of King, Lords and Commons in miniature. Although the instructions from England prescribed that the colonists "imitate and follow the policy of the form of government, laws, customs and manner of tryal" used at home, it seems apparent that procedure was much more liberal. It appears that all male inhabitants, including even indentured servants, of seventeen years or above could vote. The suffrage was not confined to forty-shilling freeholders. The voting took place in the "towns, boroughs and hundreds" and was viva voce or by show of hands. Governors or chiefs of particular plantations probably had a good deal to say as to who should go to the Assembly from the bailiwicks. The government was in general carried on by men of social standing. The servant class was not rising to any political heights. Thus there was the same combination of class influence and democracy that was then current in England.

The second colonial experiment was a radically different one. A small congregation of Separatists sent a part of their number to America under peculiar circumstances. London capitalists were interested in finding steady, earnest, reliable people to undertake the difficult task of setting up wilderness posts. A number of Separatists had refused compliance with Elizabethan laws for religious conformity and had fled to Holland. They were, however, patriotic Englishmen who wished for a spot in the homeland where they would be free to worship as they pleased. After much negotiation some of them agreed to go to America to operate a concession for the London promoters. As there were far too few of them, others who were not of their religious persuasion were enlisted, and all set sail eventually in the famous *Mayflower*. The concession was to be located on land belonging to the London Company and to be part of "Operation Virginia."

The leaders of this venture were the pastor and elders of a congregation, and their concept of political ordering was that of a community of believers managing their affairs in congregational meeting. At first they seemed to think that their plans needed no formulation and that all would be simple. Two complications arose, however. First, the colonists were blown off their course and arrived at a part of America not within the bounds of the London Company. Second, the leaders realized that those among them who were not of their religious persuasion were not going to think as they did about many things. Therefore, before they landed they came to the conclusion that they must formulate a document of political agreement.

This Mayflower Compact, signed by all responsible adults, was an agreement to form a "body politic" in which all would abide by the common will. This "body politic," congregational assembly, town meeting, or what you will, then chose annually a governor and later a council or board of assistants. All could vote who were admitted as freemen, and substantial, steady men— probably mostly church members—were so admitted. When Plymouth Colony, as it was called, grew so large that various other towns were established, the old congregational meeting with a ruling council of elders was succeeded by a lawmaking body consisting of representatives from the towns, who chose the governor and assistants and made the laws. Thus there was an executive and what amounted to a bicameral legislature, again somewhat reminiscent of King, Lords and Commons.

The third experiment was, like the second, primarily religious in origin but more complicated in conception and operation. A group of substantial Puritans, feeling the hostility of the Anglican hierarchy and the pinch of a rising cost of living, began to contemplate a move that would provide religious and social independence and greater economic resources. They therefore formed a chartered company as for business enterprise but really designed to create a Puritan society where those of that mind might construct a Holy Commonwealth. The Puritan stockholders of this corporation, the Massachusetts Bay Company, decided to migrate in a body, carrying their charter with them. There would be no London managers as in the case of the Virginia Company. In 1630 they completed these plans, and more than a thousand recruits crossed the sea with them.

At first the stockholders through their general court or stockholders' meeting planned to place the government in the hands of a so-called governor and board of assistants. However, the stockholders were so few in number and the Massachusetts Bay colonists so numerous that it soon became apparent that so small a group could not maintain control. Freemen were therefore presently admitted, but only church members were usually so privileged. They attended the general courts and participated both in the election of officers and in the making of law. As the number of towns increased, however, it became increasingly difficult for the freemen to come to the general courts; the towns therefore demanded a representative system, which was granted. Thereafter representatives of the towns made up the lower house of the general court, with the governor and board of assistants functioning as in Plymouth. Gone was the chartered-company government of stockholders, gone in part was the government of the elders. In its place was the ever more familiar pattern of executive and bicameral legislature.

At the same time yet another type of colonial experiment was in the making. One of the Calvert family, who had become a Catholic, had been interested in colonial projects for some twenty years without much success, financial or otherwise. Now he took advantage of a favorable political relationship with King Charles I to try again. This time his objective was to combine a business project with an effort to make a refuge for his Catholic co-religionists, who had no legal existence in England and were therefore distinctly at a disadvantage. He secured from the King a charter, not for a company as had the London Company promoters, but as an individual grant to himself.

In other words, Calvert—or Lord Baltimore, as he was about to be styled—wanted to establish feudalism in America. The charter he received was in fact largely a feudal document, giving him the right to establish a domain like that of the Bishop of Durham in northern

England, on the Scottish border, in which he was to have power to legislate with the advice of the local landholders. He proceeded to rule his "barony" by appointing a governor who was to call together the citizens and propose a set of laws to them for their assent. But America was not hospitable to feudalism. The assembled freemen were not interested in merely listening to proposals of the proprietor and, after giving their assent, going home. They were more positive in their attitudes and wanted the right to initiate legislation in the Maryland legislature as well as to approve prepared programs. On the insistence of the inhabitants, therefore, feudalism gave way to the lawmaking of a characteristic legislative body. A representative lower house of assembly chosen by the landholders joined the governor and his council in the rule of the colony.

This same process was repeated again several times. During the Restoration proprietary grants were given to the Duke of York and certain supporters of the Stuart fortunes. New York went to the Duke after its capture by Colonel Richard Nichols. New Jersey became the property of Sir George Carteret and Lord Berkeley. Carolina was granted first to several proprietors close to Charles II. Pennsylvania was a payment to William Penn and his heirs, creditors of the Crown. Georgia was a grant to the philanthropist Oglethorpe, to permit him to attempt an experiment at rehabilitating social unfortunates.

The types of government these proprietors proposed showed the trend. While the Duke of York attempted to manage the affairs of the Dutch inhabitants of his new colony without a legislature, none of the other proprietors had similar hardihood. They adopted the now prevailing pattern, and their appointed governors with their councils worked with the popularly elected houses in making laws. True, the Carolina proprietors essayed a paper feudalism with ranks and conditions of men, and Penn and Oglethorpe sought to be benevolently paternal, but not for long. Governor and legislature, like King and Commons, was the English formula strong enough to command almost a uniformity.

In organizing town and borough government, county and local units, British experience was again the guide. To be sure, there was little of the close corporation oligarchy characteristic of English municipal government in the colonial cities, towns and boroughs; no one in that free environment would accept such distinctions. But the cities were chartered, and freemen were admitted who elected those who ruled over them. Nor was it forgotten that the ancient custom of British burgesses was to speak their minds freely and to value highly the "liberties" contained in their charters. In New England town government was closely patterned after the congregational meeting and its political customs. The town meeting in which all citizens came together and deliberated in their tax levying and ordinance making became a great institution. In several colonies the British county with its board of justices, sheriff and coroner was taken over, and for lesser units the parish ruled by its vestry was adopted. Here the justices were presumably chosen by the governor, but in effect they formed self-perpetuating boards, and the parish vestries enjoyed like privileges of self-perpetuation. These were institutions more of the aristocratic southern colonies. But throughout the variety the pattern was British.

By 1732 thirteen of the numerous English-American colonial projects had in a measure stabilized themselves along the Atlantic seaboard. These colonies were to have an experience different from others in Canada and the Caribbean. The century and a half of colonization had involved the drafting of a continuous series of documents ranging from Raleigh's charter of 1584 to Oglethorpe's grant in 1732. Not one of these projects lacked some form of written basis. Monarchs, ministers of the Crown, merchants, churchmen and proprietors had produced brainchildren that were of record in various London offices and other English muniment rooms; but some of them had been composed on the American side of the Atlantic. The colonists early undertook to supply their own basic documents, and in a much more systematic way than their political directives had been produced in England.

The Pilgrims started the American process of compact writing on shipboard off the "stern and rockbound" coast in 1620, but not until a year after Virginia had begun statute writing. Then the Virginia House of Burgesses had put in operation the formal process of lawmaking, amidst such faint counterparts of the pomp and circumstance of the English Parliament as sickly Jamestown could supply. Settlements in Connecticut, Rhode Island, New Hampshire, Maine, New Jersey and New York drew up compacts for their own ordering, and all thirteen colonies and some that eventually were consolidated with them devised their own lawmaking bodies. There were at least two score of these charters and covenants supplied to or created by the colonies, and the volumes of session laws passed by their legislatures numbered in the hundreds. A steady stream of statutes began in 1619 and has never ceased. Blueprints for the American Leviathan were a constant concern of the industrious American draftsmen.

These thirteen colonies found themselves in a position so multifariously unique as to spur them on to the careful composition of other documents defining political responsibility. The distances that separated them from Europe in space and time, and their tradition of political behavior, insured that large measure of self-government that required the documents above described.

Leviathan as conceived in England was largely a creature of the imagination, one deemed to exist without exact specifications, never visible in space, a spiritual rather than a material entity. It could be discovered only by living in the realm and absorbing a mass of custom, such as the common law, parliamentary enactments and judicial decisions like those Lord Coke had brought together in his *Institutes*. But nowhere was it officially visible. The English rejoiced in their *unwritten* constitution.

Such was never to be the colonial or the American pattern. The Americans' was to be a government of record; they would draft blueprints and prepare exact specifications for their political enterprises. When adventuring across a stormy sea and risking their fortunes in a frowning wilderness beset by hostile aborigines, the dauntless pioneers wanted something more definite to go by than somebody's memory of the good customs of the far-away homeland. Hence all the writing and, after the delayed arrival of presses, the printing.

But this situation produced a second series of problems more difficult to understand and to define, problems that placed an even greater premium upon the work of the scriveners and upon the brains of those who composed the thoughts to be indited. The colonies had undertaken self-government within the great empire, far removed from its capital. This meant that they had a government divided in location and in function. They were answerable both to the Crown and to themselves. The colonists must pay heed to British statute law as well as to their own ordinances. They must acknowledge the functions of two sets of officials —those commissioned by King or proprietor and those chosen by themselves. They might have to pay two levies of taxation. They were subjects of the Crown and of a great empire, as well as self-reliant colonials. Their independent operation was always subtly or obviously limited by the British Empire serving as surrogate. The "presence" was never absent from the subject whether in peril on the stormy sea, lost in a giant forest or carrying on the simple life of a colonial.[2]

This divided colonial personality, at one and the same time a "subject" and a "sovereign" as well as an "empire builder," produced difficulties of definition. And whenever difficulties of definition beset the colonials, there was call for the pen. The individual colonies on occasion obviously recognized the need for relationship with something greater than any one of them. Most of the time this was for allegiance to the Empire. The time came, however, when they felt themselves confronted by the need of a different surrogate, and then more complex rationalization was required. The colonists were three thousand miles away from the homeland, and they were beset by foes, first by the savage aborigines indigenous to America and soon by colonial venturers of the French and Spanish powers. In the face of such peril, they had to create a new and greater strength. Their forces had to be united to invoke a surrogate other than the Empire—one of their own making.

As early as 1643, in the midst of Indian warfare, four of the colonies created a New England Confederation. In 1690, when in the midst of foreign war they faced the French and their savage allies, they held an intercolonial Congress to plan joint effort to insure their safety. In the next century, in the face of similar peril, they planned a new order in 1754 at Albany, where their representatives drafted an elaborate Plan of Union that, had it been accepted, would have brought into being an American Dominion with a Crown-appointed Governor-General and an Intercolonial Parliament. The colonials were never at a loss when blueprints were needed. This was even more obvious when the events and circumstances consequent to the so-called

Peace of Paris in 1763 indicated that there was a rift in the British Empire that was to produce a new Leviathan constructed along novel lines according to new specifications.

During the confused years of the world-wide war which was characteristic of the last half of the eighteenth century, the British colonies on the Atlantic seaboard, oft in danger and poorly protected by the Crown, found themselves more and more frequently required to assume greater responsibilities for self-government and self-protection. They learned more self-reliance and at the same time gained increased self-confidence and increased contempt for the incapacity of the Mother Country. These twin lessons spelled the inevitability of greater independence and a major readjustment of the great British Leviathan.

Convenient precedents were furnished by the English revolutions that characterized political developments during the seventeenth century. A century and a half of colonial experience supplied a liberal quantity of knowledge. When in the 1760's, therefore, word began to arrive in America that the war-worn Empire was seeking to recoup its fortunes and pay its debts by requiring greater financial contributions from the colonies and by otherwise restricting certain fields of colonial economic and political enterprise, the colonies were ready to prepare a new stream of documentation based on English ideas and American experience.

In one unhappy period there arrived news of added customs levies, of the curtailment of cherished real-estate speculations that the colonists had hoped would ease their load of debt, of the dispatch of larger garrisons, ostensibly to protect the colonies from the Indians in recently acquired Canada, and worse still, of the proposed imposition of an internal tax, in the form of stamp duties. It was then that the colonists reached for their pens. Committees of colonial legis-

latures and associations of colonial merchants drafted
resolutions and petitions to Parliament and wrote instructions to their London agents to present them.
Strange doctrine flowed from their quills: the British
Constitution was being violated; Englishmen could only
be taxed by their elected representatives; the Stamp
Tax was a direct tax levied on the colonials without
their consent; such taxes could only be imposed by
colonial legislatures; taxation without representation
was unconstitutional—it was tyranny. In May, 1765,
Patrick Henry gave most notable expression to this doctrine in the Virginia legislature.

Another drafter of blueprints, James Otis, proposed
in the Massachusetts Legislature that the colonists be
invited to send delegates to an intercolonial Congress to
meet in New York in October. In due course delegates from nine colonies came. In the petition they
drew up are found certain words indicative of their
temper. "The increase, prosperity, and happiness of
these colonies depend on the full and free enjoyments
of their rights and liberties." The language of Locke
and the Glorious Revolution of 1688 supplied most
convenient vocabulary.

For nearly ten years the quills continued to scratch.
The British government retreated from one position
to another, but at each change there was still a tax, so
there were more resolutions, more petitions and firmer
steps marching nearer independence. The colonists no
longer accepted a distinction between the customs duties that they acknowledged to be necessary to regulate
imperial commerce, even if they would not pay them,
and internal taxes that, as they were imposed without
the consent of the taxed, they held to be tyranny. Then
came the open defiance. The tea they were presumed
to buy taxed was thrown into Boston Harbor. Smug-
gling, the Boston Massacre, this wanton destruction of
property and continued disobedience brought an end

to the Ministry's patience. A series of "intolerable" acts was passed, designed to punish the colonies, particularly Massachusetts, by crippling them in fortune and curtailing their "liberties."

The loose cooperation that had been exemplified by the Stamp Act Congress and the document it produced served as a precedent. When news of the events climaxing in the Boston Tea Party and the resulting Intolerable Acts, particularly the closing of the Port of Boston, spread up and down the seaboard, the writers again turned to ink and parchment. The so-called First Continental Congress came together in Philadelphia in September, 1774, and proposed a petition to the Crown.

And the colonists went further. On motion of Richard Henry Lee of Virginia it was agreed to break off trade with England until the grievances were redressed. A committee was appointed to draft Articles of Association for this purpose. On a fateful October day these delegates agreed upon the first political organization and regulation for what they called "our country." They did "firmly agree and associate" not to import from Great Britain until the Intolerable Acts were repealed. A committee was to "be chosen in every county, city, and town, by those who are qualified to vote for representatives in the legislature" to "observe the conduct of all persons" and to report to the public any violations of this association through the press.

This was the first sketch of the American Leviathan. A group of delegates from the several colonies made regulations and prescribed mechanisms, democratic in concept, to operate them. These drawings were a composite of a variety of sketches suggested by the colonial legislatures and their committees on correspondence. As yet the pen was mightier than the sword.

When the British government retaliated by increasing the garrisons in the colonies, the clash of arms took place in the spring at Lexington and Concord, and a Second Congress returned to Philadelphia. The events of the winter of 1775-1776—particularly the organization of a Continental Army under George Washington, the creation of a navy, the siege of the King's garrison in Boston and the projected establishment of diplomatic relations in Europe with Britain's enemies—all spelled the destruction of the imperial tie. Richard Henry Lee made a motion that independence should be declared, and a committee headed by Thomas Jefferson, likewise of Virginia, was appointed to draft the necessary document. On July 4, 1776, a Declaration of Independence was perfected and adopted.

But though independence had been declared, the problem of the surrogate remained. The colonies, though calling themselves free and independent states, had seemingly no thought of standing each alone. They wished some substitute, some overseer in place of the Empire. They seemingly had grasped that they were something other than thirteen states, that together they created something greater than themselves, some substitute for the Empire, which they must now needs define. So, in true American fashion, the Congress appointed a committee to draft a document. This companion group to the Declaration Committee, headed by John Dickinson, wrote The Articles of Confederation. Charged with drawing a blueprint for the new United States of America, they prepared the form of a confederation or league of states that, though independent, wished to appear in a new guise.[3]

The unity of these rebellious states was far from perfect, and nearly the entire five years of the Revolutionary War were to elapse before these Articles received the unanimous approval required to put them into operation. Not until March 1, 1781, when the long war was almost won, were they proclaimed as "Articles of Confederation and perpetual Union between" the thirteen states, drafted "in the Second Year of the Independence of America" under the name and the "stile" of "The United States of America." The lawmakers were careful to stipulate that "Each State retains its sovereignty, freedom and independence, and every Power, Jurisdiction and right, which is not by this confederation expressly delegated to the United States, in Congress assembled." This was to be the pattern of the new Leviathan.

The decision for independence brought a reminder of the fact that government was still to be conducted on two levels. Not only had the colonies collectively declared themselves "free and independent" states and were in the process of contriving "Articles of Confederation," but each was engaged in creating a basic constitution for its own individual operation. Each of the thirteen save two were creating for themselves a fundamental code. The two self-governing colonies, Connecticut and Rhode Island, needed merely to change the headings of their liberal English charters, but the other eleven wrote anew. They were busy with precedents drawn from British custom, colonial experience and the wisdom of John Locke. They all came up with practically the same pattern—a bicameral legislature, a governor and a judiciary—in a fashion reminiscent of King, Lords and Commons. Pennsylvania and Georgia, however, provided only one house for the legislature, and the former essayed to get along without a governor. Some of the new states were not satisfied with their work, however, and it very soon became obvious that a few of them were engaging in revision. Almost immediately South Carolina adopted a second instrument, and within a decade of the peace Georgia, Pennsylvania, Delaware and New Hampshire were likewise again at work. South Carolina and New Hampshire were also shortly thereafter to essay a third instrument.

The larger Leviathan likewise was to be subject to further adjustment. The Articles of Confederation provided for a league of states without central power, and they failed to do what those desired who craved power and respect for the new republic. Efforts to amend the Articles piecemeal failed, and an effort was therefore made in 1786 to assemble a convention that would try a united effort. This meeting was inadequately attended, and it was not until 1787 that enough men of prominence and substance in the various states were sufficiently concerned to secure the attendance of a representative group from all the colonies but one. For all of one summer these men met in Philadelphia, charged with drafting a series of amendments designed to give the government sufficient power under the Articles to make it work.

This convention concluded early in its deliberations that what the new republic needed was more than amendments—it needed a new system. These men thereupon drew up a complete new set of specifications and decreed that it would go into operation if nine states agreed. In other words, the states were invited to secede from the Confederation. The result was the Constitution of the United States, which was sent to the states in September, 1787, and eventually duly ratified by all of them.

In this document appears once more the English pattern of King, Lords and Commons in the President, Senate and House; but government is so well structured, so precise in its system of checks and balances among the equal and coordinate branches—legislative, executive and judicial—that it is apparent that there has been some French influence. At least some of the founding fathers had read Montesquieu. They had grasped the French love of theory, of codes inherited from the Roman law, just as the Normans had. After all, as Lord Macmillan cogently pointed out, there are

"Two Ways of Thinking," and while Leviathan was largely English in its formless copying of precedent, nevertheless it had its French strain, and one evidence is the greater precision of its blueprints.

The principle of the Articles of Confederation had been a very sparing delegation of power by the sovereign states to a Congress of their delegates, in which the states large and small were equal in power. The principle of the Constitution was an elaborate and complicated division of newly created power. A system of checks and balances was designed to prevent the concentration of power in any one section of the mechanism. There were to be three equal and coordinate instruments of government in the Union, and the power to govern was to be shared with the states. The Union was to be the new surrogate replacing the Empire. Instead of continuing the loose league of independent republics or creating an all-powerful centralized national government, the daring innovators created a novelty in political construction, a federal system embracing thirteen units, including four million people, and extending over a region that had a meteorological variety marked by such contrasts as Maine winters and Georgia summers. This convention was unique, unprecedented.

But this Leviathan was to have a greater claim to unique conceptualization. American political leadership that summer realized that the vastness of the domain of the new republic and the sparseness of its population demanded an additional instrument of peculiarly ingenious construction. While the Constitutional Convention was laboring in Philadelphia, the Continental Congress in New York was likewise working on a document of great significance. In the Northwest Ordinance of 1787 they were inventing a mechanism that would enable the Americans to make constant adjustments for growth in an unprecedented manner. States and empires had been reshaped before, but usually by a combination of conquest and diplomacy, international politics and matrimony, in all of which the people involved had had no say. But this new sovereignty was to be elastic in a novel fashion. Its citizens could create new states and their representatives fit them into the structure, giving each new unit a share of power equal to that of each of the several older states. The members of the Congress thus recognized and implemented a process that had been in some sort of operation since the days of the first seaboard colonies.

The possibility of new communities thrown off by older ones on the seaboard appeared early. A Massachusetts group had gone over into the Connecticut Valley as early as 1636. A hundred years later Virginia had organized a county beyond the mountains, and some of her citizens formed a real-estate company to operate in the Ohio Valley. In 1754 the Albany Congress included in its abortive plan a mechanism for organizing new self-governing units to be fitted into the colonial dominion that the conferees envisaged. During the adventurous years of the French and Indian Wars, the colonists had begun to be increasingly conscious of the great region beyond the mountains—conscious of its dangers and its opportunities. It could be a place for real-estate speculation and for home building.

As soon as the Peace of Paris was consummated in 1763, various attempts had been made to clear away Indian claims and open these lands to adventurous settlers and speculators. As early as 1768 migrants, mostly from Virginia, had penetrated the Upper Holston Valley and settled on the banks of Watauga Creek in the belief that it was part of the Old Dominion. Since then, surveyors, Indian agents and treaty negotiators had been busy and had determined that the Wataugans were not in Virginia. On a forgotten day in 1772, therefore, a group of arms-bearing men in this region assembled at Watauga. Wanting government and the means of protection, these self-reliant woodsmen were going to supply both. They drafted and signed an agreement to form an independent self-governing Association, prescribing the laws of Virginia for their governance and appointing a ruling executive committee of five. The identity of these pioneers and the document itself, as well as its date, are lost to us, but this Watauga Association indicated the beginning in what was to become Tennessee of a process that had to be recognized by the new surrogate.

This act of the Watauga settlers began a new chapter in the do-it-yourself capacity of Americans for tinkering with the new Leviathan.[4] These inventors were not working on the grand scale of intercolonial cooperation in nation making; they were designing new local units. Had the creation of new documents been only on the continental level, the republic *in posse* would have been a much different body politic than the government that did emerge. Then and ever after it was always to be a two-level contrivance. Rather than a unitary empire stretching endlessly westward and governed from the east, it was to be a system constantly expanding. New units were to be repeatedly in the making as population went westward. In each there was to be local concern with writing specifications, and such designing had to be accepted and generally authorized and directed from the capital of the new United States. At first the process was as informal and unheralded as the almost mythical act of the Wataugans. But later such action began to develop into an accepted program. Adventurous men on the borders of settlement worked in various frontier regions.

On the far northern frontier was an area in dispute between New Hampshire and New York. It had been in the process of settlement for fifty years in the eighteenth century, but as the Revolutionary conflict of arms began, these distant settlers were conscious of their situation on the Canadian border and their proximity to British military forces on the natural invasion route down Lake Champlain and the Hudson. They took a leaf out of Philadelphia's enlarging book and met in a convention at Windsor on January 15-17, 1777, when they declared themselves independent of New York and New Hampshire as well as of Great Britain, under the name and style of Vermont. Congress refused to accept them; the New Yorkers' objection to this loss of what was felt to be theirs was probably controlling. But nothing daunted, a second convention assembled at Windsor, and went to work on a constitution somewhat resembling that of Pennsylvania, which was adopted on July 8, 1777. The Green Mountain boys under the leadership of the Allen brothers were prepared to go it alone, and they did. On August 16 Colonel John Stark and the Vermont militia performed valiantly at the Battle of Bennington, where Burgoyne's invading forces received their first check.

The process started by the Wataugans in Tennessee had been continued beyond the mountains. Settlements sprang up on the Kentucky River, where Harrod's Town and Boonesboro were seats of rival enterprise. At the latter place in May, 1775, scarcely a month after Lexington, settlers attempted to found the state of Transylvania and adopted nine laws for their governance. But the Virginia legislature, alerted by the men at Harrod's Town, stepped in and organized the region as a county—the County of Kentucky. This action, however, did not permanently stop the tide of interest in statehood. As soon as Revolutionary battles were over, Kentucky turned again to planning her future and petitioned Congress for admission as a state. Three times Virginia passed laws giving her consent to the independence of her former giant county, but the Kentuckians were in difficulties among themselves. Only after holding ten conventions could they agree on a blueprint, and they did not finish it until April, 1792. This document included Pennsylvania's Bill of Rights and other features of the constitutional pattern that had been developing in the fundamental laws of the revolutionary states.

Similar activity was resumed in the Tennessee region, where the spirit of Watauga still flourished. When Virginia denied the Transylvanians a field of operation in Kentucky, they migrated to James Robertson's settlement at what was to be Nashville. There they adopted a Cumberland Compact reminiscent of the Nine Laws of Boonesboro. North Carolina was reluctant to let these people go and, after consenting once, changed her mind and refused. But the frontiersmen would not be denied. The settlers in the Watauga region persisted, and two conventions produced a constitution and the independent "State of Franklin" in 1784-1785. This move was premature, for North Carolina resisted, local leadership divided and the move collapsed. Not until 1789 was North Carolina ready to part finally with her transmontane wards.

The Revolution in the meantime had done its part in stirring interest in the frontier. Its military strategy had finally insured the United States possession of the region between the mountains and the Mississippi, even though the British proved reluctant to surrender some of the posts. More land companies were formed, particularly as veterans saw in the vast expanse possible compensation for the danger, hardship and loss of fortune that they had experienced in their patriotic effort. Land grants were to be the equivalent of the modern pension and bonus.

The growing pressure of land speculators, veterans and other settlers, together with the desire of the poverty-stricken Congress of the Confederation to raise revenue, produced the decisions embodied in congressional ordinances. These laws accepted the principle of constant growth and the necessity of adjustment thereto. Congressmen in some sense realized what was going on in the Watauga region, in the Green Mountains, in the Blue Grass area and in the valley of the Cumberland. The lawmakers could have been satisfied to open these areas to settlements and to govern them from New York as ancient empires had ruled their satrapies. But these men were willing to accept the principle of continuous expansion of self-government and to make the federal system open-ended. Whenever enough people went out beyond the bounds of the original thirteen states, they might set up for themselves and at length be admitted as states equal to the elder bodies. The American Leviathan could be constantly adjusted so that it might cope efficiently with new conditions.

Under the congressional enactments, therefore, there was to be a continuing process of organizing, not colonies to be ruled by the newly constituted federation of thirteen states, but communities that would create self-government and eventually enter the Union as states on an equality with the original units. This procedure meant that there would be a constant reviewing of the process of making self-governing communities and a frequently recurring admission of new units that perforce readjusted the combinations operating the existing system.

This territorial process was spelled out in two ordinances of the Congress of the Confederation—the Land Ordinance of 1785 and the Northwest Ordinance of 1787. The first provided for a gigantic rectangular survey of all land north of the Ohio and west of Pennsylvania and prescribed that this vast territory be sold off in sections, each one mile square regardless of terrain or location. The second ordinance directed that this area should be organized eventually in as many as five states, but in the meantime as territories. A preliminary plan drafted by Jefferson in 1784 would have allowed the settlers to begin governing themselves immediately, but the real-estate and veterans' organizations that finally secured the legislation of 1787 were more interested in the security of land titles and the laws necessary to insure them. Provision was therefore made that the first governors, secretaries and judges be appointed by Congress and given authority to make the laws and execute them until at least five thousand people had settled under their jurisdiction. Thereafter the inhabitants would have territorial legislatures of their own choice. The new federal Congress re-enacted this law in 1789.

Implementing this program, the surveyors began their work, and their first plans were ready by the time the Northwest Ordinance was completed. Congress then proceeded to sell six and a half million acres to a veterans' group, the Ohio Company, and to a speculator, John Cleves Symmes. On April 7, 1788, General Rufus Putnam directed the settlement of the Ohio Company's first contingent near Fort Harmar, at what was to be the city of Marietta, Ohio. A governor was shortly after appointed by Congress, and he and the secretary and judges undertook to put the Northwest Ordinance into operation. After a law was passed in 1790 applying the principles of that ordinance to the region south of the Ohio, President Washington appointed the officials who were to organize the Watauga and Nashville settlers into a territory that was to become the state of Tennessee. The new Congress admitted three states in its first sessions—Vermont (1791), Kentucky (1792) and Tennessee (1796).

The territorial system as it expanded was going to make use of the eighteenth-century enterprise of the French and Spanish in the Great Valley. Their settlements became the nuclei for additional territories. The French had established posts at Vincennes and at Kas-

kaskia, Cahokia and Peoria. After the exploits of George Rogers Clark during the Revolution had helped to bring these into the new United States, they were used as organization points for the beginnings of Indiana and Illinois territories, which were created in 1800 and 1809. The British post of Detroit, which the mother country held on to until the Jay Treaty in 1795, became the outpost from which Michigan Territory was set off a decade later. French and Spanish posts along the lower Mississippi and the Gulf were used as nuclei for Mississippi Territory set off in 1798. The procedure laid down in the Laws of 1789 and 1790 was in operation from the Great Lakes to the Gulf.

Those who had devised the methods for making the American Leviathan operate had indeed proved themselves most ingenious when they conceived of the organization of these territories. The concept of creating and operating frontier communities—"territories"—as a preparatory step toward their later admission as states was one of the most inspired inventions of the American political genius. It was to be one of the important instruments that maintained experimentation in developing the capacity for self-government in the midst of the nation's spectacular expansion in wealth and power. It gave elasticity to an organism that might otherwise have become rigid.

The territorial process did much to make American democracy a unique form of social control, a different type of self-government. None other has to like degree been conditioned by such a quality of frequent self-renewal as this territorial process represents. From the sixteenth century on there has been a constant creation of new self-governing units within the present bounds of the United States, and these were in one way or another ultimately integrated into the federal Union. This process of constant experiment, adjustment and re-arrangement within the framework of democratic procedure was to represent a recurring opportunity for freshening and renewal that was to do much to keep the republic flexible and vital. American democracy had its origin and its experimental grounds in the local units, colonies, territories and states. Thirty-one of the eventual fifty states were once territories, so that the state patterns were in this high proportion of instances formed in this stage. The federal government was in reality to contribute little to the development of democratic behavior patterns. These were designed in the scattered communities, not in Washington. The prospect of constant additions to the number of states meant something that few realized. Any power aggregate which might be in operation at any given time might have to be altered as new units were admitted to a share in the federal government. But what the implications of this constant readjustment might be none grasped at the time of the creation of the system. They began to be apparent when the area of the nation was suddenly enlarged. The territories were the seed beds of American self-government, but signs appeared early that they might likewise be the germinating ground for poisonous plants of disunion.

CHAPTER FOUR

OPERATIONAL ADJUSTMENTS

THE editor of the Boston *Palladium* was an enterprising journalist who was careful to cover the incoming sailing ships bringing "the latest" from Europe. On June 28, 1803, a packet docked at its accustomed wharf and unloaded mail from Havre. The letters bore the startling news that the United States had doubled its size. The *Palladium*'s pressman immediately set it up, and that day Bostonians knew that on April 30 United States envoys had signed a treaty purchasing from Napoleon the whole of Louisiana, the great empire extending from the Mississippi to the Rockies. Two days later, the news was in Washington on the desks of Jefferson and Madison.[1]

These astonishing tidings placed Jefferson in a dilemma. He had been eager to purchase land from Napoleon, but he had wanted only the city of New Orleans and a relatively small area controlling the mouth of the Mississippi. But now, working quite outside the limit of their instructions, his ministers had bought an imperial domain. To make it more embarrassing, Jefferson believed in strict construction of the Constitution, and nowhere in that blueprint could he find any specific warrant for such a gigantic real-estate transaction. Despite the dilemma, Jefferson felt the magnitude of the opportunity justified the sacrifice of consistency and scruples about strict construction. He recommended to his party leaders that they accept the *fait accompli,* and Congress agreed. As Henry Adams described it: "By an act of sovereignty as despotic as the corresponding acts of France and Spain, Jefferson and his party had annexed to the Union a foreign people and a vast territory, which profoundly altered the relations of the United States and the character of their nationality." [2]

The purchase was a precocious as well as a despotic act on the part of a very young and rather insecure government. It displayed a daring and an imagination that were hardly to be expected of so immature a society. As Henry Adams indicated, it involved some procedures inconsistent with the ideal conduct of a republic. The acquisition was to raise many problems. It was to contribute to a situation that eventually almost destroyed the republic. It at once called for adjustments in the American Leviathan and stimulated the draftsmen to lay out ingenious devices.

Jefferson, famed author of the Declaration of Independence, had once again to sharpen his pen as he undertook the acceptance of so remarkable a responsibility. For some time the President had been concerned for the safety of the young republic; he believed that it was beset by danger. The Napoleonic wars in monarchic Europe threatened the commerce and the dignity as well as the safety of the United States. But Jefferson was not so fearful of this external danger as he was of one from within.

He was conscious of disturbing internal dissension. Certain elements in the sparse population between the Alleghenies and the Mississippi had been made anxious by the recent action of Spain whereby at Napoleon's behest the port of New Orleans had been closed to the export of their produce. This decree was a disastrous blow to their prosperity, for the port was their trade outlet. Furthermore, they were alarmed at Napoleon's determination to take over the rule of Louisiana. These calamities, actual and potential, seemed to be all-too-convincing evidence that the United States was too weak to protect its transmontane citizens. Would it not be better for them to set up for themselves or join their fortunes to those of Louisiana on terms favorable to them, which might be offered by Spain or France? The Spanish-French alliance would welcome a breakup of the American republic.

Such a development would have made Jefferson's concept of the nature of the United States much more difficult to realize. He wanted to make it a body politic dedicated to the rights of man and the doctrines of the physiocrats, which held the independent farmer to be the ideal citizen. He had been fighting the Hamiltonian ideas of government by the elite in alliance with entrepreneurs. He was counting on the region beyond the mountains as a great home of an agricultural population which would vote Democratic-Republican and contain and diminish the power of the Federalists. The disaffection in the Ohio Valley and in Tennessee, based upon the damage just done to their interests, endangered Jefferson's dream of a ruling Democratic-Republican Party. He had therefore to remove the causes of the fear and apprehension. This could only be done by securing New Orleans for the United States. It was needed to protect the purity of the American Democratic-Republican Utopia against the schemes of the Hamiltonian stockjobbers.

So motivated, Jefferson had drafted his original limited instructions. When to his surprise he received the astonishing report from his envoys, he realized that here was an even greater possibility than he had dreamed of. This vast expanse would be a great locus of communities dedicated to agricultural frugality and rural felicity. There could be organized many territories and states settled by independent and enterprising landowners that would be natural Republican constituencies untainted by the influence of the seaboard cities and their huckstering promoter leadership. Motivated in part by this concept of securing a great new reservoir of republican virtue to protect the purity of American democracy, Jefferson therefore prepared a message to Congress asking for the ratification of the great Purchase. His faith was to be justified, but only after some bitter experience, for the Purchase brought danger that would nearly destroy Leviathan.

The acquisition of this great region changed the pattern of the republic. The original bounds of the United States were natural, and neat in prospect—the Atlantic on the east, the Mississippi River on the west, the St. Lawrence Valley on the north and the Gulf of Mexico and Florida to the south. These bounds circumscribed nearly 900,000 square miles inhabited by some five million people. This population was reasonably homogeneous; its institutions and its language were predominantly English. This society had come to independence in an interesting epoch in the history of Western civilization, the Age of Reason. Inspired by its spirit, the architects of the new republic had worked out a rational system embodied in the Constitution of the United States and the Northwest Ordinance, which provided a tidy system for the orderly development of self-government over a wide area by an expanding population. The United States on the eve of the Purchase seemed a homogeneous, neat and rationally organized body politic.

The Purchase added to this congruous structure an area doubling its size but so sparsely populated that it was to present a constant field of opportunity for those who were enterprising or just restless. This great invitation to activity increased the tempo of American development and raised a series of immediate intense problems that would not have been generated had the original bounds of the United States been more static.

The first of these was one of assimilation. The population of the American republic prior to the Purchase was to a certain degree homogeneous, predominantly Anglo-

American. The Louisiana Purchase introduced into its ranks some 50,000 people of different origin. At New Orleans and St. Louis were small centers of population predominantly French in their cultural background though not unmarked by the fact that Spanish rulers had been governing them for almost forty years. These people had no tradition of self-government, no knowledge of Anglo-American law or pattern of cooperative administration in which the responsibility for governance rested to such a degree upon the citizens of each community. To make the problem more difficult, these new population groups were on the border, far distant from the seat of government in Washington, in a day when communication was most elemental and so slow as to be almost nonexistent.

The Louisiana communities had been ruled by a small bureaucracy under the paternalistic direction of Paris and Madrid. Now under the treaty, they were to become self-governing states in a federal republic as quickly as possible. The terms of the treaty, in fact, were explicit: "The inhabitants of the ceded territory shall be incorporated in the Union—and admitted as soon as possible, according to the principles of the Federal constitution, to the enjoyment of all rights, advantages and immunities of citizens of the United States, and in the meantime they shall be maintained and protected in the free enjoyment of their liberty, property, and the religion which they profess." To carry out this was to be a difficult problem, because the people and their natural leaders were alien and inexperienced and there was a language and cultural barrier. The task was fraught with danger.

The problem was solved without excessive confusion because of a series of fortunate circumstances. The adjustments for assimilation designed at Washington, though ill-contrived and ineptly set in motion, were not vigorously employed. The proposed alterations to

Leviathan were detailed in a statute that provided for the appointment of an imported governor and a council of the Louisiana elite to administer the region under instructions from Washington. This program was resented from the first because it did not seem to fulfill the promise of the treaty. Neither President Jefferson nor the governor he appointed, W. C. C. Claiborne, however, were in a position either to exercise any very direct control or to use any kind of force. In fact, their personalities, the distances involved and the lack of any means or inclination to use coercive measures in effect compelled the disaffected Creoles of New Orleans and St. Louis to work out the problem by learning methods of self-government. The Act of 1804, which gave the first political framework to that great region, was utterly inadequate. This act attached all the region north of the future state of Louisiana to the territory of Indiana and placed the authority in the hands of a governor in far-off Vincennes. Such an impossible situation the residents of St. Louis and the surrounding parishes met by public meetings, resolutions, delegations to Washington and a calm continuance in their own ways until Congress supplied a more adequate statute.

These new citizens were aided in this process by the growing number of people coming into the newly acquired territory who brought their knowledge and enterprise in the arts of republican operation. After some initial friction, which fortunately produced no very dangerous clashes, and despite some plotting to revolt and secede, the problem of assimilation was solved by compromise and accommodation and by the saving grace of the federal system, which permitted Louisiana, soon admitted as a state, to keep much of her French law, particularly that regulating property. Thus the Purchase enabled the new republic to demonstrate its capacity to assimilate variant cultures not schooled in its tradition and experience. It did so by the simple device of writing statutes and instructions that were deliberately vague and indefinite and then trusting to nature.

Much more difficult were the problems created by the constant movement of population into the new area. This land beyond the Mississippi was to invite new explorers to follow the original Lewis and Clark Expedition of 1804-1806 and to invite in turn the adventurous who made up a constant migration. Men and women were eager to go in and possess the land's wealth; they were just as eager to find homes for themselves there. They assumed naturally that they would make communities, establish customs and design and operate self-government. Furthermore, they were confident that their creations would be accepted into the federal family of states and that their representatives would take their part in the government at Washington, as outlined in Leviathan's basic blueprints.

This migration of population into the trans-Mississippi wilderness almost immediately demonstrated a dangerous political consequence. The Purchase covered the same latitude as the original republic, and the variety of societies that marked the older would therefore be likely to extend over the river and continue in the new region. The differences and rivalry developed by free and slave-labor communities would be projected into the new societies.

These variant and rival cultural groupings had already conditioned political contests for control of the policy making of the Federal government. They had been kept within safe bounds, however, because the original limits of the republic comprised degrees of latitude favoring northern and southern cultures about equally. The arrangements for political expansion of the American Leviathan, perfected in 1787 by the Constitution and later by the Laws of 1789 and 1790, had operated in such a way that an equal number of slave and free-labor states had been carved out of the original quadrilateral, and an equilibrium was maintained between them in the Senate, where each state was equal to every one of its fellows.

The Purchase and the migration of population into its broad expanses changed all this. As Jefferson had hoped, it invited people of rural proclivity to settle, but the part of the area first entered by migrants encouraged the creation of communities of the southern type. Thus as new states and territories began to appear, they seemed to indicate a southern predominance which would place the leaders of that section in a position of continued political control of the federal government. Jefferson's hopes for the dominance of the rural interest appeared to be all too completely realized.

The process of admitting new states from the Purchase was to be the occasion of bitter controversy that was to threaten the permanence of Leviathan. Napoleon had hoped that this great acquisition might interfere with and hinder the growth of the republic by "separating the interests of the eastern and the western states and perhaps [preparing] the moment when they would divide into two powers." [3] He had indeed been canny in his hopes, although weak in his geography. As soon as the first state sought admission, strife began. In fact, it began with the Purchase itself. In the congressional debate over accepting the empire, Uriah Tracy, a Federalist member from Connecticut, objected that "The relative strength which this admission gives to a Southern and Western interest is contradictory to the principles of our original Union." [4] When in 1811 Louisiana presented herself for admission as the first state from the Purchase, some New England representatives were so fearful of the implied danger to the northeastern states that Josiah Quincy of Massachusetts shocked the House by declaring, "If this bill passes, it is my deliberate opinion that it is virtually a dissolution of this Union; that it will free the States from their moral obligation; and, as it will be the right of all, so it will be the duty of some, definitely to prepare for a separation, amicably if they can, violently if they must." [5] These were ominous words, but few heeded them and the admission of Louisiana, consummated in 1812, was but slightly delayed.

After the end of the War of 1812 the tide of migration westward welled up and a sheaf of blueprints was drafted. Four new states—Indiana (1816), Mississippi (1817), Illinois (1818), and Alabama (1819)— were admitted from the regions operating under the acts of 1789 and 1790, two from each. By 1818 the Missouri territory, acknowledging St. Louis as its metropolis, was ready for statehood, and the land between Louisiana and Missouri was ripe for organization as the Territory of Arkansas. The tide of settlement thus seemed to be directed to the southwest and to an area where southern institutions and folkways could be readily transplanted. The old Federalist interest, of like mind with Tracy and Quincy, and younger enterprising representatives of northern constituencies could not look with equanimity on permanent southern dominance, and they decided to fight.

They chose as their weapon the evils of slavery and its inconsistency with the American ideas of liberty and equality, and they endeavored to secure a proviso that slavery should not exist in Missouri. As the population in the northern states was greater and their representation in the House larger, the opponents of the admission of Missouri as a slave state attempted to mobilize the superior northern representation in that body and insert this proviso. This move precipitated a legislative battle that roused a storm of temper and bitterness. A cleavage between northern and southern interests appeared to be strong enough to bring about the disunion that Quincy had prophesied, and it caused Jefferson to liken the angry debate to the terrifying sound of a firebell in the night. Surely the purchase of Louisiana had opened Pandora's box.

The northern majority in the House of Representatives, using the language of the Northwest Ordinance of 1787, twice voted to prohibit "slavery or involuntary servitude in the . . . State, otherwise than in the punishment of crimes, whereof the party shall have been duly convicted." Twice the Senate refused to accept this prohibition. At this time the old colony of Maine, long an unhappy noncontiguous county of Massachusetts, applied for admission to the Union as a state with Massachusetts' consent. This application gave the Senate the opportunity to arrange a harmonization of interests. Missouri and Maine would be admitted, one a slave and the other a free state, so the equal balance would be maintained in the Senate.

Subsequently an amendment to the act admitting Missouri, bearing the name of Senator Thomas of Illinois, was adopted by the Senate; it provided that in the balance of the Louisiana Purchase area lying north of thirty-six degrees and thirty minutes north latitude slavery would be "forever prohibited." Enough of the northern majority in the House was persuaded to accept this compromise to enable it to be enacted on March 6, 1820. The battle, however, was not over. The Missouri convention that undertook the task of framing the constitution inserted among its proposals an elaborate set of provisions guaranteeing slavery in the state. These included restrictions on the use made by slaveholders of their property and a declaration that it was the duty of the new state legislature to prevent free Negroes and mulattoes from settling in Missouri.

This elaboration aroused northern ire, and for a time it appeared that the state might be refused admission. Again the Senate, under the leadership of Senator Henry Clay of Kentucky, worked out a compromise, requiring Missouri to agree that no citizen should ever be excluded by Missouri from the enjoyment of any of the privileges and immunities to which he might be entitled under the Constitution of the United States. To this the Missouri legislature agreed, though it was pointed out that future legislatures could not be bound.

Still another compromise had to be agreed to before Missouri was admitted. During this period of legislation the presidential election of 1820 had been in process. The law enabling Missouri to frame her constitution had been enacted on March 6, 1820. The constitution had been approved in Missouri on July 19, and the new state proceeded to organize. It chose a governor and legislature and a group of electors for president. These gentlemen met in the capitol of Missouri at the same time as the other electors and reported their votes for James Monroe. However, when the electoral votes were counted in Congress in February, 1821, Missouri had not yet been admitted, and the whole issue was still in doubt because of the proposed constitutional provisions relating to slavery and to free Negroes. Clay therefore suggested another compromise; at the conclusion of the counting of the electoral vote it was announced that the result was the re-election of Monroe, both with and without Missouri's vote. Shortly after this, on March 2, 1821, a resolution was passed admitting Missouri if the new state would agree to the construction of its constitution required by Congress. These conditions were accepted in June, and Monroe proclaimed Missouri a state on August 10, 1821.

This heavily documented process, beginning with Missouri's petition for admission in 1818, had been elaborated over three years and two Congresses. It involved the ingenuity of a number of designers. Their work added to Leviathan the mechanism of compromise. By 1819 it had become all too clear that the federal Congress was a divided body, representing two interests that might on occasion conflict. The Senate was likely to be southern in sympathy, while the House represented the growing preponderance of population in the northern states. Unless there was to be conflict and stalemate, a new adjustment was required. The Missouri question had been the occasion that stimulated the invention of the mechanism of compromise negotiation between the two houses.

Fortunately the political genius of the United States had thus asserted itself in this statesmanlike season of document writing; it quieted the storm by providing a division of the Purchase area between slave-state and free-state settlers. Out of what remained of the original quadrilateral, still not admitted, and out of the Louisiana Purchase, a number of states might be carved, half of them slave and half free. This concept of equal division did not then seem so absurd as it does now, because much of the Louisiana expanse was not thought to be habitable. Midway within the next quarter of a century Arkansas and Michigan came in as another pair, slave and free. The Missouri Compromise of 1820 was the successful answer to the first problem of expansion presented by the Purchase. The capacity to compromise was established as a prime ingredient of American political behavior. More blueprints with the specifications for the newly adjusted Leviathan had been drafted, accepted and filed.[6]

The 1840's ushered in new complications. The restless eagerness of certain Americans to move and their continued desire to gain more territory were having a disconcerting effect. When Jefferson was looking toward Louisiana, he was also concerned over Spanish Florida on the southern border. During the period of worldwide war in the Napoleonic era, Florida—then maladministered by the Spanish—was a threat to the security of the neighboring communities in the United States. Here gangsters holed up; here was a refuge for fugitive slaves; forays were made across the border into Georgia,

Alabama and Mississippi. Jefferson had tried to buy Florida, and during Madison's day local interests organized secession movements that led to annexation of parts of West Florida in 1810 and 1813 when Louisiana, Mississippi and Alabama reached the Gulf coast. Spain realized that she would do better to sell Florida before she lost it altogether, and in 1819 the region changed hands. Congress made it a territory three years later. By the mid-1840's it was a candidate for statehood and began thinking of a constitution.[7]

In this same hectic period Americans had gone over into the Texas region of the Republic of Mexico, initially largely on Mexican invitation. Over the course of the years since 1821 the settlers' discontent had grown. The result was another resort to documents. A declaration of independence, a constitution, an independent government and a revolutionary armed rising made Texas an independent republic by 1836. The hope of many of the promoters of this revolution had been annexation to the United States. Such an arrangement, however, promised the addition of at least four potential slave states, and northern interests postponed annexation until 1845. Then eagerness to expand; ties of kindred; fear that the British might get undue influence over, if not possession of, this financially embarrassed republic; the political needs of an accidental President and his secretary of state, John Tyler and John C. Calhoun—all these combined to bring Texas into the Union. In 1845 the republic was admitted as a state, without any novitiate as a territory. Florida's requests were heeded in the same year. The admission of these two slave states was offset by the acceptance of two free states, Iowa (1846) and Wisconsin (1848), one from the Louisiana Purchase and the other from the old Northwest region. The remainder of the latter area was made the territory of Minnesota in 1849. These moves required five more basic documents, together with some auxiliary legislation.

But this was not the extent of territorial expansion in this unbelievable decade. There was the Pacific to be reached. Oregon, claimed in part by Great Britain, and California, belonging to Mexico, were irresistibly beckoning Americans. For a time it seemed as if the Republic would go to war with Great Britain and Mexico to "rectify" its boundaries. "Fifty-four-forty or fight" was a popular slogan. But even the fabulous James Polk had a canny reserve about two wars at once; there was an easier way to acquire Oregon.

Since the fur trading days of John Jacob Astor and his associates, adventurous Americans had now and again been in Oregon. After the War of 1812 there had been an agreement with England that the region should be open to joint occupation. During the years that followed, a trickle of the adventurous had crossed the great American desert in the wake of Lewis and Clark and gradually marked out the Oregon Trail. Marcus Whitman and other missionaries to the Indians did their part, and Willamette Valley settlements had been established as neighbors to certain Hudson Bay Company posts of the British in the Columbia Basin. In the 1840's American pioneers repeated the well-known drama. They held meetings, drew up blueprints to record their plans for self-government and set up for themselves. Polk—with his mind on Mexico, Texas and California and sniffing battle in the Southwest—decided to accept a British offer that the region be split between the two countries. Thus Oregon was secured and in 1848 made a territory.

In the meantime Mexico, resentful of the annexation of Texas, would make no settlement of the border situation with Polk and threatened hostilities. The American President sent troops to Texas to protect American interests and there inevitably occurred the incident that precipitated war. The seemingly rather formidable Mexican Army was defeated; after some difficult negotiations Mexico agreed to cede New Mexico, Utah and California, in part as war indemnity and in part as purchase. Immediately the problem of government arose.

The political situation was a complex one. New Mexico was almost unpopulated save in the Rio Grande Valley, where Spanish settlements had been in existence since the seventeenth century. The oldest such settlement was the capital at Santa Fé. California contained a series of Spanish mission stations established in the eighteenth century, together with several presidios or garrisons and a number of enormous haciendas, or cattle ranches, owned by a few great land owners who had benefited from a policy of generous land grants designed to induce settlement along El Camino Real. Finally, in the Rockies north of New Mexico, an American community had been recently established in the vicinity of the Great Salt Lake, hitherto known only to fur men and the few who had been marking out the overland California route branching off from the older Oregon trail. Into this latter, rather inhospitable, region had penetrated an American religious group, the Church of Jesus Christ and the Latter Day Saints, commonly known as the Mormons. This Church re-enacted the well-known drama begun by the Pilgrims at Plymouth. The Mormons had created a religion and a church; as they were never happy in the company of "Gentiles," they too decided to found a state. Theirs would truly be a wilderness Zion, and to establish it they went off into the desert, where in 1846 the likelihood of any neighbors save Indians appeared small. In the desert the Mormons created an elaborately and efficiently organized theocracy. However, they found themselves annexed to the United States by the treaty ending the Mexican War; and with the Gold Rush beginning in 1849, they further found themselves on the main highway to Golconda. Instead of working out their salvation in isolation, they were figuratively operating on the sidewalk of a well-traveled thoroughfare and with all the privacy that such a location implies. They were constrained to work out a concordat with Washington.

In settling these problems of racial, religious and political assimilation, the statesmanship of the republic was put to new tests. Again there was resort to documents. The need for blueprints became pressing because of additional discoveries of gold in California and the rush to the gold fields of would-be miners and those who would fatten on them. Such a horde could not be handled by the rudimentary alcalde system of local government as practiced under Mexican rule. After a brief period of military rule, the Americans in California, with some stimulus from Washington, chose a constitutional convention, drafted a fundamental law and applied for admission as a state, planning, like Texas, to skip the territorial phase. The Mormon Church did likewise and applied for admission as the state of Deseret. There were so few people in New Mexico that it did not seem to matter much how its inhabitants were governed, but some government nevertheless had to be provided; enterprising Americans began working on a territorial instrument.

The need for action was further complicated by the fact that the new state of Texas was claiming all of New Mexico west to the Rio Grande and was seemingly ready to march in and take it. Just at this time, in March, 1849, General Zachary Taylor, Old Rough and Ready, hero of the Mexican War, was inaugurated as President. He believed that he should protect New Mexico from Texas and urged California to prepare for statehood. At times he seemed willing to use troops in New Mexico, even to assume command of them himself. He also sent an agent to California to encourage her drafting of a blueprint.

It was obvious, of course, that the same difficulties

that had arisen over the Louisiana Purchase would now reappear. The North and South were on no better terms and continued to be jealous of any power advantage accruing to either. Evidently some document of adjustment must again be composed, particularly as the old compromise formula was exhausted; the policy of equal division in the Senate had come to its end. Among the possible new states—California, Oregon, Minnesota, Utah, and New Mexico—there was no immediate and only one potential slave state—New Mexico. The others appeared to be surely marked for freedom. The South therefore prepared to halt the advance of new states unless some concession could be achieved.

Southern leadership in Congress demanded acceptance of the principle that slaves might be held anywhere in the newly acquired possessions. This their opponents refused, and they had the votes in the House to make that refusal stick. On the other hand the South could probably prevent new states from being admitted at all. Was the process of community building to be brought to a halt? Would there be a division of the new republic over this question, a disruption by the secession of southern states, who were unwilling to be outnumbered in the federal system?

When in December, 1849, Congress met in regular session, the issue was there before it. The need for decision as to government for California, Utah and New Mexico must be met. No party, no section, was in control of Congress. President Taylor was a man of no political experience, surrounded by a weak cabinet. He was even at odds with his Vice-President, Millard Fillmore of New York. Taylor himself, Louisiana slaveholder though he was, seemed most influenced by Senator William H. Seward of New York, a "Wooly Head" Free Soil Whig rival of the "Silver Gray" leader, Fillmore. It was a confused situation growing worse, and southern spokesmen began planning for a southern convention to mobilize the South for possible united action.

Documents were in evidence. The people of California, in convention assembled, had drafted a free-state constitution. So had the Mormons. But few were willing to consider statehood for Utah; that region and New Mexico were to be organized as territories. Legislation to this effect was being worked on by various draftsmen. If there could be no further admission of states in pairs, what sort of procedure could be formulated to insure that the process of expansion could continue and the Republic be kept intact? Two northern Democratic Senators—Daniel S. Dickinson of New York and Lewis Cass of Michigan—had been working on one. Cass had made it his platform when seeking the presidency in 1848; he had secured the nomination, but he had been defeated by General Taylor running without a platform. This proposal was to let each territory decide for itself when it applied for statehood whether it wished to permit slavery or not. This was the great principle of democracy—popular sovereignty, "let the people decide."

The congressional session spanning the period of December, 1849, through September, 1850, was one of the most distraught the republic has ever experienced. Henry Clay came back to lead it to a compromise. John C. Calhoun summoned his last feeble strength to assert the rights of the South, and then he died. President Taylor breathed threats of using troops and hanging traitors—and died. The pacific Vice-President Millard Fillmore presided in his stead. The southern Nashville convention fizzled out. On his part, Clay failed in his effort at a compromise omnibus bill. At length a spunky young Democratic Senator, the Little Giant from Illinois, Stephen A. Douglas, marshaled various elements in a weary Senate to pass, by various combinations, five bills that no one group would have supported as a program. By this strenuous legerdemain, the Compromise of 1850 was enacted into law.

The new principle to determine governmental expansion was to allow the drafting process to be transferred to the territories more completely than before. The frontier solons and their constituents could have their work in California ratified and those in New Mexico and Utah could be authorized to come to their own decisions as to the future of slavery within their bounds. This outcome meant that the free states would have a preponderance of one in the Senate, and thus theoretically their interest would now control both houses of the federal lawmaking arm; this section would also be in the majority in the national party nominating conventions. The South was reconciled to this state of affairs by certain concessions. The execution of the fugitive-slave law was placed in federal hands, and slavery was not to be interfered with in the District of Columbia. Any question of the legality of slaveholding in the territories in the Mexican Cession could be referred to the pro-southern Supreme Court. Furthermore, there were many people and politicians of southern origin and sympathy on the Pacific shore, and the congressional delegations from this region were likely to be sympathetic. With such a sectional division in the Far West, southern leadership had perforce to be content for the time being. Again crisis had been averted by legislative ingenuity.

In these early years of American evolution the great factor had been growth, and the problem of the politically ingenious had been the invention necessary to keep Leviathan adjusted to function in an area of ever-increasing variety of geography and population. The community to be served had developed from a scattering of population along the Atlantic seaboard to the more than twenty millions that now inhabited the ranges from sea to sea. The early charters had boldly defined this scope, and now it had been realized. The republic did stretch from the Atlantic to the Pacific.

The designers of this constantly adjusted Leviathan had adopted several principles of operation. The first had been a federal system made up of units that were to be increased as the area and the population expanded. A second principle of invention had been determined by the range of latitude and its influence upon culture. This had been the principle of parallel admission embodied in the Missouri Compromise. But the ecological factors that permitted parallel expansion had given out as settlers approached the high plains, the Rockies and the Pacific. Here geography encouraged scattering rather than systematic parallel advance. To meet this change, the principle of popular sovereignty, affording practical autonomy to communities far distant from the older nucleus east of the Mississippi, had been introduced. This had been embodied in the Compromise of 1850. Would the engine adjusted to the revised blueprints and specifications carry the load required by the stress and strain of growth? The incurable romantics of the early fifties seemed to have all too few doubts.

CHAPTER FIVE

INCREASING FRICTION

O N A January day in 1854 American newspaper readers were startled by a bristling manifesto: "We arraign this bill as a gross violation of a sacred pledge; as a criminal betrayal of precious right; as part and parcel of an atrocious plot." The bill in question, for the organization of the territory of Nebraska, was the latest of the blueprints devised to keep Leviathan efficient enough to fit the needs of the ever-expanding American population relentlessly pressing toward the Pacific. There had been protests in 1812, in 1820 and in 1850, but never had there been such a combination of violations, betrayals and plots, such a cumulation of charges in so small a number of words!

The process of federal lawmaking was becoming ever more intricate as the nation grew and Congress increased in size, embracing more interests and more aggressive politicos. In reality it reflected the growing complexity of Leviathan. For the republic, despite its ingenious mechanism for orderly development, was showing certain signs of structural disintegration despite the legislation of 1850. It was becoming increasingly difficult to agree upon the documents required in ever larger number, and it was ever more apparent that new political techniques were needed.

To the superficial observer quite the contrary seemed to be the fact. A great system, now spreading its operations from the Appalachians to the Pacific, from Canada to the Gulf of Mexico, had been in being since 1787. In

territory after territory, from Ohio to Oregon, a governor, a secretary and judges, appointed from Washington, had administered and interpreted the law and, in
the initial stages, made it. Finally, the laws enacted by
these officials or by the territorial legislatures were subject to the possible scrutiny of Congress. The territorial
governor was instructed by the federal executive, and
congressional appropriations cared for a considerable
portion of the expenses of the communities. Further,
settlement and land acquisition depended upon the
surveys of the Federal Land Office and the negotiations
of the Federal Office of Indian Affairs. In theory, the
ultimate power was in Washington through appointment, approval, appropriation and assignment.

As is so often the case, however, there had developed
a variance between statute law and actuality. Quite a different situation evolved in the territories than that con-
templated by the federal authorities. The territories
were situated on the rim of organized settlement, far
distant from the Capitol, in a day when slow communication made distances seem even greater. Then too,
within the several territories the spaces were frequently
vast, the population sparse and heterogeneous, the settlements small and isolated. Often territorial officials found
themselves lost and isolated in some rude capital village,
with little means of communication with the widely scattered population they were presumed to govern or with
the home government from whom they were to receive
orders and to whom they were to report.

Territorial politics was becoming a new type of
technique for self-government. The population governing itself was of a specialized type. These distant
marches attracted the adventurous, the individualistic,
the ambitious, the visionary, the restless, often the ne'er-
do-well and the unfit. All saw great opportunity in a
new start in a new land. Not infrequently this combination of qualities brought into play an unscrupulous dis-

regard for law and order and seemed to encourage violence and to stimulate erratic behavior.

The stakes for which the territorial politicians and
those who voted for them played were frequently high.
There was good land in abundance, often mixed in with
less desirable tracts. The requirement that holdings
must be acquired in squares regardless of contours and
physiographic conditions meant that the best acres must
be sought early. But frequently those who prospected
could not immediately occupy or register their claims
in some land office. A premium was therefore placed
upon claim jumping, and this caused many a battle.

The opening of each territory and its lesser units also
meant that there were valuable franchises, charters and
licenses at the disposal of the early lawmakers, and
those who controlled the first councils and legislatures were in a position to apportion valuable favors.
These favors were often worth a struggle and various
forms of sharp practice. The unscrupulous and demanding could and did use methods of persuasion that
might be demoralizing.

Another striking element in the territorial situation
was the fact that each was a potential state that would
eventually have not only state officers but senators and
representatives in Congress and delegates in national
nominating conventions. If the politically ambitious
could establish leadership in these distant enclaves, they
would secure constituencies that would give them
power in national councils. Many politically ambitious,
therefore, sought preference by getting in on the ground
floor, so to speak. This was complicated by the fact that
many second-raters who had failed in other communities came out, desperate and even more determined not
to fail again.

All these characteristics could produce situations in
which there was superpressure on the part of many determined to improve their status by assuming roles of

importance in the new community. A great force of importunity was thereby created, which was difficult to manage and which made it most unlikely that the ordinary rules of political conduct current in the older communities could be enforced.

Therefore, over the years of territorial experience prior to 1854, there had emerged a political technique that was frequently chaotic and, from the Washington point of view, almost impossible in terms of federal supervision. Governors were sent out who could exercise no control. Legal processes were established through courts that could not enforce jurisdiction. Juries were difficult to assemble, criminals were hard to apprehend and almost impossible to incarcerate. Elections were irregular and returns tampered with. Legislators had little competence in lawmaking. Citizens were frequently too scattered to find it convenient to fulfill their civic responsibilities. Under circumstances such as these, settlers on many occasions lived either without government or took the law into their own hands. They formed protective associations to prevent land speculators from defrauding them or thieves from stealing their horses; they executed summary justice; they protected themselves against Indians. In effect, they organized themselves and made and enforced their own rules. The flood of documents they produced was both copious and weird. These frontier Leviathans were shaped by strange genetic instructions.

When the question of the specifications for Nebraska's Leviathan began to be debated, there was a series of new conditions developing that impressed upon the draftsmen a keener sense of the realities of the situation. The United States had now reached the Pacific. The Nebraska area, instead of being a dead end on the frontier, was in the midst of a great potential center of development. It was also on the most likely route for a transcontinental line of communication; it was on the

California road to gold.

This situation complicated immensely the territorial problem posed by Kansas and Nebraska. The California trail to fortune was blocked by a series of Indian tribes who had been established there by solemn treaties pledging them security as long as the waters ran. Would these sacred pledges be permitted to stop the onward sweep of the tide of civilization? Somehow an Indian barrier, created when it was thought the aborigines were pocketed in a dead end, must be removed now that it was found to block a great highway.

Likewise the needs of the masses of western migrants passing through to California as well as the local settlers must be met and would bring profit. There would be much business for transportation facilities such as turnpikes, bridges, ferries and taverns; above all, railroads must be provided and serviced. Real estate operations, supply depots and banks would be needed. Truly, here was to be a paradise for those gifted with enterprise. Therefore, the question of who was to control the first government, who would write the basic documents, was unusually important, for these officials and legislators would have the opportunity to direct real estate operations, grant charters and franchises, and otherwise guide the sources of profit to the "right people."

Two new fields of territorial activity that were largely unprecedented were further to complicate the process of document contrivance and territorial politics. The proposed territory was physiographically of a new type. Here ended the wooded and semiwooded region, and here began the vast expanse of grasslands with which Americans had so far hardly been called upon to cope. Furthermore, the age of machinery had begun, the railroad and the reaper were now available and this mechanization was changing man's concept of the need of work, the necessity of capital and his augmented powers of coping with nature.

But there was a more fundamental change. The republic had outgrown the Leviathan that had been provided for it in 1787, 1820 and 1850. Probably no one, however, realized this fact; therefore no one could either sense the need for readjustment or prescribe its nature. It had to be done blindly.

In 1789 the republic could be thought of as a geographical rectangle, with ecological differences that divided the society into two divisions that could be projected westward from the Atlantic shore to the region of the hundredth meridian. Beyond that point it was no longer possible to find similarity in the determining environment, yet beyond that point stretched half of the continental United States. In the 1850's the expanding population had reached a limit.

Not only was the environment changing, but the population was changing as well. The population of 1790 was relatively homogeneous, predominantly of English origin with some proportion of Scotch, Irish, and Continental European stock, a condition that had been characteristic during the eighteenth century; the immigration rate was not high, most Americans were native born, one fifth of the population was Negro. By the mid-1850's this proportion had changed. Immigrants were coming in from all parts of Europe, particularly from Ireland and Germany, at a rate that in 1854 reached 427,000 per year. By 1860, 4,100,000 of the population of 31,000,000 were white foreign-born and only 4,400,000 were Negro. Within this population, which early in the nineteenth century had been relatively homogeneous, there had developed a cleavage. This was the cleavage between the native and the foreigner. Americans were conscious of aliens, and newcomers on occasion were made to feel that they were "second class."

The changing ecology and the changing population together were conditioning new politics. This new politics was to complicate immensely the continuing process of specification writing. When the original designers of Leviathan had accepted elections as the means of providing for the choice of the membership of the federal House of Representatives, they took over a device used in the states for electing legislators. They had not foreseen the development of an extraconstitutional system of political party machinery that would be invented to insure the expression of the national will. Machine politics evolved slowly and did not really operate until the phenomenal growth of the population had been under way for some years.

In the 1820's and 1830's political leaders realized that perhaps the least satisfactory feature of Leviathan's operational mechanisms had been the instrument devised to choose the president. It had never really worked, and in 1824 it peculiarly led to chaos. Some renewed recourse to ingenuity was perforce called for. Those operating the "engine" had learned that, because of the growth of the population and the increase in the number of voters, careful organization was becoming essential to insure successful election campaigns. A most enterprising and perceptive group of them therefore developed and made increasingly effective the Democratic Party between 1828 and 1836. They were clever and did their work so well that it seemed in the early 1850's that, barring accidents, this ingenious group and their chosen successors were slated for indefinite control. They were actually to rule, with the exception of two brief intervals, from 1829 to 1861—thirty-two years.

This Democratic Party and the various less successful organizations, such as the Whigs, that attempted to oppose it were in reality not national parties, as the term is now understood; in fact, even the Republican and Democratic groups of today are not as national and centralized as is commonly assumed. They were and are really federations of state machines, and these machines are generally very independent and often hard to handle, as any national chairman can testify. In the period just before the Civil War there was hardly any central organization at all; instead, there were some three score and more state parties acting with great individual independence.

Men chosen by the voters, in a haphazard series of elections operated by such disorganized parties, undertook to direct the federal system ostensibly as representatives of the states. As such, they must apportion patronage and appropriations as well as answer demands for more specifications for Leviathan. To this latter end they had constantly employed diplomatic negotiating and bargaining. Legislation was more like treaty making than statute writing, and it was often done in an atmosphere of bad temper and antagonism, especially as the capital city, Washington, was so badly equipped and so unhealthful.

Their task was the more difficult because federal relations among the states were so complicated. Few of the states were coherent or integrated units of opinion, and a large proportion of them were confused by various and conflicting internal interests and views. Such differences often crossed state lines.

The great increase and spread of population strained the political machinery operating the federal system and keeping up with the constant need for basic documents. The Democratic Party had been in power almost continuously through three decades. Its strength lay in its appeal as a people's party, in the heroic Jackson legend, in a swashbuckling expansionist foreign policy, in its effective political organization, but particularly in its laissez-faire philosophy in domestic affairs. On questions of subsidy the party leaders, sensing some of the variety of interests and attitudes endangering the party's control, had avoided the issue by maintaining the federal government as one of very limited powers. The

Democrats attempted to encourage nationalism by an aggressive foreign policy. In domestic policy, they were more and more sympathetic to regionalism, leaving the creation of basic documents more and more to territories and states.

But no party in this country was ever to remain in power for much more than the life of a generation. As the 1860's approached, the ruling Democratic Party was more and more harried by the resentments of those who had been thwarted by its laissez-faire policy and of those disappointed in their ambitions for leadership and office, and of course by the rising generation inevitably at feud with its elders. The stage was set for schism, and it came.

A new political group was ready to take advantage of these signs of discontent and rebellion. The old opposition party, that of the Whigs, had never been very effective, in part because it took little advantage of the controversial issues of conflicting attitudes and merely tried to promote the cohesive idea of nationalism. It was now due to be pushed aside by a new party that would make capital of division. New leaders realized that the majority of the voters lived in regions where promotional, territorial and antislavery attitudes existed in profusion and confusion. Heedless of danger, they were determined to make some catch-all appeal. Combining moral indignation against slavery with promises to various promotional interests, and stressing the theoretical concept of the right of the majority to rule, they might develop an appeal strong enough to break the long-continued power of the South and of the Democratic Party and to take over the task of writing the specifications for the changes in Leviathan demanded by the fast-expanding society.

The Democratic leadership saw this opposition swiftly rising, but it was incapable of coherent action to meet it. The Democrats were faced with a dilemma.

The free-state Democrats saw the need of concessions to save their ranks from the onslaught of a new combination but their southern associates had to refuse these concessions because they themselves were in danger. They had as their local opponents the southern branch of the Whig Party, which would lose most of its northern wing to any new party and could therefore go all out for southern interests. If the southern Democrats agreed to concessions in national platforms to placate free-state opinion, they would be accused by their local opponents of betraying the South and might well be driven from the state governments. Rather than lose local control, the southern Democratic leaders might well sacrifice their national power, a phenomenon not unknown in American political history.

A second feature in the new politics was a different concept, imposed by the changing conditions, of the locus of power. The old politics had been based on the sharing of political power by two groups fairly equal in strength and well established in an equality that might be considered as reasonably stable. But the changes cited were not directing the expanding population in parallel extensions; rather, they drove the bulk of the westward migration to the northwest, to the neglect of the southwest, and they concentrated the recent foreign immigrants in the northeast and northwest. The new type of foreign migrant was by and large unwilling to enter the southern communities as a slaveholder or as an associate or competitor of slaveholders. Such migrants wished to change the nature of Leviathan. These new blueprints would emphasize the difference in the two societies that had hitherto been dealt with politically in a not-too-dangerous fashion.

The demand for new specifications was made more emphatic by a nativist movement that developed as a reaction to the increased foreign immigration, with its religious overtones produced by the large number of

Roman Catholic newcomers. The Democratic Party had been prepared to deal with this problem by fraternizing with foreigners and enlisting Catholics. Such action, however, placed a weapon in the hands of the party's opponents, and as nativism and hostility to Catholics grew with the increasing immigration of the 1840's and 1850's, there were bound to be political repercussions. This was particularly true because the same changing ecology and population produced new demands upon government for legislation to facilitate the settlement of new communities and to develop new sources of wealth.

The Democratic Party under traditional southern management could not respond, since the South did not want settlement extended west of the quadrilateral in which the balance between slave and free states could be exacted. Therefore the frustrate would attack the laissez-faire Democrats as subservient to slave interests and apologists for immorality. In the North they could be denounced as catering to foreigners, as obedient to the Pope. It was only a matter of time before these basic changes in environment and population, emphasized by the factors of westward expansion and industrial concentration in urban areas, led to a political reorganization—the formation of new political combinations with new techniques. Without ecological facilities for further parallel western institutional projection, the cherished equal partnership of the two great societies was in difficulties.

The hazards threatened by political reorganization were to be increased by the emotional state of the republic. So much mobility, the accession of so much new energy—the expenditure of the force required constantly to create new communities—meant that there was a nervousness and an erratic imagination, stimulated further by the introduction of machines that brought people indoors and caused their muscles to soften and their health to be impaired. It was a day of dyspepsia, tuberculosis, malaria, pellagra and hookworm, with occasional epidemics of cholera and yellow fever, to say nothing of alcoholism and social diseases. It was likewise a romantic age, and the American imagination had some of the characteristics of a powder magazine with the heads off the kegs and with blazing knots sending off showers of sparks.

Because of all these factors, a great political reorganization was due. The Democratic Party had said no too often; it had thwarted too many plans for federal aid and action. It was only a matter of time and the discovery of potent political ammunition before there would be a political realignment of some sort in which the dominant southern influence would be the object of attack. The South's power to write or refuse to write specifications had to be destroyed. All this was "in the air," so to speak, when the confused question of organizing Nebraska entered politics.

The process of drafting documents necessary to create territories and states, now invoked to provide for Nebraska and Kansas, had already been put to frequent political use by those contending for place and power. In renewing this process, there was the constant danger of awakening sectional controversy. The symbol involved that offered the most material for political contest was the question of whether or not slavery could be admitted into the new communities. Even in the Northwest Territory, where the famous Ordinance of 1787 had forbidden slavery, controversy had not been ended. In some parts of the region slavery had been an accepted institution and, regardless of the ordinance, was continued for a time. It was only eliminated at length in Illinois in the 1820's by the narrow margin of a few votes.

The process of directing the territorial probation and eventual admission of new states by an orderly stream of documents had not proved to be the program of precision that its designers had planned. There was something in the atmosphere of the frontier that could encourage lawlessness and a species of anarchy that could not be controlled by statutes or proclamations. This tendency to political violence was encouraged by the most recent deviation in the program initiated by the Compromise of 1850. For the easily operated concept of creating states in pairs of cultural opposites the change in Leviathan's structure had substituted a very vague and tricky process. The older device, admission in pairs, had been a true safety valve. The more recent "popular sovereignty" invention proved to be dynamite. This change in policy turned the whole process of creating new communities over to those who might get there first. To them were given the responsibilities of making the basic laws, of granting the franchises, of setting the patterns of behavior. The new documentation of 1850 had greatly complicated the process of political evolution.

The growth of the nation thus reached a point in the early 1850's when organization of the last segment of the Louisiana Purchase, the Nebraska region, was inevitable. But Nebraska was entirely within the area that, under the Missouri Compromise, was dedicated to freedom, while in the region to the south and west of it another principle had just been established. Here the squatters, not the Washington authorities, were to rule. Two systems were now in operation—one in the Mississippi Valley, the other in the Mexican Cession and in the Pacific Northwest. Two systems merely spelled confusion worse confounded. This double standard produced disaster.

The basic difficulties were twofold. The growing population was not uniform in its spread, and the area into which the southern system might be extended in terms of prior experience was in very short supply, if in fact it existed at all. The division of power in the federal Leviathan depended upon the number of states with free or slave labor, and if the number of slave-labor states was not to be increased, the possibility of the equal division was at an end. This would change the nature of the republic. The southern group could not help but believe that this was to its disadvantage, even to its danger, and southerners might be expected to use their power to arrest the menace.

Scarcely two years after the enactment of the Compromise of 1850 the question of further territorial blueprints was back in Congress. In the short session of 1852-1853 an act was passed organizing the northern half of the old Oregon region, that portion in the Puget Sound area, as the territory of Washington. At the same time a bill was debated that would have extended territorial organization over that portion of the Louisiana Purchase lying between 36° 30′ and 43°, which embraced the future states of Kansas and Nebraska and the eastern portions of what are now Colorado and Wyoming. This was called in one bill the Territory of the Platte but was more generally designed as Nebraska. Since both of these regions were north of the Missouri Compromise line, no mention of slavery was made in these documents. Whatever element of controversy there was was stimulated by ostensible concern for Indian rights. The Nebraska bill passed the House, but it failed in the Senate because on the last day of the session the Senate for various reasons would not give it final consideration. It was significant that the result would have been otherwise had four southern senators voted to advance the bill.

The pressure of population and promotion moving westward was so continuous that the Nebraska question was bound to stay before Congress until it was settled, and it was becoming dangerous. An orderly process of legislative drafting of blueprints could no longer be counted on. The difficulty foreshadowed in 1850 was to be multiplied many times scarce four years later and was to bring ruin in its wake.[1]

In December, 1853, companion bills to organize Nebraska practically identical with the one debated in the previous session were introduced in both houses. These measures, according to legislative custom, were sent to the Committees on Territories in the two bodies, presided over by the two Illinois veterans, Stephen A. Douglas and William A. Richardson, both Democrats and close associates. Neither bill referred to slavery. Both chairmen were much interested in advancing this legislation and girt their loins to accomplish the effort, which at first did not seem to promise much difficulty. To secure their objective they had to operate one of Leviathan's most intricate mechanisms.

The process of lawmaking had been made more complex by the constantly increasing size of the republic. As the thirteen states had grown to thirty-one, the Senate grew to 62 members and the House numbered 234. The Senate was still able to proceed along simple behavioral lines. It met in a small room and operated on the basis of unlimited debate, and there was not much that could be done by maneuver or political device. Each senator felt himself as *primus inter pares*. Senators knew each other reasonably well, and as each could talk as long as he wanted and as so much of the procedure depended upon the unanimous consent of gentlemen, oftentimes only patience and good lungs were required for the long speeches and the ponderous negotiation necessary to secure or destroy laws. In the House, however, the situation was different. Rules that might do for 62 would not suffice for 234, if anything was to be accomplished. The rules in the House were more numerous, more explicit. In the House more depended on leadership. This double century of politicos had to be marshaled, and where there are organization, detailed rules of procedure and numerous personnel, there are bound to be complicated maneuvering, manipulation, smart practice, surprise tactics—in sum, politics, and complicated politics at that. Such possibilities whetted the appetite, and partisanship made use of that fact. Rivalry was stimulated, smart operator vied with smart operator, tempers flared, emotions boiled—the nation watched; the press reported, often in exaggerated style; the public in some instances raged. It was a romantic age; and the complicated system of lawmaking made Leviathan increasingly difficult to operate; and the difficulty of operation made a devastating contribution to the approaching conflict.

Douglas and Richardson had to pilot the Nebraska bill through both of these houses. Douglas had expected little difficulty. But how mistaken he was! In the Senate he was only one of a group of jealous prima donnas, and some of his associates resented his presidential ambitions and his domineering ego. He was only five feet five, but he compensated for his short stature by a swaggering manner. It earned him the title of "The Little Giant." He made up for his short legs by his loud voice. Further, he had begun to run for president too early; he had stepped out of turn; he must be disciplined. Two obstacles appeared almost at once in the way of his success with Nebraska. One of his colleagues, Jesse D. Bright of Indiana, a rival in the northwest, as usual was assigned the task of making up the committees. Whether by accident or design, he gave Douglas a Committee on Territories with which he would have difficulty. He had a committee of six; two of these were Whigs and another was Sam Houston. He could get no support from the Whigs, so he was dependent on the favor of Houston for a majority; and Houston was a maverick, who would cooperate only on his own terms. Besides, the Texan had not yet reached Washington; in fact, he did not appear until January 3.

Then Douglas had some other bad news. His colleagues, Butler of South Carolina and Hunter and Mason of Virginia, who were chairmen of the committees on judiciary, finance and foreign affairs respectively, and Atchison of Missouri, President pro tem., because of their positions were the most influential Senate members in shaping legislation. They kept house together on F Street near the Patent Office and were known as the F Street Mess. They had not voted for Nebraska in the previous session, and the bill would not pass if they repeated this omission. Douglas now learned through Atchison that they would not support his bill unless it were so amended that, despite the Missouri restriction, slave owners could take their property into Nebraska.

Atchison's terms put Douglas in a dilemma. Atchison and his associates were in effect demanding the repeal of the Missouri Compromise. This Houston and the Whigs would not agree to. Therefore, if Douglas were to get any bill on the floor that could pass, he had to be an extremely ingenious draftsman. This was going to be difficult because of the composition of the Senate. That body then consisted of sixty members, of whom thirty-seven were Democrats, seemingly a safe majority. But only sixteen of these were from the South, and they were not enough to carry a bill that would admit slaves into free territory. How could a measure be framed which would get thirty-one votes? Even if the thirteen southern Whigs all voted with the southern Democrats, it would not be enough. The needed majority must be made up from two parties and two sections.[2]

Within a month from the opening of the session Douglas thought he had hit upon the answer. He prepared a formula that made no reference to the Missouri Compromise but was phrased entirely in the language of the Compromise of 1850, the only language Houston would accept. The bill, which he reported on

January 4, 1854, the day after Houston's arrival, enlarged the proposed territory to include the remainder
of the Louisiana Purchase. The subject of slavery was
covered in the following language: "And when admitted as a State or States, the said Territory, or any
part of the same, shall be received into the Union,
with or without slavery, as their Constitution may prescribe at the time of their admission." All questions involving title to slaves and questions of personal freedom were subject to final appeal to the United States
Supreme Court, and the fugitive-slave law was extended
over the territory. As the bill expressly stated, "in order
to avoid all misconstruction, it is hereby declared to be
the true intent and meaning of this act, so far as the
question of slavery is concerned, to carry into practical
operation the . . . proposition and principles established by the compromise measures of 1850," and "all
questions pertaining to slavery in the Territories and
in the new States to be formed therefrom, are to be
left to the decision of the people residing therein,
through their appropriate representatives." [3]

The presentation of Douglas' revision of the 1853 bill
gave other interests ideas about political uses to which
they might put the measure. Senator William H. Seward, a leader of the Whig Party, shrewdly grasped some
rather intricate possibilities. He urged some of his
northern Whig associates to lead in attacks upon Democrats by encouraging public meetings of protest and
sponsoring legislative resolutions demanding that northern senators and congressmen oppose the bill. In later
years he described the more Machiavellian role he
played. He suggested that southern Whigs place their
Democratic opponents at a disadvantage by assailing
them for dodging repeal, and at the same time to pro-
claim the Whigs as true friends of the South by opposing the dodge or by offering a repeal amendment to the
act. Beyond this, Seward had an even more subtle in-

tent. He wished to make the bill as obnoxious as possible to northern voters, for this would help northern Whigs discredit the Democrats. Although Whig Senator Archibald Dixon of Kentucky offered such a repeal amendment, he claimed many years later that he could not remember Seward's influence.[4]

Dixon's move gave the cue to a third group to engage in the politics of the bill. The Free-Soil senators and representatives moved much more directly than the subtle Seward. Sumner offered an amendment reaffirming the Missouri exclusion, and the Ohio men, led by Giddings and Chase, drafted the "Appeal of the Independent Democrats," arraigning the bill as "a gross violation of a sacred pledge." This manifesto was designed to and did set off a chain reaction that gave northern leaders their desired opportunity to mobilize the anti-southern voting strength of the more populous North.[5]

While the Whigs and Free-Soilers were planning these moves, elements in the Democratic Party had become increasingly dissatisfied with Douglas' dodge. Some Calhounite lawyers thought it would not admit slavery to Nebraska. Then, too, the repeal amendment of Dixon further embarrassed southern Democrats because it served to expose them to a charge that they were acquiescing in a subterfuge and so gave advantage to their Whig opponents. Simultaneously doubts were rising in the minds of certain northern Democratic senators and members of the administration, none too friendly with Douglas, that the matter was being badly handled, in a fashion that might easily split the party again. Therefore, various Democrats, including Pierce and his cabinet, began seeking a new formula that might insure united Democratic support and the passing of the much-desired bill.

The Calhounites, Douglas and the President finally achieved a phraseology to which the rather uncertain Pierce committed himself in writing. Nebraska would be opened to slavery by the declaration that all laws of the United States that were not locally inapplicable should have full force and effect in the new territories except the Missouri Compromise legislation prohibiting slavery. This was expressly excepted because it had been "superseded by the Compromise of 1850"; it was declared "inoperative and void." Also, two territories were created instead of one, one west of a slave state and the other west of free states. This division, reminiscent of the arrangement of 1820, gave the measure more of an air of compromise, and Pierce agreed to give the bill his support.[6]

The second revision of the bill and the "Appeal" were launched almost simultaneously on January 23 and 24, and they brought immediate results. Such a wave of indignation swept through the North at this blow to liberty that the possibility of support from northern Democrats was threatened; and if there were to be a serious revolt among them, the seemingly overwhelming majorities in the Senate and House might disappear, for in both bodies there were more Democrats from the North than from the South.

A further matter for concern was the discovery by the Calhounites of a great and seemingly unexpected indifference to the measure in the South. Many in that region just did not believe that climate would permit any more slave states, and they were not interested in efforts to open territories that would only create more free states. Furthermore, they did not trust Douglas' popular sovereignty. To many it implied that a host of free-state people unhampered by any slave property might move right in and elect a territorial legislature that would immediately exclude slavery. Such a proposition was a tricky device to get more free states with no possible advantage to the South. Many so-called Compromise or Union Democrats in the South held these views.

Thus the Democratic strength seemed to be melting away, north and south. The fate of the bill, therefore, hung on selling the idea to the South, particularly by appealing to the southern Whigs, and on whipping northern Democrats into line behind an administration bill. For these purposes, the second revision—the January 23 bill—was proving unsatisfactory. Further effort had to be made to create still another formula that would attract enough support from northern and southern Democrats and southern Whigs. Nothing more could be expected from Douglas through the Committee on Territories, and the possibility of northern support was dwindling; a series of caucuses was therefore arranged to include all Senate supporters or potential supporters of a Nebraska bill. Many hands other than Douglas' set to work; there was much discussion and more drafting.[7]

Douglas presented the fruits of these deliberations to the Senate on February 6. Once again he had avoided the word repeal, this time accomplishing his object by striking out the words "which was superseded by" and inserting "which is inconsistent with the principles of the legislation of 1850, commonly called the compromise measures, and is hereby declared inoperative and void."

The substitution of the idea that the Missouri Compromise was inconsistent with the Compromise of 1850, rather than that it had been superseded by it, aroused a new phase of debate. Much time was taken up in a semantic wrangle in which the changes were rung on "supersede" and "inconsistent with" and on the virtues of "inoperative" and "repeal." Finally Douglas promised he would try once more to get a better phraseology, and once again the bipartisan pro-Nebraska caucus was assembled.

It labored mightily between the day's adjournment and noon the following day. On February 7 Douglas brought back a new agglomeration of words hammered out in caucus. Kansas-Nebraska, it was stated again, was not to come under the Missouri Compromise legislation. It was declared that the enactment of 1820, "being inconsistent with the principle of non-intervention by Congress with slavery in the States and Territories, as recognized by the legislation of eighteen hundred and fifty, commonly called the Compromise Measures, is hereby declared inoperative and void." This draft also incorporated some words that indicated a new understanding regarding popular sovereignty. There had been much objection from the South because there was no statement specifying at what point in the experience of a territory the exclusion of slavery might take place. Also there was still dispute over whether slaves could now be introduced into the new territory. The following maze of words was presented: "it being the true intent and meaning of this act not to legislate slavery into any Territory or State, nor to exclude it therefrom, but to leave the people thereof perfectly free to form and regulate their domestic institutions in their own way, subject only to the Constitution of the United States." This was understood, particularly by the southern members of the caucus, to mean that the whole question of the introduction of slaves into Kansas and Nebraska would be left to the Supreme Court. With this understanding, the Southerners accepted the new draft.[8]

The foes of the bill in the meantime were trying their hands at the pen, in the hope not of changing the bill materially but of embarrassing its supporters and creating campaign material for the pending congressional election. Senator Edward Everett made a grandstand play by bringing in a giant petition against the bill, signed by 3,050 clergymen and weighing ten pounds. Senator Chase moved an amendment explicitly repealing the Missouri restriction, daring Douglas and his allies to do directly what they were trying to do by indirection. They refused by a vote of 30 to 12. Chase then moved to grant territorial legislatures explicit power to exclude or abolish slavery. These amendments forced the administration to vote against the repeal of the Missouri restriction and against popular sovereignty. Despite the embarrassment caused thereby, they did so. The only amendments of significance that were made were proposed by Clayton, a Whig of Delaware, and Badger, a Whig of North Carolina, the first of whom moved to exclude all foreigners from voting in the territories. This stipulation was added at the insistence of those conscious of a rising nativism developing in the South, particularly among the Whigs. Part of southern apprehension regarding popular sovereignty was fear that the territories would attract large groups of recent immigrants with free-soil sympathies. The second amendment explicitly forbade the revival by this action of the old Mexican laws against slavery that had applied to the region before the Missouri Compromise had been enacted.[9]

The most significant event in the complex procedure proved to be the series of bipartisan caucuses of senators that registered the fact of the almost complete union of southern Democrats and Whigs in support of the measure. This unanimity of sentiment had been crystallized by the virulence of the onslaught upon the South in opposition to the *de facto* repeal of the Missouri Compromise. When the South found itself thus attacked, its emerging sense of danger was so strong that practically all the senators from below the Mason-Dixon line stood together. Had there been any sufficiently alert to recognize the significance of this stand, they would have realized that it was prophetic of the events of 1860-1861 and the Confederacy. Under the stress of this emotion, the Southern lawmakers were found supporting almost unanimously, regardless of party, a bill to which a substantial proportion of their constituents were either initially indifferent or opposed. The southern Whig senators broke definitely with their northern brethren. Only Clayton of Delaware and Bell of Tennessee seemed to cherish the hope of maintaining a national Whig Party. Thus a bipartisan coalition was formed to support the bill. In this final move Douglas had participated, but considering the number of Whigs involved, he could hardly have called the tune. The control of his party had vanished.

During the course of this negotiation, which lasted from late December until February, the opponents of slave extension, particularly among the northern Whig and Free-Soil senators, undertook a hard fight. Under the rules of the Senate authorizing unlimited debate and often requiring unanimous consent, they could do little on the floor but offer embarrassing amendments, require them to be voted on and talk indefinitely. When the bipartisan caucus had revised the efforts of Douglas, the Committee on Territories, certain southern Democrats and President Pierce, there was no longer any doubt that after weary hours of oratory the bill would pass the Senate. About a month later it did, at 5 A.M., March 4, by a vote of 37 to 14, with nine absent senators, only three of whom were opposed. However, it took nine southern Whigs to enable the bill to be passed; the Democrats could not mobilize enough of their majority to accomplish it. The result was achieved by hard-working draftsmen who turned themselves semantically inside out. In the Senate the battle had been fought with words, with formulae; and the necessary votes had thereby been achieved.[10] This was the grand manner, the manner of the forum. But in the House it would be different.

CHAPTER SIX

APPROACH OF TERROR

THE HEATED contest in the Senate was to prove simple when compared with the House phase of the battle for the law. In the "more numerous" body of Congress the weapons were not so much debate and oratory as they were promises, the manipulation of rules and the marshaling of disciplined party organization. In this struggle the technique of lawmaking achieved a new measure of complexity that was to strain Leviathan in a fashion hitherto unknown, threatening the engine's capacity.[1]

The Nebraska bill passed the Senate on March 4, but so shaken was Democratic party discipline and so uncertain were the House managers of their strength that they did not dare attempt even to take it up for days. Not until late in March, after an unhappy New Hampshire election that the Democrats lost, did the House managers make any effort to advance the bill. Even then the New York *Herald,* hostile to the Administration, suggested that the Democrats would not have acted had they not feared the Whigs might anticipate them. The latter saw what good campaign material this bill was and wanted to hurry on the acrimonious debate sure to follow. At length Richardson moved tardily on March 21 that the bill be taken from the Speaker's table.

Richardson was immediately met by unpleasant setbacks. An effort to get the Democratic members into a binding caucus that would have insured him united party support failed because too many refused to attend. Then his effort to get the members of the House into the usual seat of informal and unrecorded action, the Committee of the Whole House on the State of the Union, so that he could have this bill referred to the Committee on Territories, was rejected by 108 to 84. Something was up, a revolt was simmering; in fact, the press had been predicting it. And on this March 21 it occurred. Richardson had had due warning, for during the Senate debate the House had not been unmindful of Nebraska. A Nebraska bill had been before Richardson's committee since the third week of the session, but this group was not asked to do anything for the time being. Not until January 23 was any action planned. At that time Douglas and Richardson agreed to report a new bill simultaneously in both Houses. But Richardson had struck a snag in his committee. The principal reason was the fact that the bill provided a political hazard for so many members; most of them were concerned because they were on the eve of or in the midst of their re-election campaigns.

The rising tide of indignation in the North was frightening to many Democrats, who now had to face angry voters, indignant at the contrivers or supporters of this measure. Furthermore, the nature of the Democratic majority in the House proved troublesome. On paper it was so huge—158 to 76—that there might seem to be no conceivable problem. But the difficult hurdle was that of the 158 Democrats, 92, by far the greater part, came from northern constituencies. Many of these were likely to be in serious trouble if they could be held party to the "atrocious plot" to repeal the Missouri Compromise. This danger was reflected in the House Committee on the Territories, made up of Douglas' most loyal associate—Richardson of Illinois—four southern Democrats, one from border Missouri, only one other Democrat from a free state—William H. English of Indiana—and two Whigs. The original plan to report out a duplicate of Douglas' January 23 version of the bill on that day was blocked when English and the Whigs objected. They persuaded Richardson to delay the report until January 31, so that English could file a minority pronouncement.

The discussion in the House committee defined the strategy of the contest that was to ensue. English represented a large proportion of the 92 northern Democrats. These men resented the semantic gymnastics used to deal with the slavery question. They wanted a forthright statement of the doctrine of popular sovereignty, of self-government in the territories, acknowledging the complete control over the slave question by the territorial governments. They felt they would have a chance in the coming election if they were fighting a positive battle to extend democracy, whereas if they were forced on the defensive by charges of destroying the Missouri Compromise, they would be in grave danger. English essayed to be their spokesman on the House Committee on Territories and proposed an amendment: "Provided that nothing in this act shall be construed as to prevent the people of said Territory, through the properly constituted legislative authority, from passing such laws in relation to the institution of slavery, not inconsistent with the constitution of the United States, as they may deem best adapted to their locality and most conducive to their happiness and welfare; and so much of any existing act of Congress as may conflict with the above right of the people to regulate their domestic institutions in their own way be, and the same is hereby, repealed." This amendment stated popular sovereignty in terms all could understand. The House Committee would not accept it. Would the House?

Richardson was going to have no easy task in piloting the Nebraska bill through the lower chamber. The

final version of the bill as it came from the Senate put
northern Democrats at even greater disadvantage because, while it declared the Missouri Compromise void,
it gave no specific authority to the territorial governments over the admission of slavery. To make matters
worse for some of the Congressmen, the bill excluded
unnaturalized foreign immigrants from political participation in the organization of the territories. Not only
did this provision exclude numerous potential free-
state voters, but in various districts it also aroused
foreign-born voters against the Democrats.

From the day the Senate passed the bill there was
revolt in the air. New York took the lead. The willing-
ness of the Pierce administration to award patronage
to the followers of Van Buren, who had bolted in 1848,
had made some from the Empire State particularly
resentful. These were determined to show their strength
and tie Richardson's hands, at least for the time being.
Had the normal course been followed, the bill would
have gone to his committee, from which he could have
reported it out at any time and moved the previous
question. If this motion were seconded by a majority,
debate was ended and the bill must then be voted on
at once. In other words, if the majority of the Democrats held together, they could pass the bill at any time
without debate. It must therefore be taken out from
under Richardson's control. The New Yorkers consequently planned to move that the bill be referred not
to his committee but to the calendar of the Committee
of the Whole House. As there were fifty bills already
there awaiting consideration, it was too late in the session to expect the House to reach this particular one,
numbered S22. The only possibility of passing it, therefore, would be under a suspension of the rules, and this
took a two-thirds vote. The Democrats had a two-thirds
majority, but it would be within the power of less than a
double dozen to prevent such action, and the bill could

be pried loose thereafter only with their help. In other words, this group, not Richardson, would have control of the bill.

Fifty-five of the restive Northern Democrats were ready to make trouble by voting against Richardson and eleven others by staying away; of these, twenty-one were from New York. When Francis B. Cutting, a New York hardshell, therefore, moved that the bill be placed on the calendar of the Committee of the Whole, only twenty-six of the ninety-two northern Democrats followed Richardson, including but one from New York, and the chairman was defeated by a vote of 110 to 95. For the time being at least, the Democratic majority was shattered. Of the thirteen delegations controlled by the northern Democrats, only Pennsylvania, Illinois and California showed any real loyalty. New England, New York and New Jersey failed utterly. Even Michigan and Indiana, bailiwicks of Cass and Bright, fell away. Ohio and Wisconsin would have little of the measure.

This defeat was a blow that was to challenge all the ingenuity the Administration, Douglas and the bipartisan southern coalition could muster. Probably few wanted to prevent the organization of the territories, but many either desired a different bill or hoped to get something for themselves out of the measure's passage. In fact, the revolting northern Democrats were fighting not so much to defeat the bill as to change it. They wanted a return to Douglas' first bill of January 4, or else the insertion of the popular-sovereignty amendment of English, or something like it. Furthermore, they wanted to strike out the immigrant-exclusion amendment. Richardson's task was to secure not merely the passage of the bill, but its passage without amendment.

Thus three forces were at work, with the sixty-six revolting Democrats in the center. The opposition sought to get them to join in defeating the bill. The Administration and the congressional managers were trying to get them to return to regularity. The revolters themselves were battling to get their terms accepted. Here history draws the curtain. The evidence of what went on in the minds and emotions of these sixty-six still remains hidden, if it exists. What experiences these sixty-six had, what pressures they suffered, how they reacted, what they wanted and either got or didn't get, whether some reasoned it out or reacted to pressure from home, how many were moved by moral indignation or were swayed by party loyalty—these questions indicate the clue to the real history of this phase of the bill's passage, yet the answers are not known.

It is, of course, well understood that the President and his cabinet made some efforts with patronage promises, offers of administrative favors and with persuasive arguments, but they were handicapped by the fact that much of their patronage had been used up. Furthermore, the unstable President and his so-called organ, the Washington *Union,* blew hot and cold. Some effort was made to reform the ranks by appeals to party loyalty, and Douglas sought to persuade, to order, to overawe—in fact, he used all the tactics his ingenious mind and dynamic personality could contrive. Who was promised what, and why shifts were made, are still almost wholly unknown. We have only the bare results. Ultimately, only eighteen Democrats could be persuaded to return to the ranks of regularity. But in the meantime a new strain was put on Leviathan, and the effort exerted to get the Kansas-Nebraska bill through the House added a new dimension to the political skill needed to operate the lawmaking process.

Whatever the controlling means required, the work seems to have been done by May 2, for on that day Richardson announced that on May 8 he would attempt the difficult task of digging the bill out of its grave on the calendar of the Committee of the Whole. To do this, he must carry eighteen consecutive motions to lay aside each of the bills that were ahead of the House version. On the date set, he rose. He announced that he was moving that the House go into the Committee of the Whole House on the State of the Union where without recorded votes he would seek to postpone all the bills on its calendar which were ahead of the House Nebraska bill, H.R.236, and then proceed to substitute the Senate bill for it. The House was not eager for the test and the numbers assembled were so slim that Stephens of Georgia instituted a call of the House whereby after roll call the sergeant-at-arms issued warrants for those absent and unexcused. Finally the necessary members were assembled and the vote was taken. The work had been done and the motion was adopted by 109 to 88. Seventeen at this time had returned to the fold; eleven had changed their votes and six who had been absent now voted Aye. Ten others of the recalcitrant stayed away. The majority of the converts had been made in New York, Pennsylvania and New Jersey, supplying eleven of the seventeen. Little progress had been made in the West.[2]

This great hurdle cleared, the managers could proceed with a strategy that was to become more complex with each day, until it achieved a degree of complication that made its success in the end one of the great accomplishments of the American operators of Leviathan. At the conclusion of the vote the House moved into the committee role. Speaker Linn Boyd called Edson B. Olds of Ohio, an expert at presiding over the Committee of the Whole, to the chair and himself disappeared into the mass. Richardson thereupon moved that the first bill on the Committee's calendar be laid aside. This was resisted. First one obstructionist sought to have it read; it took time to obviate this move, whereupon another House leader, Houston of Alabama, sought to save time by moving that all the bills prior to Nebraska be laid aside; this move was defeated. Then a snarl was caused because Richardson had moved to lay aside the wrong bill. After some delay over points of order, the right bill was cited and the members called to vote. As this was in the Committee of the Whole, no record was made of individual votes. Two tellers were appointed, one to count the Ayes and the other the Nays, and the members formed in a double column and filed by these men to be counted. The first bill was laid aside by a vote of 103 to 82. There followed seventeen other such motions, which were all adopted with varying votes; in three instances no tellers were demanded. Occasionally there was an interruption, as when one member moved that tellers be appointed for every two bills, so the tedium could be cut in half. Once there was an effort to adjourn. Finally the eighteen bills were laid aside, and the House Nebraska-Kansas bill, H.R. 236, was reached. This was not the Senate version, which was way down the list; it was the copy of Douglas' second bill, which Richardson had reported on January 31. Washburn of Maine and then Campbell of Ohio moved to lay this aside too; they were defeated by 105 to 85.

Richardson was now in a position to move that the Senate bill be substituted for this House edition, and debate really began. The next two days were filled with speeches in long sessions lasting until late in the evening. On May 11, as there was no sign of any slackening of debate, Richardson had to move in again. He was pressed for time because the House had set up a special order some weeks previously to begin consideration of the Pacific Railroad bill on May 16. This measure would take days to consider and, together with the appropriation bills, would probably block any further consideration of Nebraska unless that matter could be disposed of before the railroad bill was brought up. Richardson had either to secure a vote by May 16 or somehow to obtain a two-thirds vote in support of a move to suspend the rules and get a postponement of the special order, and hence more time for Nebraska, before the Pacific Railroad bill was taken up.

He began his effort by moving to end debate on the Nebraska bill at noon the next day. This step was the signal for a prolonged series of maneuvers such as only the United States House can produce. The foes of the bill sought to lay this motion on the table, but the majority was sustained. During the roll call Richardson was bombarded by demands that he grant more time, even if only a day. But he refused to budge. He declared that eighty speeches had already been made, more than had ever before discussed any one question. He insisted on the seconding of his demand for the previous question on his motion to close debate next day. There followed a thirty-six-hour battle, with an exhibition of all kinds of legislative ingenuity.

Campbell of Ohio, opponent of the bill, for instance, rose and spoke: "Being slow of mind, I have not been able to make up my mind on [Richardson's] motion, I therefore ask to be excused from voting." This request was refused. Then there were various moves to reconsider this vote, and finally the whole matter of Campbell's "slow mind" was laid on the table. However, before Campbell had expressed his doubt, Edgerton had moved a call of the House to insure enough members to second Richardson's call for the previous question. This move of Edgerton's again ran into trouble. Representative Sage of New York, foe of the bill, now wanted to be excused. This request was refused, but then Campbell wanted this vote reconsidered. This took another roll call, and so it went. At 2:45 Stuart of Michigan moved to adjourn; when this move was defeated, the House again undertook Edgerton's call of the House. Thereupon Drum of Pennsylvania moved that when the House adjourned, it adjourn until the following Saturday. This required another call of the roll of 234 members, which usually consumed more than fifteen minutes. Drum was defeated.

By now it was 3:20, and Sage returned to the fray. He moved to adjourn. This was defeated by roll call, and now Edgerton's demand for a call of the House initiated some two and a half hours before was finally defeated. The House, speaking in a parliamentary way, was back to Richardson's demand for the previous question on his motion to end the debate the next day. At 3:53 Goodrich of Massachusetts moved to adjourn, whereupon it developed that there was no quorum. Richardson therefore moved a call of the House; pending a vote on this, Sage got another roll call on adjournment. When Sage was defeated, Richardson, still needing a quorum, moved another call of the House and this time, after defeating another motion to adjourn, got the call. During its progress, Drum of Pennsylvania tried to stop it, and Crocker, Whig of Massachusetts, tried an adjournment. After these moves were defeated, the call began and the House then had to consider the excuses of the absent. An excuse from Appleton of Massachusetts was voted on favorably by roll call, and then an effort was made to stop the call since it was now 6:30 and enough absentees had come back from dinner. After another negative vote on adjournment, a further roll call was secured that dispensed with the call. The House was then back to Richardson's demand for the previous question. The House next had to suffer through two calls perpetrated by Sage, one on a motion that when adjourning the house adjourn to Monday and another on a simple move to adjourn. When these were defeated, Goodrich renewed the move for a call of the House.

At this point Maurice of New York developed a yearning to be excused from voting. To stop a roll call on this, Clingman of North Carolina made a point of order that the motion for a call of the House took precedence. The Chair therefore declared Maurice out of order. Campbell appealed from the ruling. Wheeler, hard-shell Democrat of New York, moved to lay the appeal on the table. Maurice thereupon asked to be excused from voting on this latter motion. The Chair again declared him out of order, whereupon Maurice appealed. This appeal the Chair refused to entertain, ruling that he could not deal with two appeals at once. And so it went. At 8:06 Flagler, New York Whig, tried an adjournment, but again the monotonous roll call checked off Nay. The House now had to vote on Wheeler's move to lay on the table the appeal on the question of whether Maurice was in order. But this was not to be done until two more roll calls on adjournment.

Finally Wheeler's appeal was defeated at nine o'clock, not quite an hour later. Then Maurice was up, moving that this vote be reconsidered. He was ruled out of order. Campbell appealed, but this was laid on the table by roll-call vote. The house was therefore back to Goodrich's renewal of Richardson's call of the House. Two more motions for adjournment were defeated, and at about 10 P.M. Meecham of Vermont moved to be excused. He was declared out of order, and Sage appealed. At this point Richardson came back to take command. His motion to lay Sage's appeal on the table was carried, and about 10:30 P.M. Richardson made his first concession. He modified his motion to close debate by substituting the words "five minutes after its consideration that day was resumed" for "twelve o'clock," for it was almost Friday then. This turned off nobody's oratory.

At 1:15 on Friday morning, after the House had been in session twenty-five hours, Banks of Massachusetts varied the diet a little by moving that Richardson's motion to get at the bill so long pending be laid on the table. The opponents of the bill made Friday a repetition of the day before; dilatory motion after dilatory motion had to be voted down in these never-ending roll calls that continued in unbroken succession until 11:30 P.M. of Friday. They had been going on for thirty-six hours.

This filibuster was a terrific experience. Richardson was ostensibly in charge of the administration forces, but he was beset by platoons of opposition generally operated by Whigs such as Russell Sage who later was to attain vast fortune by the ruthless methods of the "Robber Barons" and who seemed now to be getting into practice. To make the confusion greater, Senator Douglas came on the floor of the House and ordered and denounced, threatened and called strategic plays. He tried to boss the Speaker, ordering him to change his rulings (without success, however) and telling congressmen what to do, thus stirring up greater strife, since the House did not take too kindly to Senate direction. Also a number of the members attempted to keep up their strength and endurance by resort to alcoholic stimulation. A number became full and foolish, quarrelsome and irrational. One Virginian, Edmundson, very drunk and heavily armed, undertook to start a fight with Campbell of Ohio on the floor of the House. Fortunately no blood was shed; the only casualties collapsed in their chairs in drunken stupor as the weary hours piled up. The end came presumably because human endurance was at an end. The House adjourned its thirty-six-hour session without reaching any decision. It resumed briefly on Saturday, May 13, at twelve o'clock and continued the debate on Banks's motion to lay Richardson's motion on the table; then it adjourned at 2:05 P.M. At sometime during this week end some final understandings were reached.

Prior to this filibuster neither side had had any success with the device of the party caucus as a disciplinary rank-closing instrument during that session. Mem-

bers would not caucus—not the administration forces,
nor the anti-Nebraska Democrats, nor the bipartisan foes
of the bill. The Senate had finally solved its problems by
caucus, but the House could not get it in operation.
However, after the terrific experience of May 11-12 the
anti-Nebraska Democrats met. They learned from Richardson that he was willing to negotiate. Nineteen thereupon agreed to vote for a suspension of the rules so that
the Pacific Railroad bill could be postponed and the
debate prolonged a week. Perhaps they also secured the
elimination of the clause excluding foreigners. At the
same time they refused a caucus with the anti-Nebraska
Whigs to plan an effort to defeat the bill.

On Monday, May 15, therefore, Richardson withdrew
his demand for the previous question and offered a new
resolution setting the end of the debate for Friday,
May 19. When this was defeated by 141 to 61, he
moved to suspend the rules so that the consideration of
the Pacific Railroad bill could be set aside and debate
on the H.R. 236 be ended on May 20. This roll call
brought the desired results, 137 to 66. Nineteen recal-
citrants who in no other significant way would aid or
advance this bill now voted for the suspension of the rules
and supplied the votes necessary for the required two-
thirds. Not only had they been persuaded and perhaps
induced, but they could not be unconscious of the inex-
orable march of the days. They were well aware of the
heavy calendar of pending measures, in which so many
had a stake. It was obvious that a majority would vote
for the bill; why not have done? It was here that some
support came from New England and the West. Seven
from New England and nine from the West made the
two-thirds possible.

The debate continued all that extra week, seemingly
without any diminution. One hundred speeches were
eventually made, but the House seemed only to be getting its second wind. During this period of general de-

bate, speeches had been limited to one hour each. Now that this general debate was over, a new danger appeared. The bill would be open for amendment, and though each man could speak but five minutes, a multiplication of amendments at the hands of the ingenious might make this an endless process. Also, as the Senate operation had shown, a number of these amendments would make it necessary for members to record votes very embarrassing to them in the current campaigns. As the added week had showed no signs of any slowing up of oratory, the House managers decided on a most unusual move. They were determined that there should be no more fighting with amendments. They were prepared to slug it out in a final battle of influence and parliamentary maneuver. This meant that they must manage to bring on a vote immediately after the end of the formal debate, without permitting any opportunity for amendment.

Richardson finally accepted a proposal that Alexander H. Stephens, Georgia Whig, had been pressing for more than a week. The 119th House rule provided his instrument. Under it a privileged motion would be made in the Committee of the Whole to strike out the enacting clause of the bill under consideration; this would kill it. As this motion was privileged, it had to be voted on without debate as soon as made. If it passed, the Committee would then have to rise and report to the House that the bill was dead. Stephens proposed that the friends of the bill take such action, only to turn around in the House and refuse to accept this report of the Committee of the Whole. If such a vote to reject the report was successful, then, under the rules, the House must vote immediately, without further debate or opportunity to offer amendments, to pass or to defeat the bill. The bipartisan majority would then pass it. If this scheme worked, the managers would at long last insure the approval of the bill without fear of any further significant delay. Richardson and Stephens, Democrat and Whig, mounted their guns.[3]

On Monday, May 22, there was to be the showdown. When the House assembled at noon, Richardson moved that the House go into the Committee of the Whole. This was agreed to and the Speaker gave place to the Chairman, who again was Olds. Stephens then arose and offered his privileged motion to strike out the enacting clause. At first the opponents were sullenly going to refuse to vote, but finally twenty-two passed before the negative teller. The Committee thus struck out the enacting clause. Would they follow through in the House?

They did after some efforts at delay by dilatory motions, and at eight o'clock that evening the House refused to concur in the report of the Committee. Then the question was put on the engrossment of the bill. At this point Richardson submitted S. 22 without the Clayton amendment (excluding foreigners) as a substitute and moved the previous question. This was seconded and the main question put. After defeating a motion to adjourn, the House agreed to substitute amended S. 22 for H.R. 236. The engrossment of the bill was then moved, and motions to lay on the table and adjourn were defeated. It was then voted that the bill be engrossed and read a third time, and then came the crucial test. "Shall the bill pass?" It was agreed to by 113 to 100. The majority achieved on May 8 had held. By 11 P.M. it was done. Only a few more futile gestures were attempted before Richardson secured the adoption of a final motion reconsidering the vote by which Nebraska had passed and laying this motion upon the table. The bill would soon be on its way to the White House.

The overwhelming Democratic majority in the House had been shattered and made impotent. Only 100 of the 158 Democrats voted Aye. Of the thirteen New

England Democrats, only three had supported the bill, although seven more had contributed to make the two-thirds vote possible. In the Middle States, Pennsylvania made the best showing. Eight of her sixteen Democrats voted for the bill consistently, five others obliged to insure suspension of the rules; eleven were voting Aye at the end. Of the twenty-two New Yorkers, thirteen soft-shells and nine hard-shells, only one, and he a hard-shell, was consistently faithful. Ten voted to suspend the rules or were absent on that crucial ballot. In the end, four hards and five softs supported the bill. No New Jersey men voted for the bill consistently; all revolted against it on the first test; two finally supported it.

In the West, in Illinois, Douglas could command only three of his five colleagues. Of the ten from Indiana only four were constant, although all aided to suspend the rules; seven finally voted Aye. Ohio, Michigan, and Wisconsin were of little or no help except to secure the suspension of the rules. The small delegations of Iowa and California were perfect in their support, but their combined voting strength was only three.[4]

In the end only eighteen of the sixty-six rebels had been won back: eight in New York, five softs and three hards; three in Pennsylvania; two in New Jersey; three in Indiana; and one each in Ohio and Michigan. Of these only three names are remembered: Francis B. Cutting and "Boss" Tweed, hard-shells, and Jim Lane of later Kansas notoriety. Of the thirteen state delegations controlled by Democrats, only four remained loyal: Pennsylvania, Indiana, Illinois, and California. Of the ninety-two northern Democrats, forty-four voted Aye, while forty-three voted Nay and five were absent. All the southern Democrats save two, Millson of Virginia and Thomas Hart Benton of Missouri, voted for the bill on the final showdown. But as the Democrats could only muster 100 of their 158 votes, the final victory was won, not by Douglas and his Democratic cohorts, but by a bipartisan coalition marshaled by the Georgia Whig Alexander H. Stephens, who devised the ingenious maneuver that in the end put the bill over. The eighteen Democratic rebels who had been persuaded to change and vote Aye were not enough. Had it not been for the support of thirteen southern Whigs, the now impotent Democratic majority could not have carried the bill.

Thus the act came into being. It bore little resemblance to the bill for which Douglas had struggled in the short session of the preceding Congress. The Calhoun faction, southern and northern Whigs, Free-Soilers, the Administration, and certain hard-shell Democrats had all made use of this measure in one way or another, and the final bill was the work of many hands and the fruit of much strategic planning. Its real history is the analysis of how a bill ostensibly to organize a territory had been made an instrument of the fundamental political reorganization that the disintegration of the old parties had made inevitable. The story of these political maneuvers is one of the most intricate of the chapters in the history of the construction of Leviathan.

In this fateful legislative session the Democrats had officially accepted squatter sovereignty, but Douglas himself had lost an essential portion of his northern support without improving his position in the South. A significant segment of the northern Democracy had left the party. Likewise a real antisouthern coalition, which could capitalize the voting superiority of the more populous North, was insured; the seed of the Republican Party had been planted. A new power was in creation that was determined to remodel Leviathan. Finally, and not usually noted, was the fact that in this winter of political discontent the southern members of Congress for the first time organized and presented a well-nigh solid political front and among them traditional party divisions were largely laid aside. It was but a few steps onward to secession, the Confederacy and the disruption of Leviathan.

The Kansas-Nebraska Act was one of the least successful examples of American political ingenuity. It not only failed to accomplish its primary objective, which was to permit the process of building new communities to continue peaceably and efficiently, but it caused the creation of a new political organization dedicated to destroying the carefully constructed power balance maintaining equilibrium between North and South.

Antisouthern political leadership, as the plot charge so vividly demonstrated, seized upon the repeal of the Missouri Compromise as an example of southern ruthless determination to rule regardless of northern and national welfare; it was the crack of the slaveholders' whip. There was a remarkably widespread resentment, which resulted in the formation of a northern party that skillfully exploited antagonism to the South and slavery. It began winning victories in the spring of 1854, and by the presidential campaign of 1856, American ingenuity had managed something new, a sectional party, appealing only to northern interest, counting on the fact that migration had now produced such a preponderance of free-state voters that their mobilization would carry the presidency and Congress. The success of this northern uprising was rapid. The Democrats were defeated in the congressional elections in 1854-1855, and had the new Republican Party won two more states—Pennsylvania and Indiana or Illinois—the Republicans would have gained the presidency in 1856.

A second unexpected and equally disastrous by-product of the Kansas-Nebraska blueprint was the explosive settlement of the territory of Kansas. Those entering Kansas had reached a stage in territorial development that was new and that opened an entirely unexpected phase of the old process of community organization. In order to settle Kansas, men had to cope with new conditions, hitherto unknown in the territorial experience. These new conditions shaping Kansas society, as James C. Malin has pointed out, were the transportation revolution of the nineteenth century, the rounding out of the continental land mass of the United States and the location of the territory in a region where men crossed a great river fed by tributaries, passed the last fringe of the forest belt and emerged on the grasslands, a new and unfamiliar environment for those who approached it. These conditions of time, space and experience were causing the Kansan settlers to undergo a compulsory and disturbing revision of behavior. There was a resultant confusion and insecurity that induced emotional exaggeration and erratic conduct beyond that usual in territories and which was to complicate the processes of cultural adaptation and social adjustment always indicated by migration to new territory.[5]

These processes were exaggerated in Kansas because of yet another circumstance. The normal process of selection that controlled the migration of population westward was interfered with by a peculiar set of factors. Normally, when a territorial domain was opened up, its settlers were dominated by individual impulses and motivations. But in the case of Kansas, organized and advertised efforts were devised to bring specially selected settlers, not as individuals, but as members of groups identified with definite intense purposes and conditioned by motives of social hostility. These new conditions necessitated the invention of new political techniques.

Even before the Kansas-Nebraska bill was enacted, a group of Massachusetts enthusiasts had incorporated the New England Emigrant Aid Company with the purpose of encouraging free-state settlers to go to Kansas.

Contrary to widely held opinion, the company did not pay people to go or even bear their expenses; it arranged block bookings and provided advice and "conductors" for migration in companies. Several such parties were piloted to the company's real-estate development at the townsite of Lawrence. One or two parties were likewise organized in the South, but it was more difficult to interest slaveholders with their Negro property to come to a region that meteorologically was to prove difficult. The extreme cold of Kansas winters was especially hard on the slaves who were moved up there. Southern interest in migration on the part of groups of slave owners could not be made to flourish.

Though these organized groups produced a relatively small part of the inhabitants of Kansas, their emotion-rousing potential was high. The fact that a few groups were brought in selected quotas from the faraway sections of New England and the lower South spread the folklore that many such companies had come. It was an age when motivation was highly colored by Romanticism and religion, and these selected settlers came to protect rights and to conquer sin, to fight evil and to prevent wrong.

Had the process of natural selection of emigrants exclusively prevailed, the migration would have covered a population that was reasonably familiar with territorial Mississippi Valley conditions; but this interruption of the process by the infusion of these unconditioned groups produced an exaggerated cultural conflict and a much more difficult social adjustment.

These difficulties of adaptation produced a political situation that almost exhausted the capacity of the territorial system. This pattern of government, instituted in 1787, had been predicated upon the premise that in distant regions a naturally selected scattered population would manage its own affairs in a series of stages that would require a minimum of supervision, interference or even knowledge on the part of the federal government. The settlers would carry on literally by themselves and make, live with and, on occasion, correct their own mistakes. But Kansas was different. Every phase of its territorial operation was spotlighted and watched; it was projected upon a distorted national screen. There were no adequate means of communication or management to make supervision efficient. The federal officials in Kansas were therefore called upon to produce an order that was neither typical nor possible.

The territorial phase of Kansas experience, therefore, is perhaps best understood in terms of a cultural rather than a technically political conflict. The elements in this cultural conflict are not clean-cut but confused. Under ordinary circumstances, men and women representing midwestern culture would have opened up the new region. They would have been reasonably adaptable. Inevitably, there would have been rivalry, contest and confusion, but it would have been kept within the limits set by transmontane customs. The infusion of organized migrants from further regions brought people who were unschooled in the ways of new settlement, unadaptable and, what was worse, bound helplessly to resist adaptation. To complicate matters further, other groups appeared who were, through no fault of their own, to arouse prejudices and stir up strife: these were people of foreign birth, some of them Catholic, as well as Negro slaves and freed Negroes.

These groups with their conflict-rousing potential found that potential increased by environmental complications. Most of the migrants were from forest-belt and corn-culture experience, who now must face life on the grasslands, out on the open prairie. The weather, the lack of wood and the difficulty of the initial breaking of the soil, together with the more subtle influence of the monotony of the interminable flat plains, had a disturbing and confusing influence on the newcomers, and it could be demoralizing. This situation produced a new temptation to strife because the forest-conditioned settlers wanted to engross the wooded areas and leave only grassland to later comers. This demand for the limited areas of wooded land made the inevitable contest for choice real estate more intense than usual. This bitterness was inflamed by the tardiness of the federal government in making the surveys and furnishing the land plats without which titles could not be registered nor deeds issued. During the first two years of the territorial experience, many had to depend on their own prowess to defend their claims against the ubiquitous claim jumper.

Another phase of territorial confusion added to the turmoil. In every territory there was a natural scattering of towns. Most frequently their locations were dictated by the natural features of the region, such as advantageous river sites. Real-estate speculators had an obvious stake in these places, and so it was not difficult to foresee rivalry, squabbles and other disturbing conflicts. In Kansas there was not only a variety of natural locations that could stir ardent supporters to initiate rival claims, but the new transportation possibilities provided by the expected railroads, transcontinental and otherwise, also invited a new form of contention. The proponents of a railroad site might well seem to be at war with the advocates of a river site. The troublemaking possibilities of these town-site rivalries were further augmented by the fact that New England migrants were developing one site while other antagonistic groups were at work building up rivals.

These situations greatly complicated the operation of the federal system of territorial control and the drafting of instructions, laws and proposed constitutions. The authorities at Washington appointed the executive and judicial officers of the territory and then expected of them the impossible. Government in the strict sense could not be imposed upon settlers on the banks of the Missouri and the Kansas, particularly by officials sent from the East. If any controlling influence was to be exercised, it could be effective only if the appointees in question were experienced men enjoying to some degree the confidence of the local citizens. This the officials seldom were equipped to command. There was therefore a basic conflict within government itself. The territorial citizens represented by a legislature of their own choosing were required to cooperate with officials appointed from elsewhere, not only in making the laws governing the usual statutory matters, but also in distributing franchises, grants, charters and other bases for economic development, some of them of great value. Striving for these latter privileges there were often bitterly conflicting interests, made more bitter in their rivalry by the fact that the appointive officials on occasion had special interests of their own or represented eastern interests. These varieties of conflict could be clothed in the simple language of contests of principle over freedom and slavery. A new politics had indeed to be invented.

This confused conflict may be related to the general complex of federal-territorial relationship by allusion to another situation—the national political reorganization that was taking place in the fifties. Kansas became a football in that contest and was violently kicked around. This game became the more difficult because so many of the interested parties could have no knowledge of Kansas or its realities. This situation had its reflex in Kansas particularly in the matter of the formation of parties and in the forming of party issues. Those who were busy creating the anti-Democratic coalition that eventually became the Republican Party found certain of the erratic, lawless and brutal phases of Kansas territorial behavior excellent propaganda, and the term "Bleeding Kansas" became part of the official Republican line. The use made of the Kansas situation in the East caused many prominent politicians in that region to take a personal interest in the territory, to correspond with people there, to send agents thither and on occasion to go there themselves. So not only was there the public relation between official Washington and the territorial politicians and other citizenry, but there was also this unofficial advice, prompting or interference.

Out of this a complex emotion developed, rousing a demand for self-government and a protest against interference, while at the same time national patterns were imposed that caused local issues to go under cover although they were still potential agents of even greater confusion. Citizens acted ostensibly in the name of national issues when they were really motivated by local objectives. Under such an analysis the whole simple picture of an antislavery—proslavery contest disappears. Here we see a struggle for self-determination in terms of cultural conflict and social adjustment, confused by outside interference and misuse.

The confusion and propaganda of these new political techniques—so useful to the rising Republicans, so destructive to the badly split Democrats—greatly complicated the process of drawing up and adopting the constitution necessary to make Kansas a state. Four constitutional conventions were called and four constitutions were drafted and sent to the voters, one of them twice. Congress, however, would not accept three of them, and it was not until the fourth try that the voters came to any real agreement and adopted the instrument that Congress finally found acceptable. Admission then could only be attained after the first seceding states had left. Kansas followed Minnesota (1857) and Oregon (1859) into the Union in January, 1861. The nineteen free states were now definitely predominant in the Union of thirty-four states, and the returns of the census of 1860 that were then being published pointed in only one direction. The slave states were to be more and more in the minority column.

Even before the question of Kansas statehood had been resolved, the territory had produced a terrible instrument, a weapon of mad and perverted ingenuity, with which an emotionally disturbed man undertook to create a distorted, frightening Leviathan. In the course of the Kansas turmoil one of the zealous free-state operators was a crazed cattle drover, John Brown, who believed himself an instrument of the Almighty to free the slave. He had gained a reputation for ruthless butchery at the Pottawatomie Massacre in Kansas and had secured through this reputation the means to lead a slave uprising in Virginia. Some northern antislavery zealots financed an expedition into the South designed to make slavery so dangerous that the southern states would have to abandon it. Brown's plan was to set up cities of refuge in the southern mountains; agents were to supply the slaves with arms and exhort them to flee to these fastnesses. He drew blueprints in the form of a constitution for a Negro republic that would serve as a continual invitation for slaves to run away to fortified communities from which it would be difficult to dislodge them. From these refuges, armed bands might sortie and release their fellows still in bondage. In October, 1859, Brown undertook to initiate his plan of terrorism by a raid on Harper's Ferry arsenal. The raid was a complete failure. Its leader was arrested, tried and hanged.

But the element of terror had been introduced in exaggerated form. It had been first charged in 1854 that there was an atrocious plot to be hatched in Congress and in Kansas, a plot to expand slavery. But then it had been distant, and in a region where there was really no racial problem. Now this terror had been brought to the Atlantic region and to a community that included a large proportion of Negroes. If a slave rebellion had broken out in Virginia, the results might have been frightful. No such terror resulted, nor does there seem to have been any real danger of it. But people thought such danger present, and through the South the fear spread. To make it worse it was believed that Republican office holders and Republican money were behind Brown. This, it was charged, was a plot literally to destroy the political power of the South by organized forays into the slave states. Though no evidence of significant Republican implication in such a plot is to be found, the important fact was that many believed such intervention to be the truth and that southern civilization was in danger of destruction by those who would seize the power to redesign Leviathan.

CHAPTER SEVEN

DISINTEGRATION

JOHN BROWN'S raid was frightening. Had the American democracy degenerated to the point where a political party on the make was supporting gangsters to break the power of its long-ruling opponents, by instigating a slave uprising? Was self-government as operated in the federal system about to collapse or was Leviathan to be redesigned by force? Such questions suggested to many that Leviathan's operation needed attention and adjustment. The talent of the politically ingenious, upon which the efficiency of self-government in such large part depends, was to be taxed to its utmost.

Leadership in political inventiveness had been a southern specialty. The part played by the Virginia dynasty in creating the federal mechanism was a prime factor in the South's initial success. And when these designers had passed from the scene, John C. Calhoun of South Carolina was prepared to take over the command, though his bid for primacy was challenged by Henry Clay of Kentucky, representing the new transmontane section, and Daniel Webster of Massachusetts, who essayed to inherit the role of the Adamses.

The real problem with which such leaders must deal involved the documentary requirements of the rapid growth of the nation in population and in area and the consequent constant adjustment of the power to govern caused by the steady creation of new units in the complex governmental structure. This process was made infinitely complex by the presence of millions of Negroes, most of whom were bondmen—legally salable chattels—rather than citizens. Had the United States remained static in the original quadrilateral of 1787, which had ecological resources to permit two cultures of relatively equal political strength, the republic might have let nature take its course in shaping the history of the Negro. But there was this constant growth, the consequent reshuffling of power and the struggle to possess it. Slavery became not merely a custom, but a political instrument and a lethal one.

In the beginning, slavery had been a normal incident in colonial development, determined by the fact that in so vast an area there was an inadequate labor supply. Promoters in such regions adopted any expedient they could contrive, such as introducing indentured servants and Negro slaves. When the republic was achieved, slavery existed in all the states. However it survived only where gangs of agricultural labor were needed. It would probably not have been an instrument of catastrophe in the long run, any more than it was in other slaveholding societies, if it had not been for the fact that the United States was so large, spread over such a wide variety of ecological areas, with such a various constantly expanding population, and with the slaveholders concentrated in what was to be but a corner of the republic. Then the trouble arose because at first the slaveholding region was much larger in proportion than it was to become by the mid-nineteenth century. It had originally been in control, but as it shrank in proportion it was to shrink in power.[1]

It was the fact of the change in power status of the sections of the United States that produced the conflict. This change was bitterly contested and those engaged in the conflict used any weapons they could lay their hands on. The southern leadership endeavored to slow down development or at least to shape institutional patterns in new communities to draft specifications for Leviathan in unnatural designs. To keep the power to enforce such unnatural patterns, the South endeavored to frustrate the ambitions and plans of a growing number of individuals and interests. Those whom they frustrated therefore sought political means to break their control. They sought to rally uncommitted voters, voters from nonslaveholding areas and foreign immigrants by attacking the morality of slavery and the morals of slaveholders.

In an age of revivalism and in a society that was as Calvinistic and sin-conscious as American society was, this weapon could be used with powerful effect, arousing Freudian libidos before Freud was ever dreamed of. Under its use southern attitudes intensified. At first southerners simply justified their society as a good society, more humane and Christian than the irresponsible industrial society where the employers accepted no responsibility for their wage earners, and supported them only when they worked. But under years of attack and as they saw the free-labor population outdistance them, southern leaders found their power slipping. This fact made it easy to believe that those who attacked slavery were determined, in order to gain power, to set the Negroes free, no longer under restraint in their communities. Under this possibility the southern imagination began to imagine horrors that John Brown's raid made seem real.

Particularly after John Brown's foray, the South had now come to believe that Republican victory would mean that the slaves would in some way be tampered with and the southern states put in mortal danger of rebellion, rape and enforced social equality. Against these dangers the South felt the imperative need to retain the means of self-protection. If it could not keep the old power, it must secure a new one. The need of new power was also felt in order to protect the section from a disproportionate share in taxes, and the nation

from the dominance of a new power that would be established in the increasing number of communities in
the newer United States of America. The nature of this
new power no one knew, but the South, which had held
the old power, had complex reasons to dread and fear
it and to endeavor to avoid being subject to it. They
feared a new Leviathan of northern design.

But must the South lose its power? Could not Leviathan be adjusted or, if not, could not a new but southern Leviathan be constructed? Calhoun and certain of
his sectional associates had long been concerned with
Leviathan's design. As early as the 1820's the South
Carolinian had been increasingly conscious of a change
taking place in the equilibrium of the power structure
of the republic, a change harmful to the South. He
sensed that some ingenuity was called for to maintain
the balance. He was a man of ingenious mind, and he
built upon the work of the Virginia dynasty. In the
spirit of the Virginia and Kentucky resolutions of 1798
he could advocate nullification. He worked for the acquisition of more slave territory, notably Texas. He
demanded the recognition of the right of slave owners
to take their property into the common territories and
the protection of it there by federal law. Toward the
end of his career he concluded that there should be a
reconstruction of Leviathan.

In the last year of his life he formulated his conclu-
sions. He insisted that the constituted elements in the
republic must "provide for the insertion of a provision in the constitution, by an amendment which will
restore to the South, in substance, the power she possessed of protecting herself, before the equilibrium
between the sections was destroyed" by the greater size
and power of the North.[2] This amendment was designed to insert in the federal system the principle of
the concurrent majority whereby each interest, particularly the South, would be given "the means of protect-

ing itself by its negative, against all measures calculated to advance the peculiar interests of others at its expense." [3] The operation of the concurrent majority should be implemented by reorganizing the executive branch "so that its powers . . . should be vested in two" presidents, one chosen periodically from each section. One should administer foreign affairs and the other domestic concerns alternately, the assignment to be made by lot. The approval of both executives would be required to complete the enactment of any law.[4]

According to Pollard in his *Lost Cause,* Calhoun had "hit upon one of the most beautiful and ingenious theories in American politics to preserve and perfect the Union, and to introduce into it that principle of adaptability to circumstances which is the first virtue of wise governments. He proposed that in cases of serious dispute between any State and the General Government, the matter should be referred to a convention of all the States for its final and conclusive determination. He thus proposed, instead of destroying the Union, to erect over it an august guardianship." [5]

However much Calhoun in his last days may have hoped that the sectional problem might be solved by such a constitutional convention, over the years of his long life he had been on occasion willing to contemplate direct action and to threaten nullification and secession in a fashion vigorous enough to make the issue now uncertain. As these threats hitherto had obtained what were probably their objectives—that is, concession and compromise—there seemed a good deal of doubt whether anything more drastic than threats was now needed. Would not these threats secure for the South the autonomy with security that was wanted?

Calhoun had died in 1850, leaving this variously equipped political arsenal to the South as his legacy. Since then the center of southern political gravity and intellectual activity had shifted from Virginia and South Carolina to Alabama and Mississippi, where a new generation was contesting for Calhoun's mantle. In Alabama, William L. Yancey, a "fire-eater," and an active candidate for the Senate, sounded a call for drastic action. In January, 1860, the Democratic state convention followed his lead in demanding that the national presidential nominating body insert in the party platform a plank endorsing Calhoun's demand that slave property be protected in the territories. The Democrats' indirect object was to prevent the party from nominating Stephen A. Douglas of Illinois for the presidency. The delegation was instructed to leave the convention if this slave protection plank was not adopted. Shortly afterward the legislature of Alabama passed a law requiring the governor to call a sovereignty convention if a Republican president were elected in November.[6]

In this same season of apprehension, Senator Jefferson Davis of Mississippi, in many respects the real heir of Calhoun, turned the Senate of the United States into a preconvention Democratic caucus. He proceeded from where Calhoun's resolutions of 1837 and 1847 had left off and presented a new set that in effect repeated the demand for federal protection of slave property in the territories. A full-scale debate brought the matter to no conclusion in Washington, but it set the stage for Charleston.

At the April national convention Douglas held the line for squatter sovereignty; thereupon, as instructed, the Alabamans led a walkout of the the Gulf States' delegations. The convention recessed for six weeks to attempt to reunite the party, but to no avail. In June two Democratic conventions met in Baltimore. The majority group nominated Douglas, and the "come-outers" presented Vice-President John C. Breckinridge of Kentucky and the Calhoun-Davis platform. Even at this early stage there seemed to be some calculation that Breckinridge's position as Vice-President placed him at a point of rare vantage to lead a southern coup in Washington if the section's interests seemed to demand it prior to March 4.[7]

Douglas campaigned strenuously, armed with the principle of squatter sovereignty, but the split in the Democratic Party practically assured victory for the Republicans. They went to the people with Abraham Lincoln of Illinois, a prairie dark horse, as their candidate and a catch-all platform that combined prohibition of the further spread of slavery with a protective tariff, a Pacific Railroad subsidy, and free homesteads —in a sense building on the American system devised by Clay and in part supported by Webster.

The probable success of the Republican ticket in 1860 caused certain of the hotheads in the South to threaten secession if Lincoln won, more or less daring the nation to elect him. When their threats were not heeded, the southern people fell prey to mixed emotion. Anger, fear and a sense of being honor bound to fulfill a pledge were uppermost.[8] This confusion threatened a crisis, and the politically ingenious were now really challenged to produce some sort of saving blueprint. Southern designers in studying the available plans gave their closest attention to one drafted long before. This was secession; to some a counsel of desperation, to others a shrewd solution. Over the years it had often been worked over.

Americans had been come-outers from the very beginning. Many of those who had settled New England were secessionists from life and customs as practiced in the British Isles. The founders of Connecticut and Rhode Island, discontented, had migrated from Massachusetts Bay. The American Revolution was a mass secession from the Empire, and the states ratifying the Constitution seceded from the Confederation. For many years New England interests had chafed at southern domination, and an incipient secession move came to an inglorious end with the failure of the Hartford Convention of 1815.

When the tide of population began turning to the northern sector of Transappalachia, the shoe was fitted on the other foot. After the Mexican Cession and the failure to extend the Missouri Compromise line to the Pacific, when certain southern leaders, notably Calhoun, had become apprehensive of minority status, there was talk of concerted southern action. A convention as abortive as that at Hartford came to nought in 1850 at Nashville. When in 1856 there seemed to be the threat of the election of a Republican president, the Governor of Virginia wrote to his fellow southern governors expressing concern and the need of united action if the militant foes of the South thus triumphed, prating of majority rule. But it was a false alarm.

During the summer of 1860 renewed planning was undertaken, not only in the southern capitals but in Washington itself. What should be done if the South were in a sense defied and Lincoln elected? Just what the extent of these plans was cannot now be accurately charted. The word "conspiracy" has been used off and on. Certainly there were many discussions and a variety of suggestions. Likewise there was organizing. Marching clubs of "minute men" wearing palmetto cockades were drilling in South Carolina. Blue cockades were sported in Georgia. Governor Gist of South Carolina sent his brother, appropriately named States Rights Gist, to confer with his fellow governors. Southern office holders in Washington as high as cabinet rank, and those directing the Breckinridge headquarters there, hobnobbed with members of Congress from their section. Undoubtedly plans were discussed and perhaps agreed upon; the Treasury Department was spoken of as one possible center of action. Some became con-

vinced that the South must secede and set up for itself;
but others believed that the times called for a redesigning of Leviathan in the spirit of Calhoun. Here there
was further difference of opinion as to extent and means.
Some advocated conference, others believed that there
should be secession first and conference afterward. There
was more confusion than consensus prior to election day.

Because of an historical accident, southern reaction
to Lincoln's election could immediately be given official utterance. When the Constitution went into effect
in 1789, there was no method of appointing presidential electors that was uniformly followed in all the
states; several assigned the task to their legislatures. By
1860 all had given up this method save South Carolina.
But in that state the legislature met every four years on
the day before election to appoint the state's electors.
The Governor of the state was a secessionist; he had
been in correspondence with other southern governors,
and he was ready to proceed even if most of them did
not seem to concur in the need for immediate action.
The leading South Carolina politicians had been in
conference. Gist therefore requested the South Carolina legislature to remain in session until the election
result was known. These solons were thus poised, and
when the news of Lincoln's election reached them,
within a few days they decreed an election for a sovereignty convention to which the voters would pass on
their will as to secession. The Governor of Alabama
was obliged to do the same, and some such decision was
reached in the other Gulf States. Meetings of secessionists similar to those in South Carolina were reported in
other states on the eve of the election.

The newspapers carried stories of southern office
holders in Washington mounting revolutionary cockades and preparing to go South.[9] The New York *Herald* described an "informal meeting of distinguished
Southern statesmen from the cotton and Gulf States,"

held at Charleston on November 7, representing South Carolina, Georgia, Alabama, Florida and Mississippi. This group, the names of whose members were withheld, drew up a "Great Southern Manifesto" that was published and designated a representative to go to Europe to secure aid. The French minister reported such a meeting, but he too omitted any names. The minister from Bremen advised his government that Senator Slidell spoke as though there was some planning for South Carolina's program outside of the state and an understanding that South Carolina would not secede until a representative of the state had gone to Washington to discuss matters with the President and congressional leaders.[10]

When Congress assembled on the first Monday in December, no state had yet taken any decisive action, but the South Carolina senators and certain key federal office holders in that state had resigned; it was quite obvious that barring a miracle some states would attempt secession. Would Congress find some way to readjust Leviathan to keep it from falling apart? The reassembling lawmakers immediately began working on blueprints for changes. The members of the houses had much at stake, but their emotions were mixed. We sometimes lose sight of the fact that when the lawmakers assembled no one knew who would control the next Congress, that the future management of the lawmaking process was in doubt. The Republicans had won the presidency, that was clear; but what of Congress?

A great deal hinged on the control of the lawmaking body. Southern leadership had vetoed positive legislation for so long that a great frustration had accumulated. The Republican platform in 1860 had promised an end to the negative and, it was hoped, the inauguration of an age of legislative positivism. Protective tariffs, railroad subsidies, land donations had been prom-

ised in the Republican platform, the greatest pack-
age of promotion dreamed of since Hamilton's day. A
most heterogeneous variety of northern schemers and
promoters would not casually accept any denial of such
a bonanza. Any measures that could insure Republican
control of Congress would seem welcome, even the
withdrawal of some southern legislative slave drivers.
There were probably as many that hoped as feared.

As the election returns indicated, the Senate would
surely continue Democratic* and the House would likewise be so, at least on paper. A complicating factor was
the possibility that Douglas and his small nucleus
might hold the balance of power. Such an eventuality
was pleasing to neither side. The southerners hated
Douglas and the Republicans did not wish to share
with him, to owe him that which they were determined
to have. If a few southern delegations were to withdraw, the Republicans could be in complete control,
beholden to Douglas for nothing.[11]

National political thinking since the days of Calhoun,
Clay and Webster had been done largely in the Senate.
Since the death of these statesmen, a new junto had
essayed the leadership. These men were the chairmen
of the principal Senate committees and some associates.
Since they had deprived Douglas of his chairmanship of the territorial committee, this ruling junto was
wholly southern. In 1860 its members were Robert
M. T. Hunter and James M. Mason of Virginia,
chairmen of the finance and foreign relations commit-

* Of the sixty-eight Senators there would be twenty-nine southern
Democrats, seven northern Democrats, thirty-one Republicans and
one Southern American. Support of Douglas and three northern
Democrats might enable the Republicans to control the Senate,
but such support was not likely. These seven northern Democrats
were Douglas, Latham and McDougal of California, Nesmith of
Oregon, Rice of Minnesota, Bright of Indiana and Thomson of
New Jersey. Even if Douglas and Latham would vote with Republicans, could two more be persuaded, probably in the hope of
a Pacific Railroad subsidy?

tees respectively; Jefferson Davis, military affairs; Clay of Alabama, commerce; Benjamin of Louisiana, private land claims; and Toombs of Georgia and Slidell of Louisiana, who held no chairmanships. The opposition was scattered, but concentrating as the number of Republicans increased. Its principal spokesmen in 1860 were Douglas, still a Democrat; Crittenden, one of the few remaining old-line Whigs; and Seward of the Republicans.

When Congress assembled it was voted by both Houses, though in the Senate only after some delay, that each should raise a special committee to seek a solution for the great problem. The Senate authorized the Vice-President to choose thirteen men, and the House instructed the Speaker to set up a committee of thirty-three. If any blueprint were to be contrived, it would presumably be achieved by the senators. Vice-President Breckinridge chose the Senate committee well and named to it Crittenden, Davis, Douglas, Hunter, Seward and Toombs, six of the strongest members. Could these men draft any plan to which Congress would agree?

A bewildering group of conferences undertook to find new designs. Most dynamic was a caucus of the members from the lower South. The border-states representatives likewise conferred. A group from the northwestern states went into session. The delegations from New York, Pennsylvania and Ohio, each had their discussions.[12] These designers were in fact engulfed in a confusion of thinking that it is now difficult to recapture fully. The eventual quick succession of secession, the organization of the Confederacy and the war itself make it seem that the problem was merely one of reconciling two points of view, union and secession, North and South. But this simple analysis gives no accurate picture of the confusing variety of plans and ideas whirling around in the minds of the many who attempted new designs.

The most significant element in the confusion, and one sometimes lost sight of, was the lack of anything like unity among the inhabitants of the fifteen slave states and their leaders. Despite the precipitate action on the part of South Carolina and the appearance of similar haste along the Gulf Coast, it did not take much perception to discover that less than half of the fifteen were ready to act. At least eight, including Virginia, were not going to move without some more tangible evidence, some overt act of hostility. There was significant criticism in the upper South of South Carolina's haste, criticism that focuses attention upon a problem that was to cause many repercussions during the life of the Confederacy. This was Virginia's historic position, established in the days when her dynasty was so long in power. Virginians believed themselves titular leaders of the South and resented action in which they did not play a leading role. The Old Dominion senators felt that any move that did not include Virginia was unthinkable.[13]

Virginia, though herself not ready to act, believed that the nation should turn to her for mediation. Her statesmen were planning to undertake direct negotiations with the Republicans and the northern Democrats. They were designing terms of readjustment and were indignant that the lower South had not waited. Some believed that the Gulf States were rushing off with indecent haste to create a republic of their own, which they would design and rule, leaving only the crumbs for any who might later wish to join. Virginia was not used to inferior status; this attitude was to bear fruit later. Virginia's distaste for precipitate action, if not her pretensions to leadership, apparently were shared by the seven other slave states north of the Gulf contingent, where those interested in secession seemed in a decided minority.

Even among those seemingly headed for direct action it may be doubted if all had the same final objective—namely, an independent republic, a confederacy
of slave states. One of Calhoun's ideas probably figured
larger in the minds of those in responsible places in
Washington and in the South than we now recall. He
had detailed a plan for reconstruction of the Union by
constitutional amendment to be proposed by a national
convention.

Certain of Calhoun's disciples were working for this
plan. Jefferson Davis had suggested such a convention
back in Mississippi at election time. He was hesitant to
engage in the precipitous action so epidemic in the
Gulf region. He was doubtful whether immediate secession showed proper timing. Before leaving Mississippi, the senators and congressmen of the state had
held a meeting at the capitol at which Davis spoke
against secession before Congress had had time to try
its hand. He believed that delay might bring the federal government to realize the extent of the emergency
and to consent to a convention as an instrument useful
in negotiation, as a trading device to secure Calhoun's
plan for a reorganized union. He proved to be a minority in the delegation. At a White House reception
that November, Mrs. Davis had appeared wearing an
antisecession ribbon and proclaiming that Jeff Davis
was no disunionist.[14] There was undoubtedly much
thought given to finding a solution through negotiation
in some such agency of consensus as Calhoun's convention. But there was such a variety of counsel in
this fateful winter that the real southern program and
its objectives and motivations, if there were any, are
most difficult to define accurately.

Even in Calhoun's own state of South Carolina the
purpose and the process are not too clear. There is
some evidence that the Palmetto actionists, sporting
their revolutionary cockades, were not so hell-bent for

a Gulf State confederacy; rather, they had other purposes. The Palmetto State was independent in thought and action, the real personification, if there were any, of the purity of the states' rights doctrine. She had suffered much from loss of population and capital migrating into the Southwest, from the tough slavery promoters and profiteers beyond the mountains. These newer states were in effect sucking her blood. Her cultural and economic ties were along the Atlantic Coast, and in the continental heartland where she had been developing railroad connections with the Mississippi and the Ohio valleys. There were certainly some among her public men who were thinking of a Middle Confederacy wherein these river-valley states might be allied with the upper South. South Carolina hurried forward so as to be in a position to send representatives to Washington. The upper South sought to discover what the possibilities of negotiation were, perhaps for Calhoun's plan or for some other.[15]

The confusion of counsel can be further illustrated by certain samples of the variety of the interpretations of events. Everyone who talked was not necessarily saying what he meant. Some of those who made the most violent disunion speeches were reported as "entertaining in their private conversation" the prospect of adjustment and confidentially advising their constituents not to sell real estate in Washington nor dispose of their property in northern states. They were using fire-eating as an instrument.[16]

The Secretary of War, a Virginian and so far a professed Unionist, by "reluctant steps had arrived at the opinion that it might be well, if bloodshed could be avoided, to let secession actually take place; for then, affairs having come to a crisis and both parties to the quarrel having realized the solemnity of the case, an honorable and permanent adjustment of the matters of difference between them would be rendered more practicable." Others said Floyd authorized Major Anderson to move his garrison to Sumter in Charleston harbor, in the belief that this would insure gunfire and the secession of Virginia and the border states.[17]

Former Senator John Bell of Tennessee, recently presidential candidate on the Constitutional Union ticket, believed he understood what was up. "I have suspected from the first that Yancey & Co. succeeded in seducing so great a number of the Democratic Party into the plan of dividing the party at Charleston and Baltimore by persuading them that though they might fail to elect Breckinridge, the election of Lincoln would be insured, which would give a pretext for secession to so many states, already well-disposed to do so and that when they should actually secede, the North would become alarmed, make such concessions as would be satisfactory and therefore the seceding states would return to the fold of the Union and the Democrats or Breckinridge party would have all the credit of having forced the North to do justice to the South and thenceforth claim to have been the saviour of the Union." [18]

A Floridian wrote to his brother-in-law in the North: "This whole secession movement is the work of a few persons influenced by various motives. There are some who think a separation from the North would be advantageous to the South. These have been untiring in the propagation of their views, others are ambitious of place and think their prospect of getting it would be better by overturning the government and beginning anew. Others are bankrupt and think in a revolution the past would be blotted out. Others again want Negroes and to open the slave trade. . . .

". . . Taking advantage of our election excitement and the hatred engendered by a studied misrepresentation of the North as a whole, of the predominant party, the people have been impulsively rushed into the secession movement without reflection or care for the consequences . . . it has been a raging fever, an epidemic." [19]

To add to the confusion, no idea seemed too bizarre and no imagining too irresponsible to secure some expression and attention. In this romantic age imaginations were running riot. Southern men and women of wealth and family, long schooled in the necessities of justifying human slavery, had set up a concept of theirs as an ideal society. The South was an aristocracy benevolently guided by superior people of culture and property. Southerners thought of themselves as a chivalry of unusual valor and responsibility. The continuous attacks upon their morals by boorish, money-grubbing Yankees whom they had come to despise were becoming increasingly intolerable. The idea was spreading in "society" that it was time to break away from these canting hypocrites, particularly the New England variety, and establish a new republic in which the principle of rule by an elite should prevail. Mrs. Jefferson Davis, no longer opposed to secession, was quoted in this regard. This idea had been perhaps stimulated by the recent visit in October of the charming Prince of Wales. There were those who dreamed of inviting over a royal prince to rule and of creating an order of nobility.[20]

The sampling of this confusion brings us back to the possibility that there may have been fewer southern actionists bent on independence for its own sake than has been assumed. The real motive and object of many, now largely lost sight of, was the creation of the Confederacy as a bargaining agency more effective than a minority group negotiating within the Union. As Thomas R. R. Cobb expressed it, better terms could be secured out of the Union than in it. This underlines the probability that the real objective of many more than is sometimes credited was the reconstructed Union projected by Calhoun, in which the South would have autonomy and security. This plan Hunter of Virginia reworked and formally presented to the Senate on January 11, the day before Seward was to advocate rather vaguely a national constitutional convention at some indefinite future time.[21] The hope of negotiation and reconstruction, later somewhat conveniently forgotten, makes more meaningful some stray records of expectation of speedy return to Washington by those participating in secession.

In northern circles there were confusions just as destructive of realistic action. The most prevalent was the feeling that southern attitudes were all bluff. There had been threats of southern nullification and secession now and again for forty years and nothing had yet happened. Many felt that there was something specious about these threats. "Wolf" had been cried too often. After the usual fire-eating bluster, the contenders would sit down around a table somewhere and bargain it out. The situation had always worked out that way before.[22]

Others felt that the current threat was an agitation by a fiery few and that the mass of southern people were loyal. No less a statesman than Abraham Lincoln held this view. He had started life as a poverty-stricken southerner, and he felt that a great number of southerners of similar humble origin would accept him as their leader.

A third group was not sorry to see some southern states go. Horace Greeley and General Winfield Scott were willing to let the seceding states "depart in peace." Probably certain Republican congressional leaders felt that such a course would solve a problem for them. They had not won control of Congress, but if a few southern members left, the power to make laws would then be firmly lodged in Republican hands. In their caucus on the eve of the session, the Republicans decided to do nothing.[23]

Other possible forms of reorganization were thought of. Some dreamed of a new republic made up of the northern states and Canada. Midwestern interests talked of a Mississippi Valley Confederation cut loose from the East and including the southern valley states, with New Orleans as its outlet. Some men of southern sympathies in the Far West gave consideration to a Pacific Confederacy of California, Oregon and the Puget Sound area. Northern motives, like those of the South, were mixed, and there were those who would "let the Union slide" without too great regret.[24]

In the Northern States the conspiracy idea gained early currency. Gideon Welles, soon to be Secretary of the Navy in the new order, recorded in his diary: "There has been a great conspiracy maturing for years and [Southern] men in high positions have been engaged in it. The election of Lincoln is made the occasion of carrying it into effect." [25] These sentences were written in January, 1861. Later Welles elaborated. The leaders "had been in a course of sectional and pernicious training under Calhoun and his associates, who for thirty years devoted their time and talents to the inculcation first of hate, and then of sectional division, or a reconstruction of the federal government on a different basis. . . . I have always entertained doubts whether Calhoun intended a dismemberment of the Union. He aimed to procure special privileges for the South—something that should secure perpetuity to the social and industrial system of that section, which he believed, not without reason, was endangered by the increasing intelligence and advancing spirit of the age. Many of the lesser lights—shallow political writers and small speech makers—talked flippantly of disunion. . . . The arrogance begotten of this folly led to the great Rebellion." [26]

The portrait of confusion thus broadly sketched is designed to puzzle those who read it as the confusion itself puzzled the nation that horrid winter. No matter what degree of truth or lack of it these various elements represented, there were people holding these beliefs and recording their thoughts. Was there a single conspiracy? Whether there was one conspiracy or not may be a matter of dispute, but there were conspirators and they were conspiring to the extent that so many were proposing designs for the altering of Leviathan. Some were determined on a new design and it was to become a fact. The drafters of blueprints were working overtime.

In the midst of this confusion of counsel, of deviousness of motive and purpose, the two congressional drafting committees undertook their work. Three days after the opening session, the House Committee of Thirty-three came into being on December 6.

To what degree a southern program had been developed before that time is not known. There had been conferences in the South before the assembling of Congress, but only the senators from South Carolina failed to return. The rest of the delegations from the South came, and observers noted that a number of southern members brought their families and settled in residence for the session. Soon the most specific organized action that was to develop in Washington appeared under southern auspices; a southern planning group had the most definite ideas.

The southern caucus was meeting as early as December 3. It took as its first task the drafting of a proposal for the House Committee of Thirty-three. In two sessions it hammered out a document that was presented to the Thirty-three on December 12. The caucus required a constitutional amendment prohibiting the abolition of slavery in the District of Columbia and guaranteeing slave property in the territories. Its members insisted on an amendment to the fugitive-slave law requiring the federal government to pay for escaping slaves not regained. They required a change in foreign policy to allow for the government's recovering of slaves escaped into foreign countries. There is some evidence that the adoption of some such proposal for constitutional amendment might have halted secession.

The House Committee rejected this plan on December 13. Instead, they adopted a resolution by an Indiana member regretting the discontent and hostility and proposing to grant reasonable, proper and constitutional remedies and guarantees, without specifying what these might be. As this statement was filled with words upon the exact definition of which there was absolutely no possible agreement, the southern caucus met the following evening to decide upon what should be the next move.[27]

In this caucus southern planning advanced another step. Two schools of thought had emerged. Those who spoke the loudest declared that compromise was impossible, even undesirable; the time had come for immediate secession by individual states. On the other hand, there were those who urged delay until concerted action could be arranged. These men spoke for Calhoun's idea of a convention to consult and draft a program. But in this as in so many caucuses it was the loud and fast talkers who carried the day. The more deliberate were persuaded to sign a fiery directive written by piratical-visaged Senator Wigfall of Texas and Congressman Pugh of Alabama. Jefferson Davis, who was past his hesitation, wrote some changes in the directive to make certain Slidell would sign it, and it was proclaimed to the world: "The argument is exhausted . . . All hope of relief in the Union" was gone. Each state was advised to get out, as fast as it could, of this "unnatural and hostile Union." [28]

At the same time the leaders of this congressional bloc of the lower South came to agreement upon a program. As Slidell and Benjamin told the French

Minister on December 17, the longer the South waited,
the harder the task of reorganization would be. Seven
or eight states were to secede immediately and set up a
provisional government to negotiate with other states.
These designers hoped to make a new Leviathan that
would include all states save the New England six;
these latter, they hoped, would unite with Canada.
With all the states in the Mississippi basin and in
the West, together with Pennsylvania and, they hoped,
New York, they would form a powerful mixed confederation in which the slave states would have a
majority. This plan Slidell and Benjamin preferred to
the better-known idea of a confederation only of slave
states.[29]

This program was the basis for the assertion, made
after hostilities had broken out, that a schedule for
secession had been worked out in advance and that
Senator Slidell had given this to some northern Democrats from whom help, or at least sympathy, could be
expected.

This plan, it was maintained, not only provided that
the fifteen slave states would be out of the Union before the February date for the counting of the electoral
vote by Congress, but also that forces from Virginia and
Maryland would move in and take Washington. It was
claimed that Buchanan was to be persuaded by Senator
Slidell, or forced, to resign. It was even reported that
Senator Wigfall, the fiery Texan, had planned to kidnap him and had approached Floyd, the Virginian
Secretary of War, to insure the success of this effort. The
removal of Buchanan, by whatever means, would have
made Breckinridge president—a hope held by some at
least as far back as April—and would have put him in
charge of the process of reconstructing the government.
It was further reported that New England's representatives were to be excluded by Congress.

In the meantime, according to the plan, the purged

Congress would call a convention to draft a new constitution "suited to the demands of the South." This altered Congress was to have a president ready to take over on March 4 in place of Lincoln. Was the presumption that this would be Breckinridge? Later on the excluded states would be invited to return with an inferior status. Even as highly placed a figure as General Scott believed that a hostile force was assembling in Washington; rumor had it that Colonel Ben McCulloch of Texas was to take command of this contingent.

General Winfield Scott, veteran of the War of 1812 and the Mexican War and presidential nominee in 1852, was a giant in size and experience although a tottering one. He was seventy-four in 1860 and so obese that movement was difficult. But he had gained a great reputation from his military career, and at this troubled moment he was looked upon as the savior of his country. He was of Virginia origin and was well aware of the preponderant southern sympathy of the officers under him. He was told of this southern plan for taking over the government, and he was much exercised. After a sleepless night he got up and wrote out the story. He also had another concern. Since John Brown's raid 115,000 firearms had been sent to southern arsenals to be ready if slave uprisings should break out. Quite recently Floyd had also been distributing arms, and just before Christmas he had ordered large guns sent south from Pittsburgh to the Gulf fortifications. The citizens of Pittsburgh protested most vehemently, and that shipment was stopped. Scott's military secretary believed that southern-born bureau chiefs in the War Department were providing arms for potential rebels.

Scott, with the responsibility for Washington's defense hanging heavily on him and knowing that "militia" of southern sympathy was drilling in the District, was further harassed because he felt he could not trust his officers. However, he summoned all the troops he could to the capital. He reported the plan to seize the city and the arms shipments to his superiors, who did not heed him. Finally, when Governor Hicks of Maryland sought his advice, he persuaded him not to call the legislature. Some credited Scott's vigilance and Hicks's caution with scotching the "plot."

Whether there was a plot to seize the capital, whether there was a plan for concerted secession, whether there were other plans or no plan at all cannot be stated now with complete certainty. The significant fact is that there were plans and that many people were suspicious and frightened and in some instances exhilarated by anticipations of danger. Senator Wade wrote his wife the day after Christmas: ". . . The President is doubtless guilty of treason and all here is confusion. Many believe that the South intend to seize on the capital before the 4th of March and all the Southern states go out of the Union. There is certainly great excitement but I do not feel so much faith in all that is threatened as many do. But if this is the means fixed by providence to get rid of slavery then let it come. I am resigned." [30]

It was at this point, December 18, that the Senate finally agreed to raise a committee on compromise, but this group did not begin its work until December 22. In the meantime, on December 17, Senator Wade of Ohio in a decisive speech in the Senate slammed the door on any meaningful compromise as far as the Republicans were concerned. Then South Carolina had seceded according to schedule. The Senate Committee understood only too well that unless any agreement they reached had practically unanimous committee support, it would have no influence, particularly since the program of secession was now under way. Jefferson Davis therefore proposed, and the committee agreed, that no plan would be submitted to the Senate unless a majority of the five Republicans and at least five of the other eight committee members approved.

Crittenden, the chairman, introduced his simple proposal to extend the Missouri Compromise line, 36° 30′, to the Pacific Coast. This formula promised to be the one most likely to succeed because the southern members of the committee indicated they would accept it if the Republicans would. Seward therefore had to consult Lincoln; he sent his associate Thurlow Weed to Springfield to learn Lincoln's wishes. Weed returned with a negative. Lincoln pointed out that if slavery could exist south of 36° 30′, the door would be opened to the annexation of Mexico, Central America and Cuba for future slave states. Before long the South would insist upon annexation in these regions and threaten to secede if these demands were not met. At such a time the same crisis would have to be faced again. The Republicans were solemnly pledged to stop the extension of slavery. This pledge they must keep or forfeit public confidence—and the fruits of their victory.

The Republican senators could not fail to grasp the force of this logic, and they voted against the Crittenden Compromise. For this reason Toombs, Hunter, and Davis declared themselves equally opposed to the motion. Thus on the first day of its deliberations the committee tacitly admitted failure. But the meetings continued over the Christmas holidays. Toombs and Davis offered Calhoun's proposals for guarantees of protection for slave property in the territories, while the Republicans offered to urge the repeal of the personal-liberty laws, to promise to the South a fair deal on fugitive slaves and to support an amendment to insure slave property against federal abolition in the states where it then existed. Other proposals were also made.

The most significant came from Douglas. He, like Crittenden, attempted to provide a formula. He reworked his popular-sovereignty idea into a constitutional amendment. Such an enactment would have forbidden Congress to legislate on slavery in the territories.

Nor would any territory be able to alter the status of slavery until its population reached 50,000. As soon as a territory had enough population to entitle it to one member of Congress, it automatically would become a state. No new territory could be acquired without a two-thirds vote of approval in both Houses. Enforcement of the fugitive-slave law would be guaranteed. Douglas maintained that this measure settled all the slavery questions related to the crisis and took them out of Congress forever, at the same time that it insured self-government to the white males in the territories. This suggestion was no more acceptable to the committee than any of the others.

The House committee had little better success. It eventually reported a miscellaneous conglomeration of resolutions but no program. The only matter of any significance they could agree on was a constitutional amendment guaranteeing that there would be no federal interference with slavery in the states where it existed at the time. This amendment the Senate finally endorsed but, immediately on December 31, its committee reported it could agree on no plan. As they did so, however, they requested the Senate to seek amendments to the Constitution to be framed in a national convention called for the purpose. To this the Senate paid no heed. Nor would they approve Crittenden's further motion that his Compromise be submitted to a popular vote. The Congress was not going to be able to readjust Leviathan. North Carolina, Virginia and Tennessee, however, had voted down moves for secession in various forms. The Governor of Maryland refused to summon the legislature. The Governor of Kentucky was inviting a border-states convention for conference and the legislature of Kentucky petitioned Congress to call a national convention.

During these efforts on the part of the legislative, what help would come from the executive? President

Buchanan was no Jackson, and he was not psychologically prepared to assume leadership. He was approaching seventy and his term had only three months to run. He had always been closely allied with southern leaders, and he felt they owed it to him to spare him the necessity of dealing with this problem; they should wait until March 4, 1861. As they gave him no consideration, he was aggrieved. Further, his advisers were badly split. Cobb and Thompson were secessionists and Floyd of Virginia was as hesitant as his state. Cass was feeble. Toucey was a zero. Holt of Kentucky was not yet as outspoken a Union man as he was going to be; he was alternately mourning his dead wife, communicating with her in the spirit world, and "carrying on" with a married woman of some notoriety.[31] Black was the only member in full possession of his faculties who was a strong Union supporter.

Buchanan did not believe in secession and had hoped he would not have to face up to it. The President, in common with many others, held that the answer lay in the calling of a national convention. Perhaps the policy of 1787 could be repeated in 1860-1861. The proposal of Senator Crittenden of the Committee of Thirteen had his approval, and he endeavored by diplomatic devices to promote it. He sent Caleb Cushing to South Carolina at the time of secession to attempt to persuade the promoters to postpone their action. Duff Green acted as his emissary to Lincoln a week later, to urge his support of Crittenden's Compromise. After Crittenden sought a popular referendum on his compromise proposal, the President in his special message of January 8 urged Congress to approve it. In February Buchanan transmitted to Congress Kentucky's resolutions in behalf of a national convention. But he presented no plan to Congress other than calling a convention; instead, he turned the problem over to them. He told the lawmakers that there was nothing in the Constitution or the laws permitting secession or allowing him to do anything to prevent it, unless they put it there.

The President hoped against hope that nothing would happen before the day of his release. He soon learned that he was not to have his wish. South Carolina went out, compelling him to face at least one issue. There were two forts in Charleston Harbor—historic Fort Moultrie on the mainland and Fort Sumter on a rock in the harbor—manned by a garrison of less than a hundred, all of whom were in Moultrie. General Scott wanted these reinforced. The South Carolina congressmen who, unlike the senators, had returned to Washington, wanted assurances that these forts would not be strengthened. In effect they told Buchanan that if South Carolina was to be expected to respect federal property, they must have assurance that the strength would not be increased. The President would make no pledges, but they understood him to be attempting to convey to them that they need have no fear, he would send no force.[32] On the other hand, he did not wish to be held responsible for any surrender of federal property, and he therefore gave the federal commander, Major Robert Anderson, authorization to dispose of his forces as he thought best to secure his defense.

South Carolina had seceded as planned on December 20. On that rainy night, as the news raced around Washington, there was great rejoicing in certain high circles. Despite the storm, a gay group converged on the White House to invite the President to rejoice with them. Included in this revel was Mrs. Jefferson Davis. She no longer sported her antidisunion ribbon; the President, of all people, had taken it from her a month before. This was to be the last time the President would be surrounded by these southern friends whom he had so long cultivated and whose friendship he had so highly prized. That afternoon he had heard the news at Congressman Bouligny's fashionable wedding, and he had felt no joy, only shock and apprehension.³³ Could they not have waited? Did he foresee that he must lose the friendship, even the respect, of these cherished associates and that they would soon revile him and call him "traitor"?

Yes, it was the last night of White House gaiety. Within a week his erstwhile friends would be denouncing him as a liar unfit for gentlemen to associate with. His cabinet would be completely disrupted, one of its members in disgrace, accused as a defaulter. His once firm "copperplate" handwriting would be a shaky counterfeit and he himself would be shivering by the fire in his dressing gown, trembling like "an aspen leaf," begging his advisers to tell him what to do and imploring old associates not to desert him while he fumbled in an agony of indecision and apprehension. Had Senator Slidell attempted to persuade him to resign? Was Senator Wigfall planning to kidnap him and had he learned of it? Edwin M. Stanton, his new attorney-general, later reported that his health seemed so precarious, that he was so shaken, that he believed death might be the agent who would place Breckinridge in the White House.³⁴

During this distraught Christmas week South Carolina sent three envoys to Washington to start negotiations for peaceful coexistence, perhaps for some form of new relationship that would lead to a readjustment of federal relations along lines planned by Calhoun. But they had scarcely arrived when the telegraph brought a shock. Major Anderson had found his situation at Moultrie unsafe and his command in danger of "unpleasant incidents"; he therefore moved out to Fort Sumter, his island fortress. Here there could be no encounters with "fire-eaters," nor could he be compelled to any undesired action. He made this move silently at night, during the Christmas festivities, while the celebrants were unwary.

This news arrived in Washington as the envoys of the

new "republic" of South Carolina were seeking an audience with the President. They and the senatorial junto immediately accused him of bad faith and demanded that the act be disavowed and the garrison be returned to Moultrie. They declared he had promised the South Carolina congressmen that no change or reinforcement would be permitted if South Carolina did not attempt to seize federal property. Their pressure culminated in the junto's implying plainly that Buchanan was a liar. The President thereupon became angry, refused to yield and sent the South Carolina envoys home. Thereafter they claimed that this action made war necessary; had there been negotiation, there might have been readjustment. The implication is that such negotiation could have been the basis for the drafting of a reconstruction agreement. President Buchanan, recovering his aplomb somewhat, not only refused to withdraw the troops but also sent down men and supplies on an unarmed merchantman, *The Star of the West*. The South Carolina militia fired on this ship, and it turned back on January 9. Anderson hesitated to fire, and he and Governor Pickens referred the question to Washington. He reported that he really needed no aid.

The South Carolinians, the senatorial junto and the Buchanan administration, now changed and strengthened by several resignations, arranged a truce of sorts at Charleston and shortly after at Fort Pickens at Pensacola, Florida, where another federal garrison held on. The reinforcements that had been sent to Pickens were ordered to stay off the fort on shipboard, riding aimlessly at anchor. Washington prepared an expedition to go to Anderson's relief at Sumter, should he call for aid. This he did not do while Buchanan was in command. Nobody was really ready for hostilities; the seceding states were still unorganized. Virginia was even working to assemble a peace convention.

The turning point, however, had really been passed

when the Senate Committee of Thirteen reported its failure on December 31. By the end of that week the southern senators were ready to act. On Sunday, January 6, they met in caucus to perfect the plans projected in the middle of December or earlier. They began to issue orders. The wires hummed. Senator Slidell telegraphed to the Governor of Louisiana: "No prospect of adjustment unless out of Union." Senator Brown of Mississippi wired: "Hope is dead. Secede at once." Roger A. Pryor advised Virginians that "The last hope extinguished today." One of the Kentucky Saunderses telegraphed: "All hope is lost. Disunion inevitable." Senator Wigfall had already wired that troops had been ordered to Charleston on January 6. Instructions were sent by members of the caucus to complete the schedule. A convention should have a confederacy organized by February 15, so that a government would be in operation on March 4 to give Lincoln the choice of peace or war.[35]

Vigorous campaigns for secession had been pressed in the lower South. One of the arguments used most strenuously in favor of secession was that it was the certain way to achieve reconstruction on a firmer basis, to secure southern rights and a more perfect union. The possibility of war was discounted because the North was in no condition to fight; the Democrats would oppose war and the abolitionists would be glad to get rid of the slave states. These arguments, reinforced by social pressure, prevailed in six more states, all in the lower South, and they seceded. State governors and state conventions were already at work. Federal property was so generally taken over that only Sumter and Pickens were occupied by federal garrisons.* The seceding senators continued their efforts to persuade Buchanan to surrender these

* There were fortresses on islands off Florida, Taylor and Jefferson, but they did not figure in ensuing events and never left federal hands.

forts. The conventions of the seceding states sent envoys to each other and to the states of the upper South.
A group of such envoys had already met at South
Carolina's capital during the Christmas holidays or perhaps earlier, and they had framed the program finally
followed, which was carried by the commissioners South
Carolina dispatched to the various states.[36]

It is significant that the Alabama congressmen, Pugh
and Curry, wrote, as their state convention was preparing to secede, that they were advised by associates in
the free states and the border states that secession of
some states was "an indispensable basis for a reconstruction of the Union." After such action the seceding
states would no longer feel the danger of coercion and
would negotiate on a basis of assumed independence.
Upon seceding, Mississippi sent commissioners to the
other slave states. The one sent to Maryland told a Baltimore audience that "Secession is not intended to break
up the present union but to perpetuate it." The states
were withdrawing so that they could secure constitutional amendments "guaranteeing our just rights"—pure
Calhoun.[37]

The result of this planning was an invitation officially extended by Alabama, upon the advice of
A. P. Calhoun, South Carolina commissioner, inviting a
congress to meet at Montgomery on February 4, there to
create a new government built from a new blueprint as
near like the Constitution of the United States as the
delegates could contrive. At the same time that they included a more efficient guarantee of their rights and a
remedy for their grievances, they would make reconstruction the easier. The new blueprint designers in
Secessia did more than pass ordinances of their own
drafting—they chose delegates to the Montgomery convention.

It was at this point that the British Minister, Lord
Lyons, reported to his home government on January 15.

"The plans of the secessionists are settled. They intend to have a Southern Confederacy fully established with a President and Congress, duly installed in some Southern City before the third of March. They declare that they shall then be prepared to negotiate on equal terms with the United States for a Union of the two Confederacies. Such a Union they say they should be prepared to form, provided the Constitutional arrangements were such as would prevent the vastly larger population of the Northern Confederacy having power to overwhelm by the number of their votes the influence of the South in the general Government." This too is pure Calhoun.[38]

When the general plan, which had been developed so largely in Washington, of a convention to meet at Montgomery was accepted and the secession of the six states was completed, their senators dramatically withdrew from the Congress and their representatives departed less ostentatiously. They now hastened south to take more immediate charge of the new move. When Senator Benjamin left in January, he told a friend, "We shall be back here in two months, and you will join us. New York and several other states will come in!" Mrs. Slidell told friends she expected to be back; she was not going to take her furniture or even many of her clothes. Somehow the plan went wrong.[39]

In these disastrously confused weeks the power of the congressional junto to maintain Leviathan intact had disintegrated. The ruling southern faction had, for mixed motives, seemingly abandoned the task early and turned to a new effort in Montgomery. Or was this really not a new objective but a new means to obtain the old? There was no consensus. With the ruling Democrats out, the new Republican leadership was at the moment impotent. The party's titular leader was off in Illinois and largely unknown. The congressional members themselves were unused to anything but minority

status. Seward presumably had plans for new statesmanship, probably known to some of his seceding colleagues,
but could he implement them? In the meantime there
was still hope of restoration by negotiation or at least
of peaceful coexistence.[40] The best blueprint designers
had gone to Montgomery to try a new set, and a new
group were converging on Washington to see what they
could do.

CHAPTER EIGHT

CONSTRUCTING THE CONFEDERATE LEVIATHAN

A MAKESHIFT STUDIO for drafting a blueprint was now set up in Montgomery, Alabama's capital city, in the heart of the deep South. On February 4, 1861, forty-three delegates from six states assembled. Though the map proclaimed this political center to be far from Washington, any visitor familiar with the ways of the federal metropolis on the shores of the Potomac would have felt at home. There were a number of familiar faces at the Exchange Hotel, the Montgomery House and other local establishments, for a majority of these delegates were veterans of the United States Congress.[1]

The obvious leaders were the eighteen representatives from Georgia and South Carolina, fourteen of whom had seen congressional service. Other states had not sent distinguished delegations, and some men of mark—such as Senators Slidell and Benjamin of Louisiana and Jacob Thompson of Mississippi, late Secretary of the Interior—had been defeated. William L. Yancey had been ignored. Parties had not played much part in the choice; Whigs fared as well as Democrats. In Louisiana and Alabama there were more Whigs than Democrats. In Mississippi they were equal. In Alabama and Mississippi secessionists were in the minority.

Alabama hospitably placed her beautiful capitol building at the disposal of the delegates and loaned them $500,000 to set up their enterprise. The delegates thereupon proceeded to hold their sessions sometimes in the senate, sometimes in the house chamber, and to use the state's library for the books required in drafting a constitution and statutes.

These delegates immediately chose veteran legislators as leaders. Those who played the major roles were representatives from Georgia and South Carolina. Howell Cobb of Georgia, late Secretary of the Treasury and former Speaker of the National House, was chosen presiding officer of the new body. Alexander H. Stephens of the same state, undoubtedly one of the most astute parliamentarians the old House had ever produced, provided a set of rules drawn largely from those in operation in Washington and unofficially assumed responsibility as floor leader. Christopher G. Memminger of South Carolina was appointed chairman of a committee on a provisional constitution, to work on a draft of such a document, which he had brought with him from Charleston. He was appointed on February 6; he brought back his report on the next day and the Confederate Congress adopted it on February 8.

This constitution was written in language very much resembling that of the federal document. The delegates made themselves a one-house provisional congress, assigning one vote to each state. They were to make the laws necessary to put the government into operation, to choose a provisional president and vice-president, and to draft a permanent constitution to be submitted to the states. The delegates decided to stay in office until the permanent establishment was installed. Probably no group of political designers ever assumed so much responsibility for so long with so little authorization or in the face of so little objection. Certainly, had some of the states expected that so much was to be undertaken, they would have given more care to the delegations they sent to Montgomery.*

* The forty-three men who originally gathered together at Montgomery representing the six states first to secede—South Carolina,

When the provisional constitution was perfected, the delegates turned to choosing a provisional president and vice-president. They were very conscious of the fact that only six of the fifteen slave states were present, and they knew that there was resentment among influential men in the slave states that had not yet seceded that these six had made such haste without any effort at a general conference. The various states represented at Montgomery had sent emissaries to the upper South, and now they were hearing from them in a fashion bearing on the presidential choice. In Montgomery there were several candidates. Georgia had three—Robert Toombs, Howell Cobb and Alexander H. Stephens. There were also two ardent secessionists—Robert Barnwell Rhett of South Carolina and William L. Yancey— each of whom expected the honor. In the background, home on his Mississippi plantation, was Jefferson Davis, but it was known that he would like to be commander of the army.*

Georgia, Florida, Alabama, Mississippi and Louisiana—were joined by seven from Texas on March 2. In the second session in May, twenty-seven representatives came from the next group of seceding states—Arkansas, Virginia and Tennessee—while the fourth seceding commonwealth, North Carolina, sent ten in July. In the fifth official session in December, 1861, the Provisional Congress accepted four members from Kentucky and seven from Missouri, although these states never left the Union. Despite that fact, they were represented in the Confederate Congress for its entire life.

Of the fifty who finally attended the initial session, twenty-five had had congressional experience. Of the thirty-seven who joined them later in the year, nineteen were likewise veterans. Thus, of the real workers in the Provisional Congress a majority were sometime members of the federal Congress. The rather irregular delegations from Kentucky and Missouri brought only one veteran among eleven.

* The Mississippi state convention had not expected the Montgomery convention to stay long in session or to do more than make initial arrangements. When the state legislature convened it elected two senators and a panel of representatives, thinking that a bicameral congress would soon be called to function. The long

Words from the upper South indicated that there was fear there lest some such fire-eater as Yancey or Rhett, popular in the lower South, might get the prize "of the Presidency." The Alabama envoy to Virginia was emphatic that a conservative must be the choice if the Old Dominion were to be expected to join in the new fellowship. Senators Hunter and Mason favored their colleague Jefferson Davis. On the basis of these tidings, Yancey and his Alabama support withdrew. Cobb, Toombs and Stephens, all from Georgia, more or less effectively canceled each other out, and Jefferson Davis became the unanimous choice on the first ballot with little difficulty. Georgia could not be ignored, so Alexander H. Stephens, her most conservative candidate, was chosen vice-president despite the fact that he had opposed secession.

A delegation was appointed to welcome the president-elect to Montgomery, and the Confederate Congress proceeded to set up six executive departments by statute—state, treasury, war, navy, justice, post office. As the Confederacy was minimizing all central administration, there was to be no interior department. As soon as he was inaugurated, President Davis turned his attention to appointing his cabinet, and it is significant that four of the six were colleagues of his in the Congress they had just left. Senators Toombs, Mallory and Benjamin and Congressman Reagan, together with a Charleston banker, Christopher G. Memminger, and an Alabama lawyer, LeRoy Pope Walker, were his department heads. Toombs, Mallory, Reagan and Memminger were members of the new Congress and continued to hold their seats. This government was to be truly a government of federal experts.

The next task for this steadily working Congress was another in the series of blueprints, for a permanent

---

duration of the provisional congress deprived these men of any service.

constitution. A second committee of twelve, headed by
Robert Barnwell Rhett, undertook to draft this document. On February 28 it presented its work to Congress. Thereafter this body held evening sessions as a
constitutional convention. By March 11 the work was
perfected and sent to the states for ratification.

The Permanent Constitution like the Provisional
Constitution, was largely a copy of the federal charter.
But there were significant changes. These were designed to insure the supremacy of the states. Their
sovereignty was carefully acknowledged, and the new
Constitution was specifically defined as a compact among
them. The states were guaranteed the right to maintain such institutions as they might choose, notably
slavery, although foreign slave trade was forbidden.
The Confederate government was to be one of limited
powers, *laissez faire* was its doctrine. There were to be
no subsidies, no protective tariffs, no contractor's jobs,
no financial manipulation, no legislation or taxation
for the "general welfare." The authors had suffered
under federal abuses and corruptions. They were reformers, and this was their reform manifesto, with copious excerpts in spirit, if not in language, from the Democratic Party's national platform.

The new administration now set up housekeeping in
an office building. Its members rented part of a com-
modious fireproof structure, already the headquarters
of the Montgomery Insurance Company. Here, at the
corner of Commerce and Bibb Streets, the President
and his six department heads established their offices.
They had to construct the machinery of government,
and they used federal models. In fact, they hired government clerks from Washington and encouraged them
to bring full sets of the forms used in the United States
departments. Here again care was taken to stick as
closely as possible to federal ways. The salary scale
established, however, was kept secret. The congressmen

feared that if the local innkeepers learned the amounts, they would make their charges equal the congressional per diem.

The Congress continued with other blueprints and more statutes for the new republic had to be written. As in Washington, these congressmen worked through a committee system. The principal directors of legislation were the Vice-President, Alexander H. Stephens, and the chairmen of the four principal committees— Robert Toombs, finance; Robert Barnwell Rhett, foreign affairs; Francis S. Bartow of Georgia, military affairs; and Charles M. Conrad of Louisiana, naval affairs.

These lawmakers were conscious of the possibility of war. Since they expected to depend largely on state militia, they provided for a provisional army of 100,000, made up of militia units mobilizing with their own equipment under their own officers. This force would be organized and commanded by President Davis and the War Department, under a general staff and four brigadier generals. This command was empowered to take over state forces and to direct defense, particularly at Charleston and in Florida where federal troops still held forts. A navy was projected and ten gunboats were authorized. In the meantime, the Navy department made use of such boats and yards as it could seize. Money was to be secured by continuing the federal revenue tariff of 1857, by borrowing and by issuing treasury notes. Free navigation of the Mississippi River was announced, the registration of vessels was provided for and a lighthouse board was set up. Foreign consuls were authorized and the President was empowered to initiate diplomatic relations with European governments and the United States. The Indians were accepted as charges, to be under an Indian bureau. Finally, an elaborate judiciary law was enacted and a complete set of Confederate courts, Supreme and District, was authorized. Having thus created a state as far as one can be created by legislation, its shapers paused to contemplate their handiwork, the Confederate Leviathan.

When the first session of the Provisional Congress adjourned on March 16, it can be said that few legislatures had ever before done so much in so short a time, even though much of the work had been achieved by the hands of copyists. These men had even re-created the political atmosphere of Washington. Mrs. James Chesnut, wife of one of South Carolina's delegates lamented that "Every political intrigue is as rife as in Washington" as she languished in that "den of dirt and horror," the Montgomery House, where the food was so dreadful that she depended on fruit and meals to which she and her husband were invited. She also reported that "grudges" were carried over from the old Union days. New cliques had not formed yet; the old ones were bent upon displacing each other.

Already the first rift had appeared in the Confederate lute. There was opposition to President Davis on the ground that he was a reconstructionist. Was he? Was he striving for Calhoun's proposition for a revised constitution? Certain interesting possibilities struck people at the time. Certain of the architects of the new regime, old Washington cronies, may have been hopeful that this new government might be an instrument of reconstruction rather than of independence. There was an interesting relationship, the old Senate tie, between Seward and his southern colleagues. Why had former Congressman Alexander H. Stephens, opponent of secession, been chosen as vice-president? Was it so he could woo the reluctant upper South, encourage the hope of federal negotiation for coexistence or reorganization? Or was the purpose, as in so many phases of these operations, hopelessly confused? As soon as Davis was inaugurated, he sent an embassy to Washington, including two congressional veterans in a three-man team.

The Virginia senators, Hunter and Mason, particularly the former, kept in close touch with Montgomery. George N. Sanders, on other occasions an agent of Douglas, was in the Confederate capital, and the Illinois Senator was working on the idea of a commercial union, an American Zollverein between USA and CSA. Some New York City Democrats, such as James T. Brady, were also in Montgomery, and Mayor Fernando Wood of Gotham was proposing that the great seaport set up for itself as a free city, a Hansa town, that could continue to serve the Confederacy as its banking and commercial agency.[2] After all, the Confederate system was so similar to the federal; and had not Davis said in his inaugural, "With a constitution differing only from that of our fathers, in so far as it is explanatory of their well-known interest . . . it is not unreasonable to expect that states from which we have recently departed may seek to unite their fortunes to ours under the Government which we have instituted?"[3] Such a result certain disappointed fire-eaters were determined to prevent. Rhett and Yancey were bitter about reconstruction, and Roger A. Pryor was so aroused that he came all the way from Virginia to force Davis into war and thus prevent him from negotiating the Confederacy out of existence. Pryor shortly went on to Charleston to aid in starting a fight there to achieve his end.

By March 16 the Provisional Congress had surely earned a recess. It had created a Confederate Leviathan in record time. The Confederates knew the documents were not finished, but they were not sure how far they need go. The Republicans, perhaps under Seward, were now in power in Washington. Would they give up Sumter, would they accept peaceful coexistence? Better still, would they negotiate? Seward seemed to indicate as much. Stephen A. Douglas was drafting a plan. The Confederate mission was in Washington and hopeful. Probably it was just as well to cease work on Leviathan for a few weeks; perhaps at the end of a recess new specifications could be used. To date, as Davis had declared, "We have changed the constituent parts but not the system of government." [4]

As the ingenious Confederates were putting these defining touches to the design for their new Leviathan, renewed efforts were exerted, principally in Washington, to rehabilitate the old. The work of those who had been laboring to convene a national assembly for this purpose finally bore some stunted fruit. The Virginia legislature, called into special session, had spent the latter part of the month of January in an effort to establish the Old Dominion's claim to leadership by bringing Washington and Montgomery together. As the chief instrument, Virginia issued her call for the much-considered consultative convention. She invited all states to send delegates to Washington on February 4 "to consider some suitable adjustment" and at the same time sent promoters to Washington and the seceding states to make sure that the invitation was accepted and that any hostilities were avoided until the delegates could try their hand at new designs. At the same time Virginia ordered the election of a sovereignty convention of her own on February 4, so that the state would have a body ready to decide Virginia's future position in the light of the unknown developments that were impending. Perhaps such a convention would be in a position to bargain. Virginia's move took precedence over somewhat similar efforts projected in Kentucky and Tennessee.

The response to Virginia's invitation was neither enthusiastic nor general. The seceding states would have none of it, and some of the northern states either sent no delegations or reluctantly chose men with no efficient mandate. Delegates from but twenty-one of the thirty-four states began deliberations behind closed doors at the Willard Hotel on the date set. This gathering, which included a number of men of reputation, generally somewhat overripe, chose ex-President John Tyler as its presiding officer and labored for three weeks. Finally on February 27, with but four days left of the 36th Congress, the planners threw open their doors and exhibited their production. They had taken the work of Crittenden and Douglas, endorsed it and made a significant addition. They proposed that the territories be divided between slavery and freedom by the Missouri line but stipulated that no new area be annexed without the consent of both sections. In its last hours Congress rejected this plan. At the same time it finally approved the only remedial proposal it could agree upon, a constitutional amendment that it sent to the states, guaranteeing domestic institutions in the states against federal interference. After great labor the Congress had brought forth a mouse that scurried around for only a few moments, scarcely noticed.[5]

The futile outcome of the labors of the "national convention" added to the discouragement of those who were trying to readjust Leviathan. The Congress had failed; its most effective leadership had departed to create a rival mechanism. Neither those who remained in Washington nor the sparse scattering of delegates convening in that city had been able to accomplish anything of consequence. But now on inauguration day the dramatis personae were changing. The Republicans had been peculiarly negativistic so far. The President-elect had said nothing publicly, and in private his principal achievement had been to veto the Crittenden Compromise. Douglas charged that for the last month, since the withdrawal of the secession delegations, the Republicans had had the power to take legislative steps to meet the growing crisis and had done nothing except pass a protective tariff, admit Kansas as a free state and organize three territories without reference to slavery. Now that their leader was to enter the White House, could they do anything more? Would they negotiate a reunion, could there be peaceful coexistence or would there be war? Lincoln's carefully tailored inaugural seemed capable of various interpretations. Perhaps it represented the salient fact of the moment, massive confusion, proclaiming at the same time the duty to hold federal property and approving a national convention to propose amendments to the Constitution.

Northern public opinion and purpose were no more simple and undivided than those in the South. Some were frankly glad to get rid of the South. A group were thinking of a new northern confederacy including Canada. Others like General Scott were willing to say, "Erring sisters, depart in peace." Such men as Seward wished to continue negotiation. Few at that time seemed interested in bringing the seceding states back by force; on the other hand, they would resist attempts to seize further federal property, such as Sumter and Pickens.

Two forces were pressuring Lincoln most and were working to influence his selection of a cabinet. One of these was a conservative group that wanted negotiation and the keeping of the peace; the other was a "radical" influence that was against concession to the South; some in this latter band were probably not averse to fighting. These pressures concentrated on demands affecting Seward and Governor Salmon P. Chase, senator-elect from Ohio. The radicals pressed Chase upon Lincoln and were hostile to Seward. The other interest demanded that Chase be excluded and urged the appointment of Seward, Cameron and other conservatives. The attacks of the Chase men on Seward and Cameron and of the Seward men on Chase grew so intense that Seward finally withdrew his acceptance, telling Lincoln he could not serve in a cabinet with Chase. Lincoln originally wanted them both, to insure the support of both interests. He was not willing to take the one without the other. He literally went to his inauguration not knowing whether he had the principals in his cabinet or not. Finally, on the morning of March 5, he had his way and sent both names to the Senate. Seward was confirmed with some southern support, which was significant.

The new administration was confused by the possibility that it was to have two heads and thus two policies. Seward was much more prominent and experienced than Lincoln. He had been a senator for more than a decade. Despite his antislavery views and his connection with the tags "higher law" and "irrepressible conflict," he had been a convivial associate of the leading senatorial promoters of secession. He was able to work with them comfortably; his champagne had on more than one occasion lubricated the jammed wheels of legislation and placed controversial laws upon the statute books. He was a man who loved intricate management and boasted of a capacity to work out sticky situations. He well understood how much of the politics that he and his southern friends played was bluff, how much exaggerated emotion was put on for effect. He had little confidence in Lincoln's knowledge or capacity; he planned to be premier and take charge of the President. Lincoln on his part recognized Seward's experience and expected to employ it.

Before the new administration had come into being, Lincoln had been using Seward as a source of information and advice. The New York Senator had been keeping tabs on the inside operation of the Buchanan administration through the Democratic Attorney General, Edwin M. Stanton, who had joined it late in December, 1860. Stanton is presumed to have told Seward the secrets of that troubled council table. The new Secretary of State continued his intimacy with his senatorial colleagues, even with those who were seceding, and he had probably talked much with them while they were engineering secession. He had been particularly friendly with Jefferson Davis and Robert M. T. Hunter. Now as he entered the State Department he found waiting for him the Confederate mission, a three-man embassy that included two recently seceded federal congress-men.[6]

Here the picture grows cloudy, but an hypothesis may be suggested. Seward seems to have been committed to some species of a negotiated reconstruction. He may have already discussed it with colleagues before they went South. Since he knew public opinion would not tolerate negotiations that involved recognizing Confederate independence, he had to seek other means of communication. He therefore worked on a devious project that delighted his managerial urge. He refused to see the envoys or to receive communications from them; such an act would have constituted recognition. However, through his senatorial associates Hunter of Virginia and Gwin of California and an old New York friend, Associate Justice Samuel Nelson of the U. S. Supreme Court, he secured the interest of another Supreme Court Justice, John A. Campbell of Alabama, who consented to act as a go-between.

Seward and Campbell were in agreement that slavery was on the wane. There had been protection of slave property in New Mexico, the only region not a state south of the Missouri line, but no more than twenty-four slaves existed in the region ten years later. Why break up over a dead issue; or more important, why fight over it? A way of peace must be found. Seward's policy was first to prevent any outbreak of hostilities and thus to secure a cooling-off period. In the meantime he would create a diversion by starting a scrap with Great Britain, France and Spain, with any or all of them.

Such a contest with the traditional and recent enemies of the republic would stir southern memories and loyalties to a degree that would put the South in a mood for alliance and reconstruction. To prevent any outbreak of violence, he was willing to surrender Sumter, holding on to Pickens to placate northern opinion.

Through Campbell he learned that the envoys were willing to be patient, on his assurance that arrangements were being made to surrender Sumter with dignity and "not under menace." At the same time he had been in communication with the Virginia legislature and its state convention elected on February 4. This latter body was Union in sentiment and had voted against secession, but it did not adjourn. Rather, it stayed in Richmond, ostensibly to watch events. Seward had in fact been in touch with Virginia opinion since early in the year, when he had gone to the capital city; more recently he had sent a representative.

Despite his great self-confidence, Seward was but one in an administration; there were also the President and his six colleagues in the cabinet. The Confederate and South Carolina authorities had avoided any attack upon Sumter, but they had been moving in on the fort. South Carolina had begun erecting batteries; the Confederacy had taken over the military direction and had sent General Beauregard to undertake the capture. He had arrived shortly before Lincoln's inauguration, and almost immediately the market privileges of the fort had been withdrawn. Anderson, Federal commander at Sumter, had therefore reported to the War Department that he must soon surrender or starve. This report was placed before Lincoln as soon as he was inaugurated. The new President must decide. Seward and most of the cabinet were ready to give up the fort, in line with Seward's "strategy." Believing in his dominance, the Confederacy was priding itself on its "patience." Would Lincoln follow along?

What of Lincoln? He had been painfully working toward a policy, at the same time that he was wrestling with organizing an administration and a new party taking office for the first time, conscious of the fact that much of his success in either depended upon the clever distribution of an intricate patronage. He undertook his great task under certain misconceptions. He hoped at first that the southern masses might be persuaded to accept his leadership. He himself was southern-born, of humble origin; he had friends among the southern Whigs, fellow supporters of Henry Clay. Immediately upon his election he had tried to establish contacts with them by opening a correspondence with an old congressional associate, Alexander H. Stephens. The President-elect had been willing to appoint a North Carolina Whig, John A. Gilmer, to his cabinet, had the latter been willing to accept. Lincoln had also sent friends into the lower South, for he still hoped that secession was an operation put over by a small group of fire-eating leaders and that there was a strong Union sentiment shared by the small and nonslaveholding farmers who only needed a leader. Would these men not accept him as their spokesman? He, like Seward, had been in touch with the Virginia convention. His anxiety about Virginia was intense because he believed her action would be the key to the general border-states' behavior. He was willing to make patronage arrangements that would allay any fears that he might appoint office holders hostile to the prevailing southern system. With so much at stake, he may at one time have been ready to surrender Sumter if the Virginia convention would only adjourn *sine die*.

The month of March had unrolled weeks of disillusionment. During this initial period Lincoln had learned that Sumter must be shortly supplied or surrendered. He was advised that there was no Union population in the South that would respond to his leadership.

And then there appears a mystery. Both Lincoln and Seward had been conferring with certain members of the Virginia convention. It seems probable that they hoped thereby to persuade the Virginians to adjourn and thus in effect contain the new Confederacy within the bounds of the seven states of the lower South. If such an action could be accomplished, they believed that they could negotiate a reconstruction, with the Confederacy thwarted in its expectation of carrying the whole South. To insure this adjournment, Lincoln seems to have been willing to surrender Sumter. Then, as March turned into April, he changed his mind, and historians have speculated much as to the reason.

The possibility that is here stressed is that Lincoln realized in these last few days that Virginia was not willing to continue in the readjusted Leviathan that he prescribed. He was willing to guarantee slavery where it existed and enforce the fugitive-slave law—in other words, to protect the southern way of life where it existed. He might even have been willing to negotiate about extending the Missouri Compromise line to the Pacific, providing, as the Peace Convention had stipulated, that no new territory be added without the consent of both North and South. After all, there were only twenty-four Negroes in New Mexico. But in these critical days he probably learned that Virginia demanded Calhoun's reconstruction as set forth in Hunter's proposal of January 11—namely, that the Republic must be reorganized to provide for southern autonomy, perhaps in the form of a dual executive, and a southern veto on Congressional legislation. This or any other definition of absolute state sovereignty Lincoln would not accept. He believed democracy to depend on the rule of the majority and not on the will of a minority that was at heart aristocratic. He therefore cast the die; further negotiation must be postponed until he had saved at least Sumter and the nation's face, to say nothing of making himself master in his own house.[7]

At the same time the President learned that Seward and Scott seemed to have joined forces to compel the surrender of the forts and that he would soon be a cypher in the administration, with Seward making the decisions and issuing the orders. To surrender both Sumter and Pickens at a time when crucial spring elections were imminent seemed foolish and, when the news came that the vote was going against the Republicans, suicidal. Lincoln politely told Mr. Seward off and took over. Pickens and Sumter were going to be kept. But even then Seward so manipulated matters that the expedition to relieve Fort Sumter was sent off without adequate force, perhaps so that Seward might tell the envoys, still cooling their heels in their hotel, that "Faith in regard to Sumter fully kept. Wait and see." As a consequence, the inadequately armed expedition set sail for Charleston while the armament not needed at Pickens was on its voyage thither. On his part Lincoln, despite all Seward's scheming, for the moment had given up the effort at conciliation.

The Confederacy was now faced with the problem of how to act at Sumter. Its "patience" had been rewarded by what Confederate leadership claimed was bad faith. In the South indignation seethed; its sense of honor had been violated. When Montgomery received word of the dispatch of the relief expedition, there were demands for action. Davis, under fire as a reconstructionist who was willing to sell the Confederate birthright for a mess of federal pottage, was ready, but there was disagreement among his official family. Some welcomed a clash, believing that it would finally bring in Virginia and the border states, but there were others who feared that it would rouse the North, loose its potential legions against the South and forever kill the hope of Calhoun's new union. Either lonely independence or subjugation would then follow. The former opinion prevailed, and word was sent to Beauregard to demand the surrender under threat of attack.

In the meantime reports were coming into Charleston of the arrival off the bar of an "armed expedition." Anderson refused to surrender but told the Confederate messengers that he had only three days' supplies and must capitulate at the end of that time. The news then became current that the armed fleet was increasing in force outside the harbor bar. What nobody in Charleston seemed to know was that the warship believed necessary to make the expedition successful had been sent to Florida by Seward. Finally three aides of General Beauregard and the Governor of South Carolina took the last demand to Anderson in the small hours of Friday morning, April 12. Anderson agreed to surrender on Saturday at noon, but he would not agree to withhold his fire in the meantime if it was required to aid the relief expedition. These three men, egged on by Pryor, the Virginia "fire-eater" who was also in the boat, did not report back to Montgomery, but on their own responsibility gave the order, and at 4:30 A.M. the Confederates fired on the flag.[8] Anderson fought back as long as he could and then capitulated. The two republics waited anxiously upon the telegraph that long week end. Friday brought the word of the firing, Saturday and Sunday news of surrender. In the end it came down to the accident of four particular men, clothed with the power to order batteries to fire on the flag, being out in an open boat in Charleston Harbor during the eerie dawn of an April day. They took that responsibility and determined the verdict. It was war.

CHAPTER NINE

THE REASONS FOR TWO LEVIATHANS

SECESSION and the guns at Charleston seemed to spell the crippling of the great American Leviathan. Instead of one "engine" there were now two, the second constructed along the lines of the old model by expert mechanics skilled in operating the original.

This cloud of gunpowder smoke had been let loose in the atmosphere because of confusion and misapprehension. Not only had there been the prevailing muddle of events and motives, but there had also been at least three basic misunderstandings of the realities of the situation, and these did much to prevent a peaceful solution of the problems.[1]

The first was a common misinterpretation of the nature of the federalism that was the United States. When the founding fathers had undertaken to create the American Leviathan, they had been limited by the constricted bounds of their social knowledge. They had failed to foresee how the intricate behavior patterns of an expanding society might affect their handiwork. In writing their specifications, they had described a political federalism, unaware of what was necessary for the operation of something that would turn out to be more intricate. It was left to succeeding draftsmen to add the further specifications that were required.

The federalism that had been invented in 1787 was basically not a political but a cultural mechanism. The people of the new republic were not only citizens of several states; more significantly, they were members of groups who were identified by a series of attitudes. The men and women exhibiting these different attitudes were not isolated in sections, nor were they separated by boundaries; they dwelt side by side, and on occasion the same person might be controlled by more than one attitude, or by different ones at different times. The emotional complex that was created by the variety of these attitudes and the tension that the antagonisms bred added such confusion to the politics of the day that the total eventually precipitated the resort to arms. The baffling problem was not how to maintain a balance among states, but how to preserve a balance among a number of emotional units or attitudes. It was this that proved beyond the political capacity of the time.

Of the multitude of attitudes within this cultural fed' eralism descernible during the ante-bellum days, there were five that were particularly dangerous in their conflict-breeding potentialities. Most prominent among them was a state of mind and emotion that dominated not only many within the South, but also numerous migrants from that region, as well as sympathizers with its situation who dwelt in the North. Its chief characteristic was its increasing defensiveness, its praise of slavery, its fear that southern culture was in danger of destruction or degradation. A second attitude was that dominating those eager to see the nation wax in wealth and power, who were anxious to exploit national resources, develop industry, provide transportation and promote commerce and banking. It was characteristic of the era and was found everywhere, but it was less common in the South, where the fear grew that such swift development might come at the South's expense. A third closely related attitude was an intense interest in frontier development, in the settling and organization of territories and the admission of new states. In these distant regions, financial and political fortunes could be made, and interest was feverish. The urge for political growth vitally affected state and national politics during the ante-bellum years between 1815 and 1860, as sixteen new states were created. Several of them emerged from territorial status through political turbulence, in which men from various regions fought to control the pattern of development in the new communities.

The confusion was worse confounded by two further attitudes that injected a combination of hatred and moral indignation into the turmoil. The existence of slavery in the southern states troubled many people as being anachronistic and sinful. Particularly in the Midwest many hated slavery and were moved by an intense desire to abolish it or at least to prevent its extension. Their hatred of slavery was often combined with antagonisms bred of struggles over the political and business problems of their states, against persons dominated by southern ways of thought and behavior. However, many people in New England were activated by a variation of this hostility. That region had been losing ground politically, and people with ambition or pride felt thwarted. They found that the dominant southern politicians stood most in their way, and their bitterness at their own inferiority could easily be translated into hatred of the sin of slavery and into attacks upon the slave power.

This complex series of divisive attitudes was underlined, emphasized and exaggerated by two prevailing attitudes that had no tinge of sectional location. They were found everywhere and their nature was such as to intensify the emotional stimulus projected by the divisive attitudes. These attitudes were the prevailing religious preoccupation and the romanticism so characteristic of the time. The first of these emphasized morality and duty and caused many consciences to be concerned over sin in the community. Because of it, therefore, the free-labor states harbored much hatred of slavery as a sin and contained a very active and militant group of abolitionists. Sensitive consciences caused people to fight southern political power in the name of a crusade against a national shame. In the South, on the other hand, the same religious attitude prevailed, but slavery was praised as a blessing because it enabled African heathens to secure Christian salvation. In that region attacks upon the institution by abolitionists and opponents of slavery extension were countered by denunciations of northern materialism, wage slavery, general servitude to Mammon and hypocrisy—all sins.

The intensity of these feelings was strengthened by the pervasive romanticism of the period. A rosy optimism precluded a realistic view of the perplexing problems. Virtues and vices stood unqualified. Few people would admit any dangers, and most went on sublimely with the most naïve concepts of contemporary trends. This romantic state of mind placed a premium upon exaggeration; ideas and emotions that were attractive were embraced without critical appraisal of their validity. There was therefore a minimum of that commodity labelled "common sense." Too few could be convinced that concerted efforts should be made to encourage cohesive attitudes that would counteract the divisive tendencies.

The few who were endeavoring to encourage such cohesive attitudes sought to stimulate nationalism. They stressed the increasing strength of the nation, natural pride in the creation and maintenance of free institutions. The growing sense of the success of the United States gave some confidence that nationalism might counteract the divisive attitudes enough to overcome the disrupting tendencies. Others felt that the saving formula should be an appeal to fair play under the classic theory of democracy. Government should be by the rule of the majority. That majority that ruled in town meeting and county council, in state legislature and Congress, should rule everywhere. The people could be trusted; by and large, the majority was bound to be right. All vexed questions of dangerous import should be referred to the people, and everyone should be bound to submit to the will of the majority. Yet neither nationalism nor democracy could satisfy the South. Both attitudes assumed that the southern people as a minority must be subject to the will of others—an intolerable assumption. Yet, since some reconciling formula was necessary, southern political philosophers must suggest an alternative. They had encouraged a concept of southern autonomy designed to make the enactment of certain types of legislation dependent upon some form of regional consent.

The strength of those leaders endeavoring to encourage the cohesive attitudes had been entirely inadequate for the task, and they had been further hampered by the general lack of understanding of the federalism that was conditioning their problems. The units in this unique structure, while officially political—that is, states—were scientifically cultural subsocieties. These subsocieties were only in part geographical; they also formed patterns of behavior that were not confined within definite geographical limits; they consisted in part of projections of attitudes developed in one geographical location and transferred to another.

Misunderstanding the cultural nature of the federation, southern leaders thought they were dealing with a primarily legal controversy, involving merely a harmonizing of rights, state and federal. They sought— just as if they were settling a case at law—to achieve a legal formula that would reconcile states to federal exercise of power and sovereignty. It was an era that throve on legal and political theory, on countless hours spent in oratory and in the writing and reading of those long, theoretical debates that we now consider to have been so unrealistic. Unrecognized behind the oratory were the prevailing attitudes, giving direction to such dynamics as moral indignation, thwarted ambition, fear of loss of face and power and the countless confusions of a growing nation. The political leaders had failed, as they were bound to fail, because they had oversimplified their problem and had tried to stop a flood with a sand pile.

A second misunderstanding confusing the issue was the fact that, in addition to dealing with a complex cultural federalism, those concerned had to cope with a political dualism; they had to operate two political systems, not one. For there had developed within the republic two types of democratic behavior, each based upon contrasting cultural conditioning factors. In the South climate, soil, and accident dictated a predominantly rural population that had small use for and developed few metropolitan communities and a not-too-much-larger number of towns. The tone of these communities was shaped by the English fashion of "squirearchy." Ambitious individuals aspired to be masters of estates, justices of the peace and parish vestrymen; their unit of government, as in England, was to be the county. In the colonial era a structured leadership, relatively permanent and often practically self-perpetuating, had been established on the English pattern in the seaboard colonies south of the Mason-Dixon line. This society had a distinctly feudal flavor in that there was a recognized, somewhat static, distinction between the leaders and the led, which gave weight and general acceptance to the opinions of the large landholders.

When population proceeded westward across the mountains, this system of political organization likewise went westward, and in the transmontane South the county continued to be the political unit, towns were few and the structured leadership migrated with the people. This type of community was democratic in that it was more fluid in its structure than it had been on the seaboard. There was a good deal of opportunity for new communities to be created as new land was offered for sale, and anyone with savings or credit could buy large landholdings and thus enter the local elite. The lack of entail also meant that these large holdings could be divided or estates sold to new owners. In the newer communities there was less appointive power in the hands of the county court, and there were more elective officials. Furthermore, while there was protest against "aristocracy," there was no real resistance to it, for it was too easy to raise the status of the individual, and besides, the freedom to criticize and to vote changes meant that real grievance was apt to be slight. Politics much of the time had something of the "game" status. In fact, the frequent political campaigns were occasions for community gatherings and entertainments, since the oratory of the day was emotionally exhilarating and the refreshments, barbecue and "spirits," physically stimulating. There was a tendency to take politics and religion "strong."

This type of community and this type of political behavior needed a minimum of organization and depended largely upon an accepted pattern of human relationships. There were natural, almost hereditary, leaders, whose views were influential and who were quite genuinely acknowledged as the ones to perform the simple responsibilities of government. When members of these elites vied for office, their followers lined up to be counted as a matter of course. The candidates went from crossroads to crossroads, from country church to country church, from county hamlet to county hamlet, from grove to grove; at these places they harangued the voters and their families. A good orator could hold his audience out in the sun, standing up, often for an hour or even more. It was all very personal and rather informal.

Outside the South other conditions prevailed. In the northern states the origin of the bodies politic had been corporate rather than feudal. The English municipal corporation, the trading company, the religious congregation or denominational synod—these were the patterns. Here there was town life, speculative community promotion, enterprise. Here the leadership was not permanent; it had to be created on each frontier as the small communities, in rude democratic equalitarian cooperation, met the problems of building the fast-multiplying boom towns. This contrasted with the moving of southern ready-made elites to new planting areas and the mere repetition of the plantation system. In the South there was no active communal creativeness, but merely the transfer of a structure or pattern that called forth little in the way of new leadership. In the numerous towns in the North, however, there was no accepted structure of leadership; new leaders were always appearing. Also, in the older sections population was fast growing in the ever-increasing metropolitan areas, so that often the simple personal touch dominant in the South was lost and the problem of appealing to the mass had to be met. That meant the mobilization of groups—mass appeal. Organization and regimented parties were the northern order of the day.

Beneath this political striving, and to a large degree determining it, was the fact that the great size and complex physiography of the United States then and since have hindered the growth of unity and have prevented any perfect commitment to nationalism. The republic has never completely yielded to centralization. A century ago these factors produced two nationalisms, two foci of patriotism and loyalty. Two patriotisms had developed in one *patria*. This dualism meant that two somewhat contradictory systems of righteousness, two sets of moral imperatives, though based upon a common religion, could exist side by side, though more or less uneasily, in the same republic. This double standard was more confusing, more destructive of peaceful co-existence, because of an accompanying confusion of political concepts. Those who had been creating the republic had been attempting to work into an effective political behavior pattern two basic political systems that on occasion could war with one another—namely, democracy that was both aristocracy and oligarchy.

Both North and South were dedicated to democracy, the rule of the people. But in the South democracy was coupled with aristocracy, the idea of an elite that controlled the service of a certain class of human labor as its right; democracy was maintained because it was relatively easy for men of ambition to become of the elite. There was the shape of egalitarianism. In the North, in a much less explicit way, democracy was linked with a concept of oligarchy that associated business entrepreneurs with government. These men of economic imagination, often wealthy, were accorded subsidy and protection on the theory that by their superior skill at development they would mobilize the nation's wealth and by extensive wage payments and dividend distributions provide opportunity, for those capable of grasping it, to emerge from the mass of wage workers and to become owners of property in various forms. By offering such opportunities for advancement, these men seemed the best supporters of a democracy that was based on a philosophy of equal opportunity. Oligarchy, like aristocracy, insured egalitarianism and the resultant democracy. In each section many articulate citizens came to see danger in the definitions of democracy current in the other. And the war came.

The two contending societies entered the struggle each with a fanatic belief in the superiority of the system for which it was fighting and with a dedication to the cause of preserving these values strong enough to reconcile hundreds of thousands to endure hardship and to risk danger and death. Both sides summoned tremendous energy, and for much of the war it would appear that neither could achieve victory.

The fact that there were these two contrasting patterns of political operation was one of the basic determinants in bringing on the conflict, and it is one that has continued to shape American political life ever since. The differences in democratic political behavior that had developed in the two sections had at length produced a dualism that was confounding. Words did not have the same meaning in different sections, and people were puzzled and disturbed. What really was American democracy? The two societies would expend a million men and six billion dollars to try and find out.

Yet it is an oversimplification merely to say that the several elements in the cultural federal system controlled by this dualism coalesced into two warring factions. What happened was that several of them fused into one, composed of those leaders and their followings who created the new unit, the Confederate States of America. This was not the South, it did not contain all those who supported slavery, it had within it many who really loved the Union and wanted neither to destroy it nor to achieve independence. But most of those within this new Confederacy were willing to support it, to fight for it and to risk loss of life and fortune for its maintenance. But here again the statement is too simple. For nobody really had foreseen what would happen, and no one had made a commitment of loyalty on the basis of such knowledge. The whole operation was shot through with the unsuspected and the unexpected, by accident and miscalculation, the result of the existence of two systems each officially bearing the same style—democracy.

A third circumstance that had been contributing to the destruction of the work of the ingenious designers of Leviathan was an ancient pattern of behavior that

seemingly prescribed a periodic damaging or destroying of the "engine" that was their creation.

As the scroll of years had been unwound in the centuries of Anglo-American history, a pattern of curbing
power by violence had been repeated again and again.
First, kings had been compelled to yield reforms; then
they had been dethroned and had lost their lives, one
had fled; and latterly the British government had been
forced to yield part of its empire. Constitutions, limited
monarchies and republics had been created, each with a
species of Leviathan. In several instances there had
been bloodshed and war. After two republics had been
established, and British kings severely limited in their
functioning, the idea of popular rule seemed to have triumphed. It appeared perhaps that such strife was on
the wane. But the American republic was not without
citizens who were ambitious and yearning for power.
And even in the republic power must be created. No
sooner had the United States been established than the
struggle for power began.

In the new American polity there was no accepted
theory of executive succession by primogeniture or other
inheritance to lessen the shock of periodic and frequent
changes. The founding fathers in their boundless optimism had decreed a nationwide quadrennial appraisal
in which rational men of the eighteenth-century pattern
were presumed to consider who was best fitted to wield
the powers prescribed in the Constitution for the executive and so carefully limited by the finely wrought
system of checks and balances. For a while all went well,
no dictators arose, and even the strongest of the presidents was moderate in his use of power and willingly
stepped down after brief enjoyment of it. There was an
increasing tendency to degrade the executive and to
choose men of no outstanding statesmanship to assume
the burden.

The dangers from a potential tyrant, feared by the

opponents of the Constitution and the Jeffersonians, had not materialized. In fact, southern leadership was generally dominant. Southern communities were relatively stable in their politics. There was not much travel except for the few, and most people lived humbly, depending on church, local court days, political rallies and fairs for their interchanges of ideas and upon the small local newspapers of the day or rumor for their news of the outside world. People of this type were apt to keep their senators and representatives in Congress for long periods. In other regions, where there were more variety and greater flux, greater mobility of population and more constant change, political tenure was more limited. This longer tenure gave southern members of Congress advantages in both houses.

This long period of southern dominance was by the end bringing its own destruction. Too many interests developing in the rapidly growing society were thwarted by southern negativism. The rise of the northern party, the Republicans, and particularly the imagination-stirring raid of John Brown had roused many in the South to the gravest apprehension just prior to 1860. They saw that the new party was seeking to use as a mobilization agent the widespread northern antagonism to human slavery and the sinful slave power. The southern leadership had cause for concern over this organized attack on its institutional set-up, particularly as southern leaders saw in it the implication of a possible slave insurrection involving the horrors of murder, rapine, loss of property and the destruction of southern society.

This state of apprehension in the South underlined one of the hazards of democracy. The hazard arose from the fact that contending candidates were capitalizing on fears and anxieties in their election propaganda. Thus, in southern political contests in the 1850's, these fears had become the chief campaign material. This situation had roused southern emotions the more because elections were so scattered in time. Today most of them are held in November every two or four years, but in the 1850's there was no such regularity except in presidential contests. From the beginning each state determined its own times and seasons, and even by 1861 there had been little progress on the road to uniformity among the then thirty-four states. State and congressional elections were held here and there in all months of every year save January, February and July. Election activity never ended. There was no rest or relaxation in the press reporting these contests. A type of sectional tension, a unity conditioned by fear, a new loyalty not to the nation but to the section was stimulated, until it became a firmly held conviction that the triumph of the new northern party, the Republicans, would mean the ruin of the South, the humiliation of its pride, the ravishing of its womanhood and dominance by the recently savage Negro. When the new party triumphed in 1860, this cumulating emotion boiled over.

The Southern leadership had put off believing that the South's loss of power was imminent until 1860. Then came Republican victory and the possible loss of the power that the South had so long exercised. With the Republicans in control, how could southerners protect themselves from invasion and slave rebellion? How were they to escape a tyranny that they believed threatened them and to create a new reformed power that they would control? As history had recorded, there were precedents for such actions, but none for initiating them before an overt act was committed, before a tyrannical power began to function. The action taken was new—brand new; its dominant purpose was to transfer an existing power, as intact as possible, to a place of safety where it could not be destroyed, where it might be reformed and protected and where southern citizens might continue to operate it unhampered.

Southern leadership fell back upon the ancient pattern that might involve war. They were drawing heavily upon eight centuries of precedents well known to them, particularly upon the tradition of 1776. They would declare themselves independent of tyranny as their forefathers had done. However, they were not going to do this merely in terms of Lockean philosophy or British constitutionalism, but rather through an American adaptation, which held it to be the spirit of the American Constitution that if states' rights were endangered, they might secede, as the thirteen colonies had done, and set up their own improved government to preserve their way of life as a positive good. They were reformers as well as revolutionaries. The hope and the full expectation was that such action could be taken peacefully. Originally there had been no plan of resorting to the precedent of violence in the long-established British pattern of forcing governmental change.

But events in 1860-1861 nevertheless followed the ancient design. When the South proclaimed the Confederacy, it proved to have committed an act somewhat similar to that of Charles I's unfurling his standard and calling his loyal subjects to protect the prerogative. When Fort Sumter was fired on, both sides summoned their hosts, as factions had done on occasion in England. Southern manhood rallied to the new standard in somewhat feudal fashion, with the planters leading their farmer associates almost as retainers. In the North, similar hosts rallied to the Stars and Stripes. Each force was fighting to protect something precious. As Lincoln said later, "Both read the same Bible and pray to the same God, and each invokes His aid against the other." The precedent of resort to violence prevailed.

When the telegraph and newspapers brought word of the dread events of the week end of April 12-14, 1861, a multitude stirred by emotion, lost in confusion and misguided by basic misunderstanding was roused to action. President Lincoln and his aides worked busily that sabbath, and Monday's press carried the President's proclamation. War had begun. But even with the outbreak of war, the possibility of peaceably negotiated reconstruction was not wholly dead. In that dread hour Davis believed "Separation is not yet, of necessity, final," and Lincoln told some militia, "I will not say that all hope is yet gone." This objective of a negotiated reconstruction was still widely held and it died hard. But a few battles would kill it.[2]

Lincoln in his proclamation of April 15 called for 75,000 men to volunteer for three months "to suppress combinations too powerful to be otherwise put down" and summoned Congress to meet in special session on July 4. The legislators' assembling was delayed because certain border states' representatives deemed essential would not be chosen until June. Perhaps there was some uncertainty, too, as to whether Washington would by then be in federal hands or a safe place in which to meet. Four days later a second proclamation ordered a blockade of Confederate ports, closing the new republic to trade. Before Congress met, the President summoned three-year volunteers, added men to the regular army and navy, spent millions and suspended the privilege of the writ of habeas corpus, all on his own authority.

Jefferson Davis on his part speeded up the mobilization of his small force, which by the middle of April numbered less than 20,000 men. He summoned the Confederate Provisional Congress to resume its sessions on April 29. The Congress had to complete its new Leviathan and prepare it for war. These ingenious Confederate artists now continued their efforts to improve the work of the original draftsmen. They were seeking "to preserve those conservative principles of the Fathers of the Republic" that they had found "fast being overwhelmed by popular fanaticism." [3] Yet the combined efforts of all working at Washington and Montgomery to preserve the great American Leviathan resulted in its dismemberment, the creation of a smaller model and a war.

The work of 1787 was thus undone. The statesmen of that year had decreed a distribution of power among a variety of units and agencies, with some provision for expansion and periodic redistribution of the power to govern, all done up in a neat system of checks and balances. Such a structure could only have been contrived at the end of the eighteenth century, for only then were men naïve enough and brave enough to put their trust in such a rational scheme as adequate to regulate a most confused and irrational society. During the course of the eighty years following, the census figures and the maps recording the distribution of population had given increasing evidence that the more northerly section of the society was outstripping the southern division and that there was danger that the great northern increase of population would give northern representatives preponderance and therefore controlling power in the Congress and in the party conventions. Whether this would have proven true is open to debate, but it was a romantic age of phantasy, in which such an extrapolation was easy to believe. The great stimulus of such vast regions with untapped reserves of wealth made any exaggeration possible, and the Americans were emotionally overstimulated.

It can be conjectured that these fears were groundless because it may be asserted that such a large society as that comprised within the bounds of the United States, and made up to such a degree of freely moving migrants, could never have developed under nor tolerated anything but a federal system. No central power could control such a people. But since there was a widely prevailing feeling in the South that just such control might be possible, the precedent of 1776 was

invoked to protect the southern way of life against a
northern tyranny. On the other hand, no such fragmentation, disintegration and disruption of a great experiment by a disaffected minority could be tolerated by
the North. The Federal government therefore sought
to maintain itself by force of arms. The ensuing war
would be waged by each contender to preserve its interpretation of the federal system. It was a struggle to
conserve, not to revolutionize.

The most disquieting fact was that a people so gifted
in orderly self-government had not learned how to prevent such violence. Too few people either had wanted
to avoid it or had realized what effort was necessary to
stop it. Besides, two important and powerful interests
had not really wished to prevent violence.

The Southerners promoting secession, whether for its
own sake or as an instrument for negotiating a reconstruction, believed that secession and the Confederacy
were the answers. No makeshift readjustment within
the old Union would give them the status they demanded. On the other hand, the South reaped what it
had sowed; too many northern politicos remembered
the domineering methods of southern control on the
floor of Congress and in committee rooms, in national
conventions and in the White House. This time the
blustering southern leaders were not going to be allowed to get away with it. They were not going to be
permitted to break up the league because they had lost
a match. Certainly they were not going to be obeyed
when they forbade the administration to provision its
own forts. If they would fire on the flag, they must
take the consequences, particularly as Lincoln and his
associates believed that secession was an operation imposed on an unwilling people by political leaders maddened by the loss of place and power. Not many of the
Republicans, therefore, exerted themselves to avoid
war. The election of 1860 had been inconclusive; Re-

publican failure to win Congress had frustrated the Republicans' eager desire to take over. Any adjustment proposed in this period of turmoil seemed to them to require that they surrender their great opportunity for fulfillment.

These various interests seemed to engross the available leadership and leave too few capable of exercising the capacity needed to avert war. Even Lincoln appeared almost completely absorbed in politics and patronage. These demanded all his skills, then not too well developed, and he seems to have had no emotional compulsion to expand his still latent powers of statesmanship in the superhuman task of avoiding bloodshed.

With the firing on Sumter there had come once again in the long history of the evolution of the patterns of Anglo-American self-government a moment of crisis when men must decide between two ancient designs. Should they write it out or fight it out? The decision, taken almost accidentally, would seem to have chosen the latter pattern. Two Leviathans were now in operation. One was a hastily constructed makeshift, built largely by veteran engineers to the specifications of the ancient model. The other was the original engine, operating, in spite of the loss of some major elements, in twenty-three of the thirty-four states. Both of these Leviathans must become instruments of war in the name of self-government. For such a purpose there had to be much designing and drafting of new blueprints, and such designing had to be done in a hurry.

CHAPTER TEN

OPERATION UNDER
DISADVANTAGES

AS THERE were now two Leviathans, so there were
two lawmaking agencies, two groups of men working out specifications for what were in reality two new
republics. One of the compelling reasons for the division of the United States had been the inability of
one legislative body to meet the problems arising from
this growth of a society in a wilderness. So large was
the country that for the nonce it seemed that a single
policy of lawmaking could not be agreed upon. Each of
the two rivals must decree its own. Rather than risk losing the control of Congress, the Confederacy-to-be seceded and created a policy of its own. The Republican
congressional leadership, fearing lack of control, seems
not to have exerted itself too strenuously to persuade
the secessionists to stay.

The two separate lawmaking operations that resulted
were both directed by veterans of the federal Congress.
The 37th Congress of the United States was to continue
the pattern of its predecessors in Washington, but with a
difference. It and its successors, the 38th and 39th Congresses, were in a very real sense to serve as a continuous
convention for the revision of Leviathan, both by constitutional amendment and by legislation. For part of
that time the Provisional and the First and Second Congresses of the Confederate States were to function simi-
larly in Richmond.

The two Congresses, though stemming from the same
roots, were to assume contrasting characters. The old

southern leadership was transferring to the new Congress in the South its great limitation, the negativism of *laissez faire*. The new Republican leadership, taking over the old Congress in Washington, was going to provide it with a new field of opportunity—that of innovation. Was the future of these thirty-four states and seven territories to be two independent republics, a republic reconstructed by negotiation, a Union restored by force or a new federal Leviathan?

The 37th Congress, reduced in number, met on July 4 in the special session summoned by President Lincoln under the compulsion of the guns at Sumter.* This group had to conduct its business in the midst of unprecedented confusion, discomfort and, at times, danger. The members were never unaware that across the nearby Potomac there was now a hostile, almost a foreign, state. Upon certain exciting occasions they became very conscious that enemy troops were within gunshot, and at least once they feared that a Confederate naval expedition might be steaming up the Potomac. The capitol wherein they were at work was unfinished, its dome still incomplete and its roof not tight to the elements. The great new wings stood with unbuilt approaches and unfinished façades. The capitol grounds were littered with building materials, sheds and tools.[1]

Despite new quarters, the members of the two houses were most uncomfortable. These new chambers were presumed to be the last word in comfort and efficiency. The old Senate chamber had been cramped in space, heated very inadequately and so badly ventilated as to create an atmosphere characterized as "mephitic." The

* The Senate was reduced from 68 to 49, as one senator, Andrew Johnson, stayed on from Tennessee and two were accepted from Virginia. The House was reduced from 237 to 178. In the Upper House there were 31 Republicans, 11 Democrats and 7 Unionists. In the Lower House there were 106 Republicans, 42 Democrats, 28 Unionists and 2 vacancies.

new chamber had space and boasted heating and venti-
lating machinery. But it had no windows and depended
entirely on this machinery and a great skylight. Senators complained of the lack of ventilation or of machine-
driven draughts of cold or hot air which either froze
or stifled them and imperiled their health. To make
matters worse, the basement of the Senate had been
transformed into a temporary bakery to supply bread
for the mobilizing troops, and the smoke and smell of
this culinary art seeped into the Senate and added to
the woes of the solons. It was months before the bakery
was removed; meanwhile the Senators continued intermittently sneezing and coughing.

The functions of Congress were always complex, but
the perils of civil war made them doubly so. The two
houses had to make law and support a war. They had
to raise armies and they would punish public enemies.
At times they undertook to conduct the military operations themselves, or so it seemed. They were also busy
attempting to perfect a new party organization; in 1864
they even took on some of the characteristics of a national nominating convention. In the long run, their
most significant activity was a more or less unconscious experimentation in long-range planning, whereby
through grants and subsidies and legal enactments they
were shaping what would turn out to be a new Leviathan.

The federal Congress that assembled in special session on Independence Day was in many respects a body
markedly different from its predecessors, despite the
fact that it was the thirty-seventh in the succession of
Congresses since 1789. It was a legislature reduced in
size by secession and controlled by a new party who
owed their dominance, not to the will of the voters,
but to the secession of the republic's erstwhile leaders.
The failure of the Republicans to win Congress in 1860
had an effect, not always subtle, on their behavior. The

new leadership was without previous significant experience save a very precarious preponderance in the House of Representatives of the 34th and 36th Congresses. Now these men had to create the capacity for direction required by the intricate process of lawmaking. The minority was under an equal compulsion to reorient itself. The Democrats had lost not only their majority status, but practically all of their leaders as well. Hitherto the direction had come almost entirely from southern members and from Douglas. The southerners had seceded and Douglas was dead. The northern and border-states Democratic rump was but a pale reflection of past power and legislative know-how. . .

The Republicans set to work to create their new junto. The senators who were to exercise the greatest influence in directing the course of legislation were Henry Wilson of Massachusetts and William Pitt Fessenden of Maine, who were chairmen of the committees on military affairs and finance respectively. They had to find the army and the money to pay it. John P. Hale of New Hampshire, as chairman of the committee on naval affairs, should have been another power, but his captiousness and peculiar personality made him something of a hindrance to effective legislation, and he had to be circumvented. Others of significance were Zachariah Chandler of Michigan, chairman of the committee on commerce: Lyman Trumbull of Illinois, chairman of the judiciary committee: Benjamin F. Wade of Ohio, territories: Jacob Collamer of Vermont, post offices and post roads: and James Harlan of Iowa, public lands. Charles Sumner of foreign affairs was a dramatic figure, but he generally played a star role or none and was hardly a member of any team. Vice-President Hannibal Hamlin of Maine and Senator Solomon Foot of Vermont, President pro tem., were the presiding officers. These men would take over the control that had been exercised by the southern solons—Hunter, Mason, Butler, Atchison, Breckinridge, Slidell, and Benjamin—in the 1850's.

In the House direction seemed simpler. Thaddeus Stevens of Pennsylvania, chairman of the all-powerful ways and means committee, was to become the dominant figure. Francis P. Blair, Jr., of Missouri was to direct military legislation, or attempt to do so. Charles B. Sedgwick of New York headed naval affairs. Elihu Washburne of Illinois and Schuyler Colfax of Indiana chaired commerce and post office and post roads respectively, while two from Ohio, John A. Bingham and James M. Ashley, presided over judiciary and territories. John F. Potter of Wisconsin was chairman of public lands. It had been expected that John Sherman of Ohio would be speaker; but since he had gone to the Senate, Galusha A. Grow of Pennsylvania secured the post and presided over the rules committee. New England was as insignificant in the House management as it was prominent in that of the Senate. Pennsylvania and the Midwest were pretty much in control.

The special session under this new leadership was very businesslike and moved along with a single purpose—the creation of a war machine. It abjured extraneous matters, even the private or subsidy legislation generally so much a part of Congressional attention. Lincoln's message recapitulated the measures he had taken since his inauguration. He had called for volunteers, increased the regular army, spent money, and proclaimed martial law in some areas by suspending the privilege of the writ of habeas corpus. These acts he asked Congress to confirm, and at this time the heads of the departments submitted estimates of costs. Senator Wilson had the army bills and resolutions ready and undertook to pilot them through Congress at the same time that leaks from his committee were presumably supplying the rebel spy, Rose O'Neal Greenhow, with the military information so helpful to the

Confederates in winning the battle of Bull Run. Senator Wilson was commonly believed to be having a torrid affair with the lovely Rose who, like the beauteous Peggy of earlier days, seems to have been a friend of senators. Senator Hale presented similar measures for the navy, but he and Secretary Welles had already reached an unfortunate state of misunderstanding. Hale's first act was to introduce a resolution demanding information about naval contracts, particularly those involving the numerous ships purchased, implying nepotism, if not corruption. Welles had retained his brother-in-law to make these purchases, on commission. Welles carried conviction in his denial and general demeanor and commanded public confidence.

In the House, Stevens' ways and means committee and the committee of commerce prepared to sponsor the loan and tax legislation on which Chase and his treasury associates had been working. As the outbreak of the war had found the nation without adequate legislation for dealing with secession, the House judiciary committee brought in bills to suppress rebellion and define and punish conspiracies. The commerce committee recommended one to punish piracy. The Senate judiciary committee endorsed a confiscation act, designed to do some damage to slavery, and a bill prescribing a new oath of allegiance. After some debate, the Confiscation Act was passed, though in a form that offered slight opportunity for deprivation of property or other punishment.

This legislation was marshaled through both Houses in record time under the spur of necessity. The Confederates were across the Potomac, and over a stifling week end the Union Army, accompanied by a number of senators and representatives, had gone forth to force battle and had themselves been compelled to flee helter-skelter back to Washington in a driving rain storm. Had the victorious Confederate host pursued the Union

Army, there is a possibility that Congress might not have met in the great capitol again for some time to come. However, Monday found the lawmakers back at their desks, and one scans the *Globe* of that day in vain for any very direct reference to the calamity at Bull Run.

On that day one issue was settled for the time being. There was a growing difference of opinion as to the war aims. Were they battling to abolish slavery, break the southern political power, punish the secessionists and create a radical power, or were they fighting to preserve the Union under the lead of Lincoln and moderate men? Lincoln was mindful of his Kentucky origin and most concerned to confine the Confederacy to the eleven states that had already seceded by keeping within the Union the four border states. He was, therefore, most insistent upon the second of these alternatives. Chastened by the defeat of the great army designed to ride into Richmond and end the war in ninety days, the House and Senate on that Blue Monday accepted similar resolutions offered by John J. Crittenden of Kentucky and—the only Senator from a seceding state to have remained at his post—Andrew Johnson of Tennessee. They affirmed the war objective to be the preservation of the Union.

The only real hitch in this well-managed lawmaking session was opposition to the resolution ratifying Lincoln's suspension of the privilege of the writ of habeas corpus. This proposal, reported by Senator Wilson on the opening day of the session, became a convenient instrument for the use of various Democrats, border states' members and others who had a bone to pick with the new administration. Finally, on the next to last day of the session, Senator Wilson took a bill to increase army pay and added as an amendment a clause approving and legalizing all the "acts, proclamations and orders" of the President between March 4 and July 4 relating to the armed conflict, without specifying any of them and without mentioning habeas corpus. This maneuver succeeded handily.

Such a prompt and expeditious session conducted under the spur of dire necessity was not to be typical wartime congressional behavior. Despite the lessons in expedition learned during this fearful summer, when Congress returned in December it generally resumed its old ways and the elaborate, time-consuming lawmaking ritual hallowed by long usage. Many, many hours were devoted to appropriation bills and the legislation necessary to raise and equip armies. The cost was staggering, but the mill ground ceaselessly. However, its operators attempted to do more than provide the means. Congress was determined to enter the field of administration and partisan leadership.

The Constitution makes the Congress and the President equal and coordinate in carrying out their functions. The President is primarily an administrator, but he has a definite part in legislation. Congress, while principally engaged in lawmaking, has certain administrative functions, and during the perils of war it was determined to assume more. Besides, there had grown up an extraconstitutional function, the operation of partisan politics. Lincoln considered himself the party leader, but a faction of Congress was to combat his assumption and in the end to try to dethrone him.

The President, as required by the Constitution, began his congressional activity as soon as Congress assembled. When the Houses met in December, 1861, he presented them with a program comprehensive in scope. He would provide more efficient and perfect means of warmaking. He would likewise make more effective certain nonwarmaking features of government, he would reorganize the court system, improve the publication of the statutes-at-large and secure the creation of an agricultural bureau. He soon found, however, that Congress paid little heed to his lawmaking leadership.

Therefore an impasse of a sort shortly developed. Despite this lack of meeting of minds, the relations between the White House and Capitol were for the most part decorous. The President was careful to consult the members on matters of patronage and made them feel that their advice was taken. Lincoln, therefore, had scarcely any trouble in securing the confirmation of the myriad appointments, enlarged by the needs of the army and navy. These were enormous, for the Senate had to approve the thousands of commissioned officers. The President also vetoed few bills. For the most part he and Congress went their separate ways, and in fact he seldom essayed legislative leadership except in fields of his own choosing.

In the administrative realm, matters were different. Under the Constitution, the President was commander-in-chief of the army and navy. This responsibility he was determined to undertake fully. But it was soon apparent that the congressmen would demand a significant role of their own creation. Politics thrust its ugly head into the war effort, and the ruling congressional junto undertook to use the war to further its power and to break down the President's authority. Stung by the defeats at Bull Run and Ball's Bluff, Congress was seeking a scapegoat. It seized upon the President, ostensibly because he gave important commands to such Democrats as George B. McClellan and incidentally to Charles P. Stone, while at the same time certain sterling Republicans were neglected.

The radicals made a most offensive move as soon as they returned in December, 1861. They created a Committee on the Conduct of the War that proceeded to investigate the generals, the strategy and, in fact, any phase of the conflict that attracted their curiosity or their suspicion. They endeavored to break down Democratic generals and to build up Republicans by methods none too nice. This committee functioned almost without interruption through the four war years, continuously seeking to interfere with and limit Lincoln's functions as commander of the armed forces.

Congress was likewise to undertake a third function, that of party leadership, and during the entire four years congressional tasks were constantly colored and shaped by a politics of the most intricate kind. Over the years since 1789 there had been constructed and adjusted an increasingly important part of Leviathan's complex mechanism—party machinery. The Republicans were proving much better at national party organization than the Democrats had been. A new centralized political mechanism was in the making, and a behind-the-scenes struggle was going on for its control. The radical Republicans sought to form a dominant junto, and on his part President Lincoln undertook to be leader. He held an almost mystic concept of himself as tribune of the people, and he would yield none of his claims to such a leadership. For four years he and certain Congressional leaders carried on what amounted to a war within a war, for a new politics was in the making, a politics incidental to the creation of a new political power.

The Republican Party had begun as a series of state organizations scattered in date of origin through the months of the years 1854-1855. It did not achieve any national central direction until 1856, when a campaign mechanism was created for the purpose of securing the election of a president. This attempt failed, and as was usual in those days, the new organization ceased to function for the four-year interval between contests. Not until 1860, when it was necessary to arrange for another national convention, had this committee resumed its operations.

At that time it became more than ever apparent that the so-called party was a group of state and sectional factions and that this factionalism was complicated by past political association. There were strong state machines, such as those of New York and Ohio. There were sectional interests and keen rivalry between eastern and western operators. Further, all these prominent leaders had previously been something else—either Whigs, Democrats, Know-Nothing Americans, or Free-Soilers. As such, they had at one time been antagonists of some of their present associates, and these former antagonisms often died hard and lingered to encourage jealousies and factionalism.

The nominating experience of 1860 underlined these elements of disunity. The western group, after having secured the convention for Chicago, had created an atmosphere of local pressure that had much to do with the defeat of Senator William H. Seward of New York, the favored candidate. Abraham Lincoln had won, somewhat to the surprise of the rank and file of the party. The result had been achieved largely by shrewd political operation and in response to no public demand.

Lincoln, though victorious in the Electoral College, was a minority choice in the popular vote and therefore had to create patterns of political operation without any decisive popular mandate for his personal service. He had little political machinery to aid him, his party was untried administratively and almost as little experienced legislatively.

Lincoln's first task had been to create a cabinet. He tried a harmonization of the more important elements in his intricately disorganized party. When the cabinet finally was sworn in, its members had little in common, not even a respect for Lincoln, their "chief." Within six weeks Lincoln and this heterogeneous cabinet had to organize, not merely to administer the government, but also to fight a war. Immediately the President discovered that he must cope with a radical faction, whose members were determined to destroy the political power of the South and were capitalizing on the popular interest in abolishing slavery to rally support for this objective. Their secondary design was to constitute themselves the ruling congressional junto, such as had been controlling the government for the Democrats since the days of Polk. Lincoln himself realized that they were almost as much a menace to his power and success as the Confederates. He had therefore in effect to conduct two campaigns, one to control his party and the other to defeat the Confederate armies; he found them constantly entangled.

As a leader he further discovered that the support of his own heterogeneous party, weakened by the rival pretensions of the radicals and the moderates, was not enough. Politically, therefore, he sought to create a wartime coalition, including the War Democrats. In fact, he had carefully considered taking Joseph Holt, a member of Buchanan's cabinet, into his own original council. When he transferred Cameron to Russia, he did appoint such a Democrat, Edwin M. Stanton, who had also been a member of Buchanan's ill-starred administration. In the meantime, particularly after Bull Run, in his almost frantic search for good military commanders he chose a number of Democrats, such as George B. McClellan, generally with the endorsement of Republican governors and senators.

When the fortunes of war went against the Union arms, the radical faction endeavored to capitalize on the fact that so much of the army was under the command of West Point Democrats. The failure of Union armies and the concentrated opposition of the radicals sharpened the warfare between the politicians and the President, and it also played on the easily aroused ambitions of the radical Secretary of the Treasury, Salmon P. Chase. Lincoln had to give some time snatched from his growing involvement in military strategy and the choice of satisfactory commanders to demonstrate his independence of the radicals. One of the reasons for his later

issuing the Emancipation Proclamation was to secure acceptance of his broad interpretation of his great war
power, and he maneuvered the ambitious Chase into
temporary impotence. Nevertheless, the elections of
1862 went against him, and the Republicans barely
maintained their congressional superiority. Such great
states as New York were won by the Democrats.

This situation gave the Democrats some hope for
further success independent of any patriotic "win-the-
war" coalition with Republicans. The confused war fortunes, the virtual dismissal of McClellan, and the possibility of using Lincoln as a "war-failure" scapegoat
meant that some Democrats and McClellan saw an
opportunity to capitalize on his great popularity with
the army, his "persecution" by the radicals, and his dismissal by Lincoln. The General could be made out to
be a martyr, and the Republican setbacks in the fall
election of 1862 encouraged McClellan to begin making
political appearances around the nation.

Lincoln had recognized some of the weaknesses of his
position, and he and his associates began a countermove.
In the summer of 1862 a new organization was planned
and its composition was begun. Lincoln had called in
Judge James F. Edmunds, Commissioner of the General Land Office, to aid in mobilizing a great Union
League out of a series of local chapters, which would
issue propaganda for the Union and for the support of
the war; and here we find the Lincoln germ of real party
organization. This super League would be operated
and directed to some extent from Washington and
would not be dependent on semi-autonomous state machines.

In the meantime the Committee on the Conduct of
the War had been creating a peculiarly offensive type
of propaganda under guise of investigation. As Mc-
Clellan emerged as a possible candidate, the Committee
undertook to break him down and at the same time to

vent its spleen on West Pointers. For in the Union as well as in the Confederacy there burned this hate, fed by the jealousy of the citizen soldier, against the government-trained elite. There were loud complaints that original Republicans with military ambitions, such as Frémont and Banks, were sacrificed to Democrats. Many witnesses were called, the majority of whom were unfriendly to McClellan, and the result was a report published in April, 1863, designed to dispose of McClellan permanently as a political force.

In the spring elections of 1863 the Republicans put forth new effort; they invented a new unit to be attached to Leviathan—permanent party organization. They were particularly worried over the New England states, where several governors were to be elected. Lincoln used the patronage of his office. Wealthy manufacturers, who were enormously enriched by the war, contributed heavily. The Republican National Committee, which unlike previous national committees was working hard in the midterm state elections, sent scores of speakers, including a number of generals, into New England. Then the new weapon was uncovered; Stanton furloughed soldiers home to vote where it was thought it would do the most good. All this paid off and the Republicans in general won, though by uncomfortably close margins; unfortunate indeed, on the other hand, was their defeat in Chicago, the metropolis of Lincoln's home state. A repetition of these tactics was even more successful in the fall elections, in which the Republicans capitalized on the victories at Gettysburg and Vicksburg. The northwestern states and strategic Pennsylvania were carried.

But from all this the radicals took too-great comfort. They claimed the credit and they succeeded in believing that Stanton as well as Chase was with them. Were they not now able to throw Lincoln overboard and take over the party and the White House? The man to do this appeared to be Chase, and a move in his behalf was actively pushed early in 1864. How much Chase knew about this is hard to tell, as he himself lied about it later; certainly his ambitious daughter Kate was not unaware of such a possibility. A boom had, in fact, been started as early as August, 1863, and during the winter a bitter pamphlet was issued scurrilously attacking Lincoln. This was followed by the Pomeroy Circular, designed to improve Chase's chances.

These moves had been met. The Postmaster General, Montgomery Blair, and his brother Frank launched violent attacks on Chase. Lincoln himself prepared to add to his political power by taking command of the reconstruction of the Union with all the assumption of authority which that would involve. Further, in rather obscure ways not yet wholly revealed, working in part through Judge Edmunds and his Union Leagues, Lincoln and his associates were planning to submerge the Republican Party in a new Union Party in which War Democrats might find a congenial home. The Republican National Convention was assembled as the Union Convention, and Vice-President Hannibal Hamlin was replaced as second nominee by the Tennessee war governor, Andrew Johnson, always a Democrat.

In the face of all this, Chase wilted. He had no political appeal against Father Abraham, and the radicals reluctantly had to give him up weeks before the convention. His place was taken by General John C. Frémont, the candidate of 1856, and an irregular convention actually nominated him. However, his thunder was stolen by the Democrats, who nominated General McClellan despite the Committee on the Conduct of the War. The summer of 1864 added to the complexities of the situation when Grant failed to capture Richmond and when Sherman's western campaign seemed equally unproductive of any sizable result.

It was in this troubled period that the Union National Committee thought of dropping Lincoln, and the President himself despaired of success. But various obscure negotiations resulted in a new mobilization of Lincoln's power. Frémont and Chase were mollified by the resignation of Montgomery Blair, Frémont withdrew, and then Sherman captured Atlanta. More important still, the great humanity of Lincoln had a vast appeal among the voters. The Democrats themselves helped by nominating McClellan on a platform that the war was a failure, thereby inviting McClellan's repudiation of it and making a demonstration that there was a dangerous Copperhead element lurking behind him. Finally, certain states provided for soldiers' voting in the field, and in others warriors were furloughed home; Lincoln was triumphantly re-elected.

By the advent of winter in 1864 it was increasingly apparent that Lincoln had been able to create both a political organization and a unified military command. It was also obvious that Congress had not assumed the party leadership. Lincoln's political achievement was making possible the military effort necessary to win the war. It is well within the realm of possibility that, had Lincoln not been able to win his political war and to organize a new and effective political machine, the Union armies might not have been victorious on the field. Certainly they gained no appreciable military success until he had begun to be politically more effective. For two years it was a drawn battle, and even in the end it can be said that Lincoln barely held his own. But though he sometimes bent, he never broke, and the ultimate direction was essentially his. One of the secrets of Confederate defeat and Union victory was the political failure of the one and the political success of the other. Not the least of the results of the conflict was the emergence of the well-organized national party as a significant part of Leviathan's mechanism.

CHAPTER ELEVEN

THE CONFEDERATE
LEVIATHAN COLLAPSES

LEGISLATIVELY speaking, during the war it was a tale of two cities: Washington and Richmond. While the wheels of the ancient lawmaking mill had been turning on the banks of the Potomac, the machinery of the new had been laboring more haltingly by the James.[1] The Confederate legislative war machine had in fact begun functioning in Montgomery when Davis called it in special session on April 29, 1861, two months before the federal lawmakers assembled. At that time President Davis reported that the Permanent Constitution had been ratified by the seven seceding states and had now to be put into operation. He reported the existence of a state of war with the United States, recounted the reasons therefor at length and called for legislation to defend the Confederacy against "aggression." He further reported that Virginia was in the process of secession and that Vice-President Stephens was at Richmond negotiating the union of the Old Dominion with the Confederate States.

The Confederate Congress straightway proceeded with its second period of legislation. The armed forces were enlarged. Sea power was strengthened by providing for privateers and the disposition of prizes. A loan bill was enacted. More taxes were voted, including a Confederate tariff. Its schedules were a good deal lower than those of the federal tariff of 1857, and they were designed to secure as large a revenue as possible. The export of

cotton was regulated. Payment of debts due in the North
was forbidden and the money was directed into the Confederate Treasury. The treatment of prisoners of war
was arranged for. The telegraph system was taken over
for war purposes.

The lawmakers were also conscious of certain unfinished features of their Leviathan. A patent office was established and a copyright law was placed on the books.
Virginia, North Carolina, Tennessee and Arkansas were
welcomed into the Confederacy, and provision was
made to expedite any efforts Missouri, Kentucky and
Maryland might make to that end. The necessary laws
were enacted to provide for the election of a president
and a Congress under the Permanent Constitution that
was to go into operation on February 18, 1862.

Thus the Confederates had designed their own Leviathan with efficiency and precision; its specifications were
detailed in record time in a new Constitution and a
neat set of statutes. The seat of the Confederate Leviathan had been finally established at Richmond in the
Old Dominion, as near as possible to the national capital, in which the Confederates soon hoped to re-establish
a reformed United States. The city was chosen not only
as an expression of gratitude to the Old Dominion for
joining the new republic but also because it was more
convenient to the coast, because its metropolitan atmosphere and superior hotels were attractions, and because
it was near familiar Washington where so many had received their governmental training. The designers of the
new republic completed the move of their creation to
Virginia in June. There on the eve of the battle of
Manassas the Provisional Congress resumed its work. Its
members had still to finish their construction of both a
government and a war machine.

The Congress became the guests of Virginia in Jefferson's Palladian capitol, and the executive was settled in the federal building on the south side of Capitol

Square. This custom house proved too small and the war department was set up by itself at Mechanics' Hall on 9th Street. Jefferson Davis, after some two months at the bursting Spottswood Hotel, was established in the Brockenborough Mansion rented for his use. Daily he came from Clay Street south to his office facing Capitol Square. The Confederacy suffered the psychological consequences of being ever a guest or a tenant. There always lurked the hope of resuming familiar quarters in Washington.

Lawmaking during the scant four years of the Confederacy's existence was beset and limited by numerous handicaps. In the first place, the congressmen labored under conditions of discouraging discomfort. The Provisional Congress, having but one house, fared reasonably well in the legislative chambers of the Alabama and Virginia capitols. But when the bicameral permanent body came into being, hospitable Virginia found her facilities taxed. Her lawmakers had to use their halls for extended periods, during which they tried to provide for their guests. But the best they could contrive were makeshifts. The House was assigned a reasonably adequate room on the first floor, but with the Senate it was different. When the Virginia legislature was in session, the senators were established in the adjutant general's office on the third floor, enlarged by removing the partition separating it from the next room. This chamber, furnished with long tables and innocent of individual desks, was discouraging. It was hard to reach, hot in summer, cold in winter, generally drafty. Both Houses had a predilection for secret sessions, which they held almost daily. It was difficult to keep these quarters shut off from the press or the public. Despite these handicaps, the Congress could never bring itself to build or buy a capitol of its own. At one time the members did consider renting or purchasing the Exchange Hotel for this purpose, but nothing came of the plan. They were probably too concerned with the cares and costs of waging war.

The hardships of the Congress were increased by the discomforts of inadequate living conditions for many of the members. They boarded at the Spottswood, the Exchange, the Ballard and the Arlington and at lesser hostelries, and a number resided in spare rooms or lodgings. When inflation became rampant, many on fixed incomes sought to keep some shred of dignity by renting out rooms or floors of their houses. Congressmen found it convenient on occasion to become "paying guests" in the dwellings of hard-pressed gentlefolk, a situation that could produce further tension in a city where there was already too much.

Under conditions increasingly uncomfortable and distracting the Confederate Provisional Congress labored most of the summer and, after an autumn recess, during the winter of 1861-1862, until the permanent government took over on February 18. The solons had to give most of their time to wrestling with the mounting problems of waging war. They never achieved the full strength they hoped for. Delaware, Maryland, Kentucky and Missouri remained in the federal Union, while western Virginia in effect seceded from the Old Dominion and eventually became a northern state. Certain elements in Kentucky and Missouri set up secession "states" "recognized" by the Confederacy. The Congress admitted "senators" and "representatives" from these mythical states who sat therein for the four years of the life of the Confederacy and enabled it somewhat romantically to mount thirteen stars on its flag.

The lawmakers did not find themselves as effective at waging war as they had at designing a new republic. At first they had believed that it was sufficient to accept state armies enlisted for a year under their own officers and place them at the disposal of their military President and his West Point generals. But the elements of state control were a continual embarrassment to the high command, particularly after Manassas, when so many professed to believe that the war was over and thought it time to go home. Efforts must be made to secure three-year enlistments. Financing was also proving difficult. The government had expected to borrow the ready cash, issue bonds and paper money, tax exports and imports for revenue and levy taxes in cash and in kind. But the federal blockade too soon cut off the trade that would have paid the taxes and brought in the needed equipment. The Confederate navy was slow in coming into being, and inflation was playing hob with prices. Dedication to *laissez faire* prevented the granting of subsidies that might have given some prospect of developing adequate transporation and industry. Distrust of central authority was in fact so ingrained that within a few months Congress even repealed the authorization for the supreme court which had never been established.

On February 18, 1862, the Provisional Congress of the Confederacy finished its year's labors and turned lawmaking over to the recently chosen First Confederate Congress. This legislative institution, like the federal Congress, was bicameral, with a Senate of twenty-six and a House of 105. Here, as in the Provisional Congress, the influence of veterans of the federal Congress predominated. The Senate was presided over in the early days by Vice-President Alexander H. Stephens, and later, during his frequent disgruntled absences from Richmond, by President pro tem. Robert M. T. Hunter of Virginia, for many years federal Senator from the Old Dominion. The Speaker of the House was another Virginia federal veteran, Thomas S. Bocock, who had been the caucus choice of the Democrats for Speaker in the last federal House. Some two-thirds of the House members were former Democrats.*

* That was the proportion in both Houses. In the Senate in six

These two houses operated under rules very similar to those of the federal Congress, made somewhat more simple because the bodies were smaller. A hierarchy of committee chairmen, closely akin to that which had dominated the federal lawmaking, was created and consisted almost exclusively of veterans of the Washington process.* It can be safely guessed that a visitor at Richmond, familiar with Washington, might have thought himself present at sessions of a federal Congress from which there were notable absentees.

The hazards of waging war made the task of the congressmen increasingly perplexing. Assembled without their expected strength, fighting a war they had not anticipated, they were further hampered by the Federal tactics. On the fourth day of the war the Union government proclaimed a blockade and proceeded with great energy to build up a navy to enforce it. At the

---

states there was a policy of equal division with the Whigs, one senator from each party. Arkansas and Alabama chose two Democrats. In Mississippi the affiliation of one Senator was unknown. In South Carolina and Texas the Whig party had never been organized.

* A new hierarchy of committee chairmen was created. In the Senate the President pro tem. Hunter, together with Barnwell of South Carolina, Finance; Edward Sparrow of Louisiana, Military Affairs; Albert G. Brown of Mississippi, Naval Affairs; Benjamin H. Hill of Georgia, Judiciary; James L. Orr of South Carolina, Foreign Affairs—all veterans of the old Congress save Sparrow—had things pretty much under control. Fourteen of the twenty-six had been in the old Congress, and ten were from the Provisional Congress. In the House, the Speaker, Bocock of Virginia; Kenner of Louisiana, Ways and Means; William Porcher Miles of South Carolina, Military Affairs; Charles M. Conrad of Louisiana, Naval Affairs; Lucius J. Gartrell of Georgia, Judiciary—all save Kenner veterans—had general oversight of legislation. Among the membership of the House the proportion of veterans was not so high as in the Senate. Of the 105, there were 24 members of either branch of the old Congress, while 30 had served in the provisional body. But there is no doubt that the first Regular Congress of the Confederacy, like the Provisional Congress, was the offspring of the old Congress and was dominated by its ways.

same time the Davis administration decided to adopt Jefferson's policy of economic coercion and to withhold cotton from export, hoping thereby to create a scarcity of their staple in Europe that would bring recognition from Britain and France. This conjunction of policy effectually deprived the Confederacy of many of the imports upon which they must depend. Consequently the war-making power of the southern states was further hampered by unanticipated scarcity. Theirs was an agricultural economy, with a staple crop that could not be eaten. They were also without many industrial resources, an adequate transportation system or much cash.

The Confederate government was further beset by psychological handicaps. Its members shared with the mass of their constituents a pervasive unrealistic romanticism. A belief prevailed that love of liberty, dedication to the cause, courage and gallantry, the strength of soaring spirits, all could make up for lack of numbers and equipment and for discipline. After all, were not the Yankees mean-spirited materialists with no real capacity or courage for fighting?

Even more inhibiting was the prevailing political philosophy that gave the Confederates a fanatic belief in local autonomy, a worship of states' rights. They were obsessed with a deep-seated antagonism to centralization. With this attitude was associated a negative complex that had been fostered by southern experience in the federal Congress. Here in the ante-bellum years many of their representatives had come to believe that innovation, expansion of federal function, would generally work to northern advantage and weaken the South. Many southern representatives had therefore become accustomed to opposing such measures.

The Confederate lawmakers were so afraid of implementing their new concept of an ideal republic with any operating mechanism, such as a federal or other power system strong enough to maintain it, that they allowed their creation to disintegrate before their eyes. Jefferson Davis understood the need, but he could never secure from the Congress consent to his plans for central power sufficiently sustained, or get the Congress to formulate any real alternatives of their own. Thus conditioned, after 1861 the lawmakers did not command the power of adjustment necessary to meet wartime demands for the centralization necessary to defend the Confederacy and to maintain its independence.

Nor, in spite of the veteran experience of many of its members in federal lawmaking, did the Confederate Congress develop outstanding legislative leadership. The natural leaders of the Confederacy chose the camp rather than the capitol. Jefferson Davis, whose heart was really in the field, had to labor in the capitol, oppressed by physical ills and allied temperamental difficulties, in part probably induced by the frustration of his military ambitions. So handicapped, he could not arouse the spirits of men to respond to his challenge, and within Congress itself no commanding figures emerged. There were enough legislative craftsmen competent to operate the system inherited from the old government, but there were few if any real innovators and too many obstructionists who rode doctrinaire hobbies at the expense of the needs of the hour.

Despite these handicaps, the Confederate congressmen took bold steps to maintain their armies. They conscripted men and wealth. For sixteen of the fifty months of their existence they granted President Davis permission to suspend the privilege of the writ of habeas corpus. They encouraged their agricultural economy to shift to the production of less cotton and more food. Late in the contest they started on a limited program for employing and emancipating slaves inducted into the army. Despite the fact that the total amount of coin under the control of the Confederate treasury never exceeded $27 million, the government was able to command credit amounting to hundreds of millions and to carry on elaborate military operations despite, or perhaps because of, runaway inflation. On the other hand, the Confederacy did not achieve any adequate increase of its limited industrial production, which might have been expanded by having manpower assigned to it. Neither did it advance very far in directing, creating or maintaining any adequate system of railroad communication. The South seemingly did not have the managerial personnel, or at least failed to recruit it. Nor would the lawmakers regulate blockade running and foreign commerce sufficiently to secure the needed imports. Rather, profiteers were permitted to reap their sorry rewards while the armies went without.

The Confederate Congress, obsessed by its negative complex and lacking any very effective leadership, proceeded in the somewhat chaotic and careless way that might be expected from extreme individualists. Reading the record of its operation, one is struck by the number of times it found that hasty and careless legislation needed reconsideration and amendment. There seems to have been, even for Congress, an unusual waste of time, and its members were constantly retreating into secret sessions, of which there is but the most meager record. This tendency to retreat behind locked doors was probably an indication of a basic insecurity.

Confederate lawmakers found little time for the administrative functioning or the partisan politics common to most American legislative bodies. There was no Committee on the Conduct of the War, and although there was criticism of Davis and his advisers, bitter almost beyond endurance, it was confined to an impotent minority. The majority prevented any legislative interference; the criticism was contained within the bounds of carping speech. Nor was there a second presidential election to focus partisanship. The six-year term prescribed for Davis meant that the next contest would not occur until 1867, and by then the Confederacy was but a memory. There had been an effort in the beginning to develop a Whig-Democratic coalition, but as the war dragged on, the opposition to Davis developed something of a Whiggish tinge and the President learned to depend more on his former Democratic associates.

Eschewing administration and party politics, the Confederate Congress worked almost endlessly at lawmaking. Despite the exposed position of Richmond and the frequent danger of attack, Congress continued its labors, interrupted only by an occasional recess, until two weeks before the fall of the capital. The houses finally adjourned on March 18, 1865, seemingly in full expectation of returning to their tasks. A reading of the record of these last days discloses little evidence of anything save the usual routine continuing, as though the Confederate cause was assured of its prayed-for perpetuity. Up to the very end these indefatigable and seemingly imperturbable legislators were passing war-related laws, even indulging in the usual final last-minute rush, just as some of them had done in the old days of power and security in Washington, so deeply ingrained was their legislative habit.

Despite the fact that the Congressional leadership undertook no partisan political activity as was so characteristic of the Union lawmakers, its activities were nevertheless in large part shaped by a politics of a different sort, a politics characteristic of southern folkways. This politics was a significant reason for the short life of the Confederate Leviathan. It was a type of political behavior that was the product of a confused set of factors.

The unity that the southern leadership initially assumed turned out to be specious. There were, in fact, basic cleavages that passed too largely unrecognized. Disagreement over timing appeared almost at the very outset between those who wanted to secede first and then negotiate and those who wished to negotiate in the hope that secession could be avoided. This produced the "original secessionists" and the "eleventh hour men." Then there was the disagreement about direction; there were the strategists, most with Washington backgrounds, and on the other hand appeared the local operators, prominent among whom were such state governors as Brown of Georgia and later Vance of North Carolina, mighty on their own heaths but knowledgeable nowhere else. Finally, there were the more obscure differences about objectives. Some actors in the drama seem to have been more interested, in the beginning at least, in a reconstructed United States than in an independent Confederacy.

Older than these immediate differences were ancient factional feuds. The Confederacy had been organized and mobilized by aggressive Democrats. But the unaggressive and unorganized Whig feudists continued to exist and to hate and despise. They liked their opponents no better than they had in Jackson's day, and for ostensibly the same reasons. They maintained that Jefferson Davis essayed to be a tyrant and was violating local rights. Whiggery was still a conservative, die-hard state of mind, persistent but still none too vigorous and incapable of the exertion effective party organization required. While there was no discernible pattern of partisanship in the politics of the organization of the Confederacy, there were evidences of factional division that were to continue to be influential. There was to be a constant undercurrent of political warfare.

The voting behavior in the Confederacy is difficult to discover because of the short-lived nature of the new combination and the failure of the principals to create a record. Journalists and participants were, on the whole, too preoccupied with the military campaigns and with constitutional justification to have much inclination to write about political behavior. A brief glance at the Confederate elections will also explain the historians' lack of data. The Provisional Congress organized, elected the executive and made the laws necessary to set up the new government without reference to any popular approval by ballot. The first elections that they authorized were held on the first Wednesday in November in 1861, when, by law, presidential electors and members of the House of Representatives of the new Congress were to be chosen. The electors would choose a president and vice president to serve for six years, beginning on Washington's Birthday in 1862. In the meantime the state legislatures would select two senators from each state. The first regular Congress would organize on February 18, 1862, for a two-year period of service.

In these nine months between the assembling of the Provisional Congress and the first march to the polls, war had broken out and the Confederacy had won certain victories, notably at Bull Run. President Davis had been much engrossed in the creation of an army. As he had been a graduate of West Point, an army officer in the Mexican War, and Secretary of War under Pierce, it was only natural that his military training should dominate his interest. It was also natural that he should seek the services of his fellow West Point alumni. Unfortunately, however, he was not always able to get along with his generals. His difficulties, first with the victor at Bull Run, Beauregard, and later with Joseph E. Johnston, had certain political repercussions. In fact, in the elections of 1861 Beauregard's name was mentioned as a possible competitor for the presidency. However, nothing came of the proposal; the period of Confederate enthusiasm and pride in unity was still at its height, and the election of Davis and Stephens was unanimous. There were various contests for House seats, but organized partisanship did not play a significant part. In the contest for Senate seats, Hunter was elected by Virginia, but Louisiana refused such a place to Benjamin.

As there was no second election for the presidency, there was never a real presidential campaign. The only other Confederate election was that for the second Congress in November, 1863. However, state elections took place regularly as in prewar days. In the congressional election and in some of the state elections there was slight or no evidence of anything like party label or organization, but there were differences of opinion and contests. These same differences appeared on the floors of the Confederate houses of Congress. First, there was the difference between upper and lower South. The capital was located in Virginia, and the compelling influence of the Virginians was much commented upon. There was a clash of interest between the cotton-planting states and the others, which showed particularly in the enacting of tax legislation. Most potent was the feeling in evidence almost from the beginning that this was a rich man's war and a poor man's fight. The small landowners who had few or no slaves were conscripted, while the wealthy planters were exempted so that the Negro labor supply might be kept at work and in order. Also, it was not long before islands of disaffection began to appear. In western North Carolina, eastern Tennessee and northern Alabama, as well as in western Virginia, traditional antagonism that had been long smoldering against the older sections of those states burst into occasional flame as the war dragged out and the cherished independence seemed less likely to be realized. Secret organizations fostered, and outspoken leaders proclaimed, a growing sentiment for reconstruction. By the congressional elections of 1863 much of the Confederacy was occupied by Union forces and trans-Mississippi was cut off from the rest. It had been very clearly demonstrated that the senators and representatives early admitted from Kentucky and Missouri represented nobody, while it was all too obvious that various congressmen from Tennessee and Louisiana had lost their constituencies.

When the congressional elections of 1863 were over, out of a House of one hundred, only fifty-three were returned to the Second Congress; the other forty-seven had been replaced by newcomers. Some, of course, had not run again, but many had been defeated for reelection. In these contests the unpopularity of such war measures as conscription, taxes in kind, currency depreciation, martial law and the suspension of the privilege of the writ of habeas corpus had been featured. So was Davis' lack of popularity; even the Vice-President was denouncing Davis as a dictator. The governors of Georgia and North Carolina were on the verge of treason in their refusal to work with the Confederacy. In Georgia only one of the ten congressmen was sent back. In both houses the enemies of Jefferson Davis were very vocal. Albert G. Brown, Senator from Mississippi, was the President's longtime enemy; so was Henry S. Foote, formerly of Mississippi, now representing a Tennessee district in the House. There was also a recognizable Union bloc. The issue that had been most effective against those in office had been the demand for a negotiated peace. The desire for a reconstructed union was becoming more apparent. It is possible that a majority of the new Congress may have had Whig antecedents. Only the fact that Davis had the support of most of the members from districts where federal troops were in control maintained his majority.

Despite his usual success in securing the necessary congressional support, Davis's experience with the second regular Congress was not happy. His nerves were shattered and he was frequently ill. Worse, he developed no capacity to placate his enemies. The increasing gravity of the situation, however, kept a majority more or less ready to support him. Only in the last few weeks of the presidency did congressmen en masse openly defy him. During the entire four years there was a contest within a contest, and in part the Confederacy was defeated from within.

During the brief experience of the Confederacy there was thus much politics but little organization. Local factions, personal feuds, the vendetta of individuals, the bitter search for scapegoats when things went wrong —all these marked the worsening fortunes of the Confederate government and the growing despair of the people. Confederate Governors Joseph E. Brown of Georgia and Zeb Vance of North Carolina seemed to be contemplating another secession and state independence. To make matters worse, the Lincoln administration was endeavoring to organize such southerners as were loyal to the old government, as many were convinced that the war was really being fought to preserve aristocracy. At Lincoln's behest Andrew Johnson was building a new power in Tennessee, and various agents were trying the same thing in Louisiana, Arkansas and North Carolina.

Despite these difficulties, political behavior went on functioning, but haphazardly and chaotically. Deterioration of morale was reflected in a growing confusion of faction. Real discipline had never been developed in government or politics. In the army, for instance, the men elected many of their officers below the grades of general. Whatever operations were successful in fighting or politics had to be carried through by spirit and mass enthusiasm—training and discipline were too seldom achieved. This was also true in the legislatures and in Congress; no partisan caucus discipline developed. Moreover, as the fine flower of the "chivalry" was killed or invalided and the ranks of the squirearchy were decimated, local elite leadership broke down, and there appeared signs of a psychological revolt on the part of the yeomen against fighting to preserve the status of the rich. Finally, no spiritual leadership exerted by a personality appeared in civil life to galvanize southern loyalty to the cause. Davis could not do what Lincoln did. Lee might have done so had he had the motivation to try. The Confederacy, which had started incomplete, never realized its full potential and finally fell apart—yet, despite this disillusioning experience, an election was never missed nor a result questioned; the process of self-government never faltered but pushed inevitably onward in the face of increasing difficulties.

From the start there was an absence of civilian cooperation, leadership and grand political strategy, just as there was in the military effort. Political factions operated somewhat like the independent, uncoordinated armies of the Confederacy. The political operators of the Confederate States were never able to organize parties to conduct election fights and then close ranks after stated battles. They could not seem to utilize the great Anglo-American achievement of organized and controlled periodic demonstrations of hostility—that is, partisan elections—that can be so psychologically strengthening on the principle of catharsis.

The Confederacy had therefore not been able to create a Leviathan adequate to the task of maintaining itself as an engine capable of independent functioning. The reasons for the failure of a group of political experts are intricate and difficult to retrieve. But as the modern science of society has been evolving in recent years, it has supplied data and certain conceptualizations that suggest more realistic answers.

The first of these answers has been produced by the historians themselves. They have become more acute in their powers of analysis and are less apt to be guided by easy reasoning. They are making a greater effort to abandon specious interpretations arising from the similarity of events that can be discovered to be falsely analogous. Historians are more than ever convinced that history does not repeat itself and that they should not be beguiled by a certain degree of repetitiveness in its process into making generalizations that are too easy. This is particularly true in analyzing certain basic considerations that led to the creation of the second Leviathan.

In expanding societies there may on occasion come a time when growth exceeds the capacity to govern. In Anglo-American history this has happened twice. In the eighteenth century, in 1763 to be precise, the British Empire reached that point, and within twenty years secession occurred and the seceding colonies became the United States of America. That republic reached such a point in 1848, and in 1861 a similar secession occurred. In each case the effort was described and justified in elaborate language of political philosophy. But the reality of both situations was the same, the task of government in each instance was too great for the surrogate to accomplish. The one secession succeeded and the other failed because of the complex arithmetic of strength and weakness that decrees that one sum of resources is enough and another is not. In planning their actions, the seceding states in 1861 were very definitely seeking to follow the precedents established in the American Revolution, when colonies seceded from the empire. These precedents were very encouraging. The success of the Patriots of 1776 seemed to demonstrate that a minority without large resources might win against great odds. Had not the British Empire been a more formidable foe than the northern states? But the struggle proved that there was a vital difference between the revolutionaries of 1776 and the activists of 1861.

The American Revolution and the Civil War were in many respects alike, but there were various basic differences. In 1861 no vast ocean intervened between the contenders, the greater remaining might of the old Union could be launched against its next-door neighbors seeking independence. Further, the Confederates, unlike the Patriots, could gain no foreign allies; there was no French or Spanish aid. Even more important was a vital psychological difference. The colonies had never ruled the Empire; they therefore had a choice between self-government and continued inferiority as an outpost. The Confederacy, on the other hand, was maneuvering to keep a superiority and power that it had enjoyed and that at heart it preferred to exclusion from the system it had dominated. Independence in 1861 therefore may well have lacked the compelling appeal that it held in 1776.

This difference in situation was reflected in significant ways. Most striking was the difference in attitude displayed toward power by the Colonists and the Confederates. The Patriots of the American Revolution had realized that if they would maintain liberty and independence they had to create power, power strong enough to enforce unity, to maintain cooperation and to impress mankind. They summoned the creative statesmanship necessary to achieve this power. Their Confederate emulators, however, failed to profit by their example. So jealous were the states of central power that they refused, or at least failed, to set up a strong enough power. Their fear of centralization, it may be hazarded, was sufficiently potent to cripple their capacity for the constructive statesmanship that the realization of their ostensible goals demanded.

A second answer to the question of why the Confederate society did not produce a more adequate Leviathan can be sought in what can be called the sociology of wars. At least two types of warfare may be identified by such analysis—wars between organized societies and wars within such. Wars between societies are conditioned in large part by cultural separation. The people at odds are distant, strange, to a large extent mutually unacquainted. Their common images are based largely upon folklore, propaganda and rumor. Each of the parties fits into the cultural imagery of the other as a stranger and an enemy. The parties' thinking about each other is colored by adjectives of derogation or condemnation. They conceive of each other as foreign, bad, dangerous.

On the other hand, wars within societies, civil wars, are fought by contestants who have a different cultural relationship. These are members of the same society, not of two different societies. They are dominated, not by a tradition of difference, but by a tradition of identification. Their past has been the same. They have shared the vicissitudes of the same fortune; their defeats and victories, their frustrations and their achievements have been held in common. They represent a type of social organization with political implications of ancient origin. Knowledge of such kinship organization and the various forms of family in-fighting is helpful in any understanding of any civil war, including that of 1861-1865. Investigation of such in-fighting is as revealing as the study of international conflict.

In the genealogical table of the United States may be found distant ancestral communities that were organized in political units described as kinship systems. In these societies the political associations and chains of command were based on ties of blood. The earliest communities in the Anglo-American experience appeared on the British Isles two millenia and more ago as polities of this sort. They eventually fused into the Anglo-Saxon heptarchy and then into the Anglo-Norman kingdom and its successors. When the English colonists came to America, they found some such system among the Indians, notably the kinship league of the Iroquois. In such societies genealogy is a basic science because the social organization and the position of individuals, families, and groups therein depend upon the nature of their kinship, on their relations one with the other. Positions are inherited that vary in degree of honor and influence, kinsmen have responsibility for the behavior of their relatives and they have an inheritance of custom based upon family relationship. Their basic definition of themselves is as a family or association of families founded upon blood relationship, immediate or more distant in time. In their customs, war played a significant role, it had a political function.

Fighting was used to avenge family wrongs, to defend honor, to keep reputations unsullied. It was a duty and it produced satisfaction. But society had learned that it should be controlled. The idea of a league or confederacy, as Wallace has pointed out,[2] had been used by the Iroquois. They had set it in operation to maintain emotional equilibrium, to extend influence and to keep the elements of the league in effective association. It developed into a play-off system based on clever diplomacy, designed to maintain the league in a profitable neutrality between other powers.

The original American Leviathan was constructed according to specifications that had some elements of the ancient kinship polity. The blueprint designers of 1774-1775 sought to create a league of British colonial kin, each of whom was entitled to some sort of equal share in its direction, even though it turned out that the theoretical equality was eventually confined to the Senate. This device in effect gave the South a veto and frequently the power of control. From the days of the founding there were always men of mind and influence who interpreted the union of the states in kinship terms. They believed that the members of the federal system, like those in the short-lived Confederation, should work in terms of consensus, of developing a tribal point of view, which all would support in a fashion reminiscent of kinship folkways. Men of this mind found such concepts as centralization and the rule of the majority to have unpleasant, even harmful, implications; it was as though these concepts violated the spirit of family accommodation. As differences of opinion multiplied in mid-century, these ancient family behavior patterns still survived to play some part in shaping the drama. And they continued to do so when conflict broke out.

The opposing hosts were men of the same language, of the same culture, inheritors of the same traditions. Their laws and government were the same. Their common civil training ground had been the Congress and the federal executive departments, their common military training school had been West Point; they had both taken pride in the federal navy. With the outbreak of war, the officers of the army and navy had been compelled to make a choice. The larger part of the army officers were southern, and a larger part of them joined the Confederacy. A smaller proportion of naval officers resigned. They had seen much of their service in distant waters where, whatever their state origin might have been, they represented the United States, and loyalty to the flag meant more to them than did the states they so seldom saw. Their quarter-decks were part of the homeland, and these they trod daily. When the armies fought, they were commanded by generals who had learned the same tactics and would use the same strategy studied in the same classes from the same textbooks.

The Presidents of both factions were born in Kentucky, not far distant from one another. As citizens of Illinois and Mississippi, they represented the West. Both had unpopular wives, and their social status in Washington and Richmond was not secure. Both had personal tragedies during the war, as each lost a little boy. Both suffered from ill health. Both were obsessed with waging war. Both were plagued with generals, and both took their responsibilities as commanders-in-chief with the utmost seriousness. Both had to ad-

minister in capital cities that were occasionally belea-
guered.

Both sides suffered from similar limitations that were
confusing and interfered with carrying on hostilities
that might on occasion be specious. Each had experienced an initial disappointment. The South found that
it was not a united section, the North that there was
so little southern loyalty to the Union. The South
found itself hampered by a negativism, a fanatic de-
votion to *laissez faire* that inhibited innovation. The
North, on its part, found a radical faction threatening
Lincoln's leadership and unified action. In both governmental components there was a lack of ingenuity.
The South failed to develop a managerial capacity
to mobilize resources and transportation. Despite its
greater enterprise, the North was likewise lacking when
it came to armament, as illustrated by its failure to
make the most of inventions in rifles, cannon, and iron-
clad warships. Both had disturbing opposition at home,
bordering on subversiveness. If the North had its "Cop-
perheads," the South had the Governors of Georgia and
North Carolina and the peace men. No one can ever
know what Davis suffered from Brown and Vanee.

As the implications of this civil war are pondered,
one of the puzzles that still perplexes us is whether the
Union and the Confederacy at length became "foreign
nations." There certainly developed a ruthlessness in
the fighting and campaigning, particularly by those who
directed the march to the sea and the burning of Cham-
bersburg. Was not the "rebel yell" feared as much as
might have been the roar of the Huns? Did not the soldiers on each side at length behave as they would have
had the foe been of a strange culture, despite the common culture? The answer to these questions will be di-
verse. The questions themselves complicate life for the
historian.

Be that as it may. Because the contenders in the conflict were bound together by so many ties, the shock of being sundered was particularly devastating. It greatly hindered the Union forces from mobilizing and capitalizing their superior numbers. The effect upon the mechanism of decision and the achievement of unified purpose and power in the Confederacy was devastating. The South was willing to die of negativism. Why was this? Why did not these veterans of successful political experience, well-read in history, see the need, as their forefathers had, of creating this power?

The southern people, leaders and followers, by and large loved the federal republic—they had played such an important part in creating it, in operating it and in bringing it into a position of nascent world power. Instinctively they wished to preserve it, not to destroy it, to improve and save it, and incidentally to maintain their power and status in it. Their hope was that, by creating the Confederacy, they could produce an instrument to preserve it.

But they showed a basic incapacity to grasp the realities of the situation. They did not have sufficient understanding of behavioral science to realize that they were not free agents within a simple political situation but were controlled by this complicated common cultural relationship. They were adopting a behavior that might be effective where hostile tribes with a long-standing history of hate might be operating, but North and South were neither hostile tribes nor rival nations; they were members of a political system with a long history of affection and common interest and achievement. A situation had resulted in which it appeared that certain members of the system were trying to dictate, to demand that, instead of the harmony of interest that had hitherto been maintained, the interest of one member must predominate. This attitude produced something resembling a family resentment. The other members would therefore fight the unreasonable brother to preserve the integrity of the family spirit. This latter possibility the creators of the Confederacy completely neglected.

This miscalculation produced significant behavioral patterns, and it is here that certain anthropological and psychiatric concepts are suggestive in this "brothers' war." For it must be recognized that a segment of the Confederate population large enough to be significant may not really have wanted independence as much as it wanted a reorganized United States in which its section would thereafter function with security insured by the autonomy prescribed by Calhoun. Southern men and women revered their Revolutionary ancestors. They were proud of the achievement of the federal system. They had as great a share in the nation's history as had the North; it was their joint possession. Despite secession and the formation of the Confederacy, loyalty to what they had abjured persisted, at least unconsciously, and provided a mixture of motives, an ambivalence.

Because of this divided objective, we may at least speculate whether the South could contrive sufficient singleness of purpose and a motivation strong enough to achieve an independence that basically many of the southern people did not want. Inhibited by an ambivalence of this nature, the South, unlike its revolutionary forebears, failed to create the power necessary to win. Otherwise it is difficult to interpret the fumbling and indecisiveness put on daily display by a group of experienced politicians backed by a tradition of success. They talked of one thing while thinking of another, for this was something like a family quarrel and the last thing that many in the South may really have wanted was to leave home or to be compelled to leave home—that is, to gain final independence.

When it began to be apparent that what the South was achieving was not security and a controlling influence in the home but at best an uncomfortable seat on the doorstep, there appear signs suggesting a possibility that is highly speculative and cannot be presented as a finding; but it may be offered for consideration as a stimulant to further thinking. If it be true that many in the South never really wanted independence, but reconstruction, it can be deduced that discovery of the impossibility of carrying out their original purpose may have deprived some of them of a compelling motive for trying further to obtain what appeared to be impossible. Rather, these turned to the idea of returning home and making the best of their position, still strong, in the federal system. For the freeing of the slaves, it must be remembered, increased southern power in the Congress and in party conventions, because all of the Negroes, rather than three-fifths, would hereafter be counted. It has been suggested that some southerners may, after a certain point, unconsciously at least, have wanted to lose, so they could the sooner return to the home they deeply loved.

Such return was made easier because the possible sting of acknowledged defeat was lessened by the ties of common history. While there was a good deal of hatred of the "damyankee" and there was fear of slave reprisals, there are nevertheless indications of a feeling that if the fighting would stop and everyone go home, there could be a resumption of the old relationship. After all, these opponents were not marauding foreigners, they were people of the same culture, with whom there had been an experience of long association, often very fruitful. Why not resume it? Enough of independence; here was the prodigal son's refuge. Why not seek it? There might even be some species of fatted calf. Because of cultural ties, it was possible to accept defeat without suicidal despair. After all, the family would again be intact, the brothers reunited, and they could turn to the tasks, not only of repairing the damage, but of combining energies to make their structure larger and finer.

Many of the designers of the Confederacy had really not wanted to construct a new Leviathan; they had hoped to continue the old model without certain new functions, certain "improvements" that rival planners insisted on incorporating. Failing that, they had contrived a smaller-sized copy, which proved hardly adequate for the occasion. It could not function effectively in a war for which it was not planned and, because of a lack of compelling motivation, for which its designers did not muster sufficient ingenuity to make the necessary changes in its structure.

On March 18, 1865, when the Confederate Congress adjourned, Leviathan was in full operation. Upon the surrender of Richmond on April 2, its operators speedily dispersed, and within two months the "engine" had disintegrated and could be found no more save in the piles of papers that were its archives. President Davis and certain of his associates were in prison, others were in flight and the armed forces were at home on parole. Some were already beginning to create the image of the Lost Cause.

In the Confederacy the habitual absence of sufficient capacity to create effective political machinery had been a great factor in that failure to achieve either political unity or military grand strategy that contributed so much to the final defeat, whereas in the Union the genius for organization had become increasingly characteristic. The years of conflict underlined the differences in political operation between the two sections and demonstrated a basic fact in American democracy— namely, that there have always been, and probably always will be, two patterns of democratic operation in the federal system.

Careful study of the operation of these patterns of democratic behavior in both the Confederacy and the

Union give a reassuring picture of the vitality of the American system. Despite the terrible strain and uncertainty of domestic warfare, all elections were held as scheduled in both sections, and the results were tabulated and accepted. There was no sign, even in the dread days of 1864, that there was any thought of postponing or omitting the presidential election. The vast power of Lincoln was submitted to the voters' decision whether to continue it or, despite the terrible risks involved, to swap horses in midstream.

The story of these war years throws light on the functioning of democracy in time of trouble. At the conclusion of the election of 1864, Lincoln responded to a serenade with these words: "The strife of the election is but human-nature practically applied to the facts of the case. What has occurred in this case, must ever recur in similar cases. Human-nature will not change. In any future great national trial, compared with the men of this, we shall have as weak, and as strong; as silly and as wise; as bad and good. Let us, therefore, study the incidents of this, as philosophy to learn wisdom from. . . ."[3] The essence of the proper functioning of democracy, in which public utterance plays such a part, is the application of a saving infusion of wisdom. Those who were working so strenuously on redesigning the American Leviathan were searching for such wisdom.

At the close of the conflict, as the Confederates were furling their banners and stacking their arms, Edward A. Pollard wrote *The Lost Cause*. In it he predicted a new war, not of weapons and blood, but of oratory and ink, conducted according to the art of politics with newly acquired wisdom. "A 'war of ideas' is what the South wants and insists upon perpetrating. . . . [It] means only that we shall have parties in the country. We would not live in a country unless there were parties in it; for where there is no such combat, there is no liberty . . . All that is left the South is 'the war of ideas.' She has thrown down the sword to take up the weapons of argument, not indeed under any banner of fanaticism, or to enforce a dogma, but simply to make the honourable conquest of reason and justice." [4]

This would be southern tactics as the section joined in the operation of the new Leviathan. In this "war" the South was to regain political power.

CHAPTER TWELVE

A NEW LEVIATHAN

WHILE the inventors of the Confederate mechanism were laboring with increasing ill-success to operate their creation, the Union engineers were making major alterations in the Great Leviathan. These changes were rather haphazard and to some extent accidental, for the draftsmen were working without too conscious a long-range purpose, but their blueprints were to produce changes of basic significance. They were in effect to create a new "engine." [1]

For most of the era prior to the war the Congresses had been guided by the doctrine of *laissez faire* and seemed to follow Jefferson's dictum that that government governs best which governs least. The lawmakers had generally fought off the idea that they represented certain interests whose demands should be heeded. But there had always been an oligarchic element abroad in the land, which argued that if the strong and enterprising were favored, all men would benefit. After the secession of the southern physiocrats, the oligarchs were having their day. Congress became, perhaps unconsciously, the patron of interests, the source of subsidy.

A vast lawmaking program came into being. For more than a decade many enterprisers had been petitioning Congress for subsidies. The ruling southern committee chairmen had bottled up such legislation. The secession exodus had removed these restraining hands, and the interested could be busy. They had begun their efforts in the special session in July, 1861, but as it had been there resolved not to pass anything but war measures, no results had been achieved, though some steps had been taken.

While the war objectives were being pursued, pressures were exerted by the growth of the nation and the promoters' enterprise, always alert to advantage. The ambitions of the venturesome had contributed not a little to bring about Republican control. Representatives of this element were imaginative and ingenious, and their desires were pressed upon the lawmakers. Many were looking into the future, uncertain though it might be. What kind of society, what kind of government was to be in operation after the conflict ended? What was to be the fate of the slave? What was to be the nature of the government? Was the South to be restored or reshaped? Should the new political power be different? Was it to be an oligarchy or a new form of democracy? These questions were asked and answered while Congress and the executive were creating and maintaining a vast armed force and uninterruptedly operating a democracy during four years of terrible war.

The great objectives of certain of the enterprising were to secure the increase and spread of population by the distribution of the nation's public lands and the building of the railroads needed to get people and trade to western areas. Almost as soon as the 37th Congress came into session on July 4, Samuel R. Curtis of Iowa rose and presented a Pacific Railroad bill to the House, and McDougal and Latham, both of California, did the same in the Senate. Thereupon select committees were appointed, but nothing more transpired during the special session.

When the regular session convened, the select committees were continued, but nothing happened until February. Then, on February 4 and 5, Pomeroy of Kansas and Rollins of Missouri introduced new bills in their respective Houses. The Senate and House select committees thus had several bills to choose from, and they reported out two in February and March. The House bill was to be the favored one, and as it was being debated, the Senate select committee reported out another one very much like it early in April. Under the terms of these bills a great subsidy of public lands and a bond issue were going to be supplied to capitalists who therewith were to build what one day would be the Union Pacific Railroad. There were no southern senators and representatives, as of yore, to fight for a southern route and to create a stalemate.

A second great use was to be found for the public lands. For a decade efforts had been made to open the great land treasury and to invite the people to go west largely at public expense. But there had always been a southern negative to the new free states that were bound to develop, and Buchanan had vetoed a species of homestead bill. But no sooner had the special session assembled than Aldrich of Minnesota introduced a homestead bill into the House, where it had been referred to the Committee on Agriculture. Under the ban on nonemergency legislation, it slumbered there. But no sooner had the regular session convened than the antislavery agitator Owen Lovejoy of Illinois brought it out of the Committee. But here another interest intervened, and the bill was transferred quite properly to the Committee on Public Lands. This group did not detain it long, and within a week John F. Potter of Wisconsin reported it out, but consideration of it was postponed until March.

A third bill involving the landed estate was one that had also passed Congress before but had fallen afoul of Buchanan's veto. Representative Justin S. Morrill of Vermont had sponsored this bill to donate lands to such states as would establish colleges to give instruction in agriculture and the mechanic arts. He introduced his project again into the House in December, and it went to the Committee on Public Lands. Late in May Potter reported this out, also favorably.

In due course the legislative wheels turned and three measures went to the White House. On May 20 the Homestead Act became law, and hereafter those of enterprise who would locate and live on a quarter section of land for five years might have it practically as a gift after the payment of small fees. On July 1 the Pacific Railroad Act and on the next day the Land Grant College Act were placed on the statute book by Lincoln. A new chapter in legislative history had been written. Freed from southern scruples three great subsidies had been offered American enterprise.

The necessities of war-making had, in effect, produced others. Great quantities of money had to be created and mobilized. Billions of negotiable paper, in the form of bonds, notes, and legal tender currency were poured into the economy. The special session had started the flood and the regular session had continued it as the committees on ways and means in the House and finance in the Senate reported loan acts and the Legal Tender Act of February 25, 1862. Some months later Congress created a national banking system, thus taking another step along the path of subsidy and government relation to business, marked out by Hamilton and Clay and now so eagerly followed by the Republicans. Taxes, too, were multiplied, and to compensate industry for such levies and to keep it in competition with foreign producers, the protective tariff of July 14, 1862, was written into law and the demands of the manufacturers, long so controversial, were now on the road to satisfaction.

Congress had strengthened the powers of the central government in other ways besides providing for subsidies and war financing. The enactment of draft legislation and the suspension of the privilege of the writ of habeas corpus gave the federal government great con-

trol over the lives of individuals. A new state, West
Virginia, and two territories, Arizona and Idaho, were
authorized by this first war Congress. Most significantly,
a new instrument of government was created. The
lawmakers had some realization of what the war was
teaching about the need of scientific experiment and
technological advance, and they incorporated a National
Academy of Science to advise the President on techni-
cal matters. Under this aegis the top scientists of the
nation were to mobilize and place their knowledge and
their advice at the disposal of the war government. In
all this legislation the President had taken little or no
part: he had left the congressional leaders free to go
these long ways in satisfying the frustrated desires of
many of those whom they represented. They had also
done much to redraw the design of the Republic.

Of all the lawmaking problems, however, the most
difficult and those with the greatest implications for the
future were several connected with the slavery question.
In these the President was much interested, and he undertook to play a decisive role. There was a basic disagreement between Lincoln and the congressional
junto that complicated both lawmaking and politics.
The President was much concerned with the safety of
American democracy. And in this regard he was concerned over slavery. The slave problem he would solve
by compensated emancipation of the bondmen and
their colonization elsewhere. But he was also conscious
of a problem of which the radicals seemed not to be
much aware—namely, keeping the border states, which
had not seceded, loyal to the Union. He was anxious
that the contest should "not degenerate into a violent
and remorseless struggle." His purpose was not punitive, and he wished to avoid extreme measures of punishment that might adversely affect the "loyal as well as
the disloyal." He would keep in the foreground the
"integrity of the Union." He was therefore at first un-

willing to seek the abolition of slavery.[2]

In proposing his program for waging war, he defined the war as a peoples' contest, "a struggle for maintaining in the world, that form, and substance of government, whose leading object is, to elevate the condition of men—to lift artificial weights from all shoulders—to clear the paths of laudable pursuit for all—to afford all, an unfettered start, and a fair chance, in the race of life." [3] He feared that certain basic principles of democracy were in danger. He believed that the Confederates' main purpose was to perpetuate aristocracy and to deny to the people all right to participate in the selection of public officers other than legislators. He likewise sensed that wage workers were headed for trouble, that danger was threatening them. He foresaw the possibility that capital might be achieving dominance over labor. The American way was to have a fluid mixed-class society, in which men would always be independent, knowing that even though they might work for wages, they could save and acquire property. The chief measure afforded them for defense of these rights was political participation, in the choosing, not only of their lawmakers, but also of the law-enforcement and law-interpreting agents. "Let them beware of surrendering a political power which they . . . possess, and which if surrendered" would eventually mean the loss of their liberty.[4] Oligarchic rule, Lincoln implied, whether it were that of slave owners in the South or masters of capital in the North, must be prevented.

The radical congressional leaders on their part were insistent on the destruction of slavery and the political and economic power of the ruling southern class. They therefore paid no heed to Lincoln's proposal in his annual message of 1861 for compensated emancipation. After three months had gone by without action, the President sent a message requesting that a resolution be passed, which he submitted, to the effect that the

United States ought to cooperate by giving pecuniary aid to any state undertaking gradual emancipation. This was accepted on April 10. On its part, Congress abolished slavery in the District of Columbia, with compensation to the owners, and in the territories without, and appropriated $500,000 to aid in colonizing slaves emancipated in the District of Columbia. At the end of the session Lincoln took a further step to push his plan for compensated emancipation. He sent in a bill on July 14, providing compensation to any state that might abolish slavery, at so much a head. This bill was referred in the House to its special committee on emancipation, while in the Senate, Sumner had it referred to the committee on finance. Lincoln took this step because he was having a conference with representatives of the border states to urge them to take action. Neither they nor the Congress responded. In fact, after a great struggle Congress was about to complete a new and punitive confiscation act designed by Congress to strike a severe blow at slavery.

The Confiscation Act of the special session had said nothing about treason and allowed only civil proceedings directed against property used in support of the war. This did not satisfy the radicals, who were eager to punish traitors by destroying their slave property. At the beginning of the session various bills were therefore introduced in both Houses, and after laborious committee work and prolonged debate, a bill seemed to emerge in the last hours of the session. Lincoln could approve most of this, which defined treason and prescribed punishment including confiscating property, but some of its provisions he would not tolerate, particularly one that would have confiscated the real estate of those engaged in the rebellion and would have deprived their heirs of it forever. This Lincoln believed unconstitutional, as in effect it was an attainder beyond the life of the traitor, and such action was forbidden in the constitution. He was also opposed to the provision to deprive the alleged traitors of their property without any hearing or conviction. He let it be known that he would veto the act, and congressional leaders knew it would be too late to get it passed over his veto even if they could secure the two-thirds vote, which was doubtful. Managers therefore rushed through an explanatory resolution, needing only a simple majority, to the effect that the act did not work a forfeiture of title to real estate beyond the life of the offender. Lincoln thereupon sent a message to Congress advising its members that he was signing both the bill and the explanatory resolution and regarding them as one. He also enclosed the veto message he would have used had this concession not been made.

In the end President Lincoln came to a measure of agreement with the radicals on emancipation. After his efforts to promote compensated emancipation and colonization had failed, particularly after his discouraging conference in July with border-states representatives, he decided to take the slavery question into his own hands. As soon as Congress adjourned he presented to his cabinet an emancipation proclamation freeing the slaves within the bounds of the Confederacy. If the Confederacy wished to prevent the proclamation's operation, they need only cease fighting. If they did not, the decree would become final on January 1, 1863, in those states in "rebellion." This act was a military measure by which as commander-in-chief he proposed to reduce the military potential of the Confederacy. This proclamation was issued in preliminary form on September 22, after the victory at Antietam, with promise of a definitive document at the New Year. Lincoln had cut the ground out from under his radical opponents.

The President looked upon his emancipation proclamation as at best only a partial solution of the race issue. He was mindful of the future, and he foresaw more difficulties than he is sometimes given credit for. He believed that if the slave owners themselves would accept compensation for their property to be made by government, and then engage their former property in some form of a wage relation using the compensation to pay for the hire, the adjustment would be more wholesome. He had studied the census of 1860 and had compiled statistics to show that the nation could absorb the former slaves as free labor without depressing wages or producing a competing labor force. Further, the cost would be covered if the war were thereby stopped and a long period of heavy expense were thus eliminated. In promoting this idea, he devoted much of his December message in 1862 to drawing a blueprint of the new nation with the race problem adjusted. He argued strongly for an elaborate constitutional amendment, which he presented. He assured Congress that he would follow up his September emancipation proclamation with a definitive one on January 1, 1863, but as this could not apply to the border states or free any slaves where the Union army was in control, a constitutional amendment was required. But Congress sent no amendment to the states at that time.

On March 3, 1863, this first war Congress, contrary to many others, adjourned in a quiet orderly manner. Perhaps its members were impressed with the gravity of the situation. They could, had they thought of it, have recounted the perils through which they had passed and perhaps recognized with a degree of amazement and satisfaction some of their accomplishments. Despite certain grotesque and dangerous activities of radical leadership, particularly of the Committee on the Conduct of the War, there had been an unusually significant legislative creativeness. These men had played a part in setting a pattern for the future development of the nation even while wrestling with the discouraging problems of too-constant military defeat. In this labor their relations with the President had been less than satisfactory. He would not submit to their dictation, they would not accept his leadership; instead, they criticized him and showed a marked distrust of his capacity. Each, therefore, went a separate way—he on the road to greatness, ever increasing in strength and understanding; they providing that which was necessary to fight the war and to plan constructively for a future to which they were to have some responsibility for giving an unfortunate direction. They were to stress material progress, seeking power and growth; he was to phrase and advance the understanding of the spiritual values of the American Republic.

In the process, Lincoln had sought to safeguard the essential character of the American Democracy. "We cannot escape history. . . . The fiery trial through which we pass, will light us down, in honor or dishonor, to the latest generation. . . . We know how to save the Union. . . . We . . . hold the power and bear the responsibility. In *giving* freedom to the *slave,* we *assure* freedom to the *free*—honorable alike in what we give, and what we preserve. We shall nobly save, or meanly lose, the last, best hope of earth. Other means may succeed; this could not fail. The way is plain, peaceful, generous, just—a way which, if followed, the world will forever applaud, and God must forever bless." [5]

The 38th Congress met in December, 1863, in an atmosphere somewhat different from that in which its predecessor began operations. Gettysburg and Vicksburg had been won and the Chattanooga victories were achieved. The fall elections had been encouraging to Republican hopes. But despite these successes, no Confederate armies had been destroyed, the Army of the Potomac had not captured Richmond.*

* In the 38th Congress there were 36 Republicans, 9 Democrats

There was no change in the leadership in the Senate and little in the House. Speaker Grow had not returned to the House, and his place was filled by Schuyler Colfax of Indiana. The radicals abandoned Emerson Etheridge, former Union Congressman from Tennessee, and elected as clerk a henchman of Thaddeus Stevens, Edward McPherson of Pennsylvania. The fact that the Democrats voted for Etheridge provided him little comfort. In the Senate the Democrats were playing no real role, nor was there any real partisan organization there. In the House there was a sizable increase among the Democrats, but the newcomers did not much affect the processes of lawmaking.

In fact, this second war Congress faced little of the novelty that had confronted its predecessor. Most important was the fact that Lincoln's policies were forcing it to confront the future. The President was making another assumption. His first had been that he had the power to protect the government, that as a tribune of the people elected by them, he could act in an emergency without warrant of law, raise an army, appropriate money and suspend the Bill of Rights. Later on he had assumed that as commander-in-chief of the army and navy he could free the slaves within the Confederacy. Now he announced in his third annual message that as commander-in-chief he would make the rules and regulations for the withdrawal of the army and the restoration of the Union. He had begun acting on such an assumption as soon as Union troops gained footholds in Tennessee, Louisiana, North Carolina and Arkansas. He had made assignments to military governors whom he had appointed, and they had been organizing loyal citizens and holding elections. Five chosen under such

---

and 5 Unionists in the Senate; 102 Republicans (a net loss of 4), 75 Democrats (a gain of 33) and 9 Unionists in the House. The State of West Virginia sent a delegation, and so did a small rump in Virginia; the latter was not allowed much service.

auspices were presenting themselves to the House of Representatives as members-elect from Louisiana. Then, on December 8, the President announced a policy for amnesty; former Confederates, save high military and civil officials and former United States officers, could resume their political privilege upon taking an oath of loyalty. If such men numbered ten per cent of a seceded state's voters, they could bring it back into the Union.

This message aroused the radicals again. Congress reappointed the Committee on the Conduct of the War. It refused to admit the Louisiana representatives chosen under Lincoln's plan and busied itself drafting a reconstruction bill of its own. Senator Wade sponsored a draft in the Senate that had been fathered in the House by a returned radical congressman from Maryland, Henry Winter Davis. This Wade-Davis bill would postpone reconstruction until fifty per cent of the white male citizens should take the oath, a much greater number than Lincoln's ten per cent. The scheme proposed to disfranchise the whole Confederate army, thereby depriving the South of most of its natural leaders. This bill was passed so late in the session that Lincoln could let it die by failing to sign it. This he did, but as he did so he issued a proclamation in effect offering the Confederate States a choice between his plan and the stringent proposal of the Congress. To this Wade and Davis issued a bitter reply, denouncing his act as executive usurpation of legislative functions, and they hoped for a season that Lincoln might be defeated. His success at the polls made it clear that he would continue to carry out his reconstruction plans. The test would come when the senators and congressmen chosen in the South under his rule should present themselves in Washington. Would Congress heed the radicals as they had in the case of Louisiana and refuse them, or would the executive finally triumph? That issue was not to be further resolved during the 38th Congress. In the meantime Congress declined to let any partially reconstructed states, including Andrew Johnson's Tennessee, cast any electoral votes in the election of 1864.

In its two sessions the 38th Congress added new dimensions to Leviathan. It made further contributions to the shape of things to come, the new nation that was to be. The highest protective tariff ever was enacted. Subsidies were granted to a second transcontinental railroad, the Northern Pacific, and to railroads in Iowa, Michigan, Minnesota and Wisconsin. Further recognition of the discovery of metallic hoards in the Rockies was taken when Montana was created a territory, to take its place with Idaho and Colorado as political units and potential states in the new mineral empire. Nevada became a state.

The influx of foreign immigrants was encouraged by the enactment of a contract-labor law that encouraged the importation by foreign contractors of cheap labor in gangs. Ancient ghosts were laid by the repeal of the fugitive-slave act. The abolition of slavery was finally assured by the submission of a thirteenth constitutional amendment to the states. The establishment of a Freedmen's Bureau constituted the first effort designed to aid the ex-slaves in enjoying their new freedom. Some effort was made to recognize the freedmen's civil status by permitting them to work in the mail service. A return to normal civil rights was forecast by a law preventing military and naval officers from interfering with elections in the states. Recognition of a new social responsibility was made by appropriations for pensions for disabled soldiers and the widows of those who had lost their lives, and by establishing a national military and naval asylum for the sick and disabled.

From 1861-1865, the federal government had labored under all the hazards of civil strife. The executive and the judicial as well as the legislative branches had re-

mained at work in the armed camp that was Washington, sometimes within sound of gun fire, on occasion in
danger of capture. The lawmakers had carried on uninterruptedly though often nervously, and during five sessions Congress had never missed a day from necessity.
Guns might roar in the distance and the Capitol serve as
a bivouac ground, but the legislative process moved on
without interruption. The great quantity of work required in the making of war and the remaking of Leviathan was accomplished despite the absence of any
unusually gifted leadership. Congress produced no great
statesmen itself, nor would it pay much heed to Lincoln.
But the Houses labored mightily under wartime handicaps and, without too great consciousness of any purpose
save survival, supplied blueprints for a recasting of American society.

Among many, a particularly significant question was
resolved—the question whether the federal system could
continue to function under strain on its two specified
strata; whether legislators on two levels, state and federal, could cooperate; whether state legislatures, state
governors and state courts could operate in sufficient
correlation with Congress, the president and federal
courts to make possible the bringing of such a full-scale
war to a conclusion. This test was met. The Union was
restored, and the nation rebuilt its Leviathan. It was a
tribute to the capacity of the American political designers that they could repair damage largely of their
own creation.

The reasons for their skill and their success are as
complex and difficult to discover as are those of the Confederate failure. It took more than greater numbers and
superior resources. Once again there is much to be
learned from modern behavioral science and psychiatric
suggestion. As the South was afflicted with an ambivalence that impaired its concentration of effort, the
North was quickened to a species of fanatic zeal. In this

section a potent instrument for victory had been forged
by the heat of a great enthusiasm. Those in blue knew
they were battling to prevent the destruction of the
American system, the great value Americans had created by their combined ingenuity. This force was the
more powerful because, subconsciously, it was shared
extensively in the South. And as it served to quicken the
spirit of the North, it served at the same time in some
measure to dissipate the energy of the South. At the
same time there was a touch of the Freudian in northern enthusiasm. The control that masters might exercise over the persons of their slaves could be sin at its
worst, and the destruction of slavery was therefore a
moral duty.

Another difficult problem connected with analyzing
the anatomy of Leviathan, this "artificiall Man," is the
problem of the cultural limitations of the "naturall"
men who attempt to deal with it and such of the American people in general as show interest in their labors.
These cultural limitations have been imposed by birth,
environment, association and tradition. Most of those
with such interest have opinions shaped by circumstances outside themselves. Each has started life with a
geographical relationship to the Mason-Dixon line,
either north of it, south of it or west of it, unless he is of
foreign origin. Even those who have moved from their
places of birth and dwell in a different cultural atmosphere have carried an inherited tradition to their new
abodes. If a historian marries on the other side of the
line, he may be confused by harboring two cultures
under one roof. But no matter how confused his experience with the conflict may be, it is not easy, though it
may be possible, for him to release himself from external influences that will determine his interpretation
and restrict his understanding.

If the history of the conflict is to be written with even
an approximation of truth, it is essential for those con-

cerned to understand the nature of such cultural limitations. This is particularly important because those who were drawing Leviathan's blueprints were circumscribed by these same limitations. These cultural determinants are emphasized because there is an almost irresistible impulse in the moralistic intellectual world in which so many Americans dwell to speak instinctively in terms of praise or blame, to condemn or to justify. The extent to which the balance is in favor of condemnation or commendation seems to depend largely upon the accident of who is making the analysis, upon his cultural definition. Do these limitations make inevitable a moral judgment, the casting up of an account? Is it not possible to accept the hypothesis that in the conduct of great masses of people there must, by some law of behavioral average, be as much to praise as to blame? In the long run, will not these judgments decree some sort of balance of virtue?

It seems to be a fact that emotions appear in pairs, and thus contrast like negative and positive charges of electricity, like the two sexes, like Yin and Yang. Where there is idealism there is sordid self-seeking, where there is loyalty there is callous disregard for the cause, where there is patriotism there is cynical disdain for the commonweal, where there is bravery there is cowardice, where there is unselfish sacrifice there is refusal to contribute a moment's discomfort or an ounce of effort. Where there is chivalry there is contempt for the foe. Where there is eagerness to serve there is heartless ambition. Where there is a favorable interpretation there is one to the contrary. There are always love and hate, hope and despair.

These contrasts, operating in both sections, suggest the hypothesis that the North American ecology decreed the evolution of two different societies in an environment and a cultural organization that would encourage a mutual desire for union—something akin to matri-

mony—in which two obviously different individuals
sought the satisfaction of a primal urge stronger than
their individual wills in a union that in this instance
was crowned with the fruits of their own creation:
something new, a nation. This nationalism in the end
proved stronger than their individual wills, and after
an emotional crisis that drove them to the brink of destruction, the strength of their own creation, their
nationalism, saved them from annihilation. When the
historian applies the dry scientific concepts of the behavioral sciences to an analysis of this war, it becomes
difficult to assign praise or blame or to award victory or
defeat.

The problem is further complicated by the puzzling
possibility that the contestants were fighting for the
same aim and that both achieved it. The war was a conflict to conserve the federal system and this end, which
both sides really desired, was achieved. The Union
forces were fighting for a federal system, in which the
principle was to govern that the rule of the majority
should prevail. The South on its part was dedicated to a
federal system in which the autonomy of a minority
should be recognized. It fought primarily to ensure the
South a veto in the system.

Ostensibly the Northern interpretation triumphed;
but did it? The South certainly did not achieve a veto
or an autonomy to the degree to which it desired, but its
achievement even in defeat was no mean one. When the
Confederacy returned to its allegiance after Appomat-
tox, the states came back eventually to positions of no
small power. The abolition of slavery increased their
representation in the House because all the Negroes,
rather than three-fifths, were now counted in appor-
tioning representatives. Likewise these states contrived
to keep senators and representatives in Congress for
longer terms than on the average their northern counterparts were allowed, and so their resultant seniority gave

them real control in the congressional committees. The southern representation can frequently exercise a veto and even control, as in the days of the Texas leaders, Lyndon Johnson and Sam Rayburn. Power in the nation is still divided, and the government is still a federal system. The war at length came to its end when there was no reason for it to be fought any longer. It was perhaps a war that in a sense nobody won.

A double achievement, the concluding of the war and the organization of a new political power in the process, created blueprints for a new engine. For the instrument of government, like the republic itself, was in many ways a new creation at the conclusion of the fighting. President Lincoln and a number of those in the 37th and 38th Congresses had been prolific draftsmen, endeavoring to adjust Leviathan to new conditions and to redesign it so that it could be geared to cope with and at times direct the nature of the change.

The conflict did much to strengthen the oligarchic-democratic definition of the republic, and it was accomplished at the expense of a concentration of power in the hands of a new few, just as Lincoln had feared. This concentration was to present new challenges to those dedicated to the preservation of the democratic rule of the people. But the failure of the Confederate government to play a part sufficiently effective to insure its permanence did not result in the destruction of the aristocracy-democracy concept. The emancipation of the slaves only confused the issue and left an ambiguous race relationship that no legislative or judicial action has since been able to adjust permanently or to clarify completely. The process is painfully slow, but progress is being made in working out the problem of race relationship. Yet it must be the South that finds the solution. North and South still exhibit different interpretations of democracy and have perhaps never really agreed upon a common definition. The attempt to define democracy still goes on as oligarchic and aristocratic groups, as well as interest combinations of later origin varying from time to time in composition, endeavor to direct the destiny of the people of the United States. The result of this "brothers' war" that the designers of blueprints failed to avert was a new American Leviathan.

CHAPTER THIRTEEN

PERFECTING LEVIATHAN'S NEW DESIGN

THE surrender of Lee on that Sunday in April was the long-hoped-for evidence that the war was over. But the story of the readjustment of Leviathan requires a final chapter. Though the federal Constitution and the statutes passed under its aegis over the years were once again the unchallenged supreme law of the reunited land, in the realm of state law and government adjustments had to be made and recognition of a basic political and social change had to be inserted in the Constitution itself.

In the eleven states that had seceded there was a species of chaos. No one pretended any longer that there was a Confederate government; that mechanism had simply disappeared. For the time being there was a vacuum as far as federal civil officials were concerned in seven of the states. In the other four—Virginia, Arkansas, Tennessee and Louisiana—there was confusion. On the state level, what was the condition of local government in the eleven former members of the Confederacy? In a very real sense they were occupied, and the military was the prevailing power. But in all of them there existed the full quota of state officers provided by the state constitutions, just as they had existed prior to 1861. Such state officials were carrying the whole burden of civil government with varying degrees of effectiveness in seven of the Confederate states, their activity depending on whether there were many federal troops at hand. Presumably in Florida, Alabama and

Texas their authority was more generally accepted than elsewhere. On the other hand, in Virginia, Louisiana, Arkansas and Tennessee the situation was very different. In these states definite efforts had been made by the federal government to insure restored state Leviathans.

In Virginia the effort had begun about the moment of secession. The Old Dominion had been divided by geography into sections that had exerted an influence similar to the geographical division in the nation. Within that state were two societies, and they had become increasingly hostile. Hardly had secession been completed in May, 1861, when the western transmontane counties undertook a counter secession, and on June 19 a convention of these counties proclaimed themselves the true State of Virginia, elected F. H. Peirpoint governor and provided for a legislature and a judiciary. Both the President and Congress recognized this "loyal" state, and after Congress met on July 4, two new senators and five representatives were admitted. In 1863 this "state" gave most of its counties permission to form the state of West Virginia, which was duly admitted to the Union.

The admission of this state left very little of old Virginia loyal to the United States, but a governor and a small legislature, representing mainly the areas around Alexandria and Norfolk, functioned throughout the entire conflict. When Lee laid down his arms, therefore, there was a recognized loyal state of Virginia. Compared with the dominion that had seceded, it was not significant, but it was legal and a part of the Union. Naturally none of the rest of the old state was prepared to pay it any heed.

During the conflict the federal government had recognized three other restored states—Louisiana, Arkansas, and Tennessee. In 1862, after the capture of New Orleans, President Lincoln had authorized Generals Butler and Shepley to summon loyal voters to the polls. In 1864 a governor was elected whom Lincoln recognized; but the congressmen elected, as previously pointed out, were not admitted to any effective service. Lincoln had likewise acted in Tennessee and Arkansas. On March 4, 1862, he had appointed Senator Andrew Johnson military governor of his native state and had commissioned him brigadier-general. He and the federal army had made possible the restoration of a loyal government, and for his efforts Andrew Johnson was made the second of Lincoln's vice-presidents. Similar efforts were successful in Arkansas, but Lincoln's attempts to do the same in North Carolina and Texas bore little fruit. Therefore, when fighting ceased there were loyal governments functioning in some fashion in Virginia, Louisiana, Tennessee and Arkansas although Congress had never accepted this operation save in its early stages in Virginia, Tennessee and Louisiana. In Tennessee three congressmen had been elected in August, 1861, and two, elected in Louisiana in 1862, had served two weeks during February-March, 1863.

As previously stated, Congress had refused to accept Lincoln's assumption of authority in reconstruction. Its leadership resented the steps he had taken and usually refused to approve or even recognize them; the 38th Congress admitted no representatives from Virginia or Louisiana; none presented themselves from Tennessee. The lawmakers on their part had taken a hand at Leviathan's design in the Wade-Davis bill. This Lincoln had refused to accept in place of his own plan outlined in the Amnesty Proclamation of December 8, 1863, and reiterated in his proclamation announcing the death of the Wade-Davis plan by his hand. He would yield nothing to Congress, though he realized the uncertainty of affairs in an apt statement: "So great peculiarities pertain to each state; and such important and sudden changes occur in the same state; and withal, so new and unprecedented is the whole case, that no exclusive, and inflexible plan can safely be prescribed as to details and collaterals." [1] He had written Peirpoint early in the process, "Make haste slowly. Things are improving by time." [2] Lincoln was willing to play it by ear.

The end of the war and the assassination of the President left Leviathan still unadjusted, with unfinished blueprints on the drawing boards. Lincoln could do no more. Who would complete the task and finish the redesigned Leviathan?

Prior to Lincoln's murder and the surrender of Lee, little had been undertaken in the matter of blueprint designs. Lincoln had issued his Amnesty Proclamation of December 8, 1863, and that of July 8, 1864, when he announced his disapproval of the Wade-Davis bill. Other than this, he had written a few letters and issued several commissions to military governors sent down to the states that he hoped were ripe for reconstruction. Just before his death he was considering what further documents would be necessary, and at his last cabinet meeting Secretary Stanton read to his associates a draft of a reconstruction program that he had drawn up. It was decided to divide this into two parts, one for Virginia, where separate action was held necessary, and the other for the remaining states. Stanton was to have copies prepared and circulated, so that there could be a full discussion at the next session.

Then came the assassination, and to the problem was added the implication that Lincoln's murder was planned in the South. A cry for vengeance was heard. "Treason is a crime and traitors must be punished." This watchword of the new President Andrew Johnson was so different from Lincoln's last utterance, "the sole object of the government . . . is to again get them into [a] proper practical relation [to the Union]." [3]

After a brief interval of uncertainty, Johnson and the members of Lincoln's cabinet whom he retained around him agreed to a series of documents, largely the work of

Stanton, which were in the spirit of Lincoln's philosophy of speedy reconciliation with as little vengeance as possible. As in Lincoln's proclamation of December 8, 1863, amnesty was offered to all who would swear allegiance. As in Lincoln's proclamations, the political and military leaders were excepted and to the classes therein named, Andrew Johnson, erstwhile humble tailor and foe of the wealthy planters, added those whose property exceeded $20,000. That was the extent of his vengeance. He would pardon even these and the other excepted groups if they would apply to him.

The second of the documents was an executive order continuing the recognition of Governor Peirpoint and his Virginia government and authorizing him and his associates to proceed to the "restoration of peace." The governments Lincoln had encouraged in Louisiana, Tennessee and Arkansas were allowed to continue without documentation. The procedures to be followed in the remaining seven states, where no steps had been taken, were set forth in a series of seven identical proclamations, mutatis mutandis, issued between May 29, the day of the new Amnesty Proclamation, and July 13, 1865.

In this series of proclamations the President as commander-in-chief of the army made known the terms under which he would withdraw the troops and thereby restore a republican form of government to the states lately in rebellion. In each of these states the President appointed a provisional governor who was to arrange for a convention chosen by such voters as would take the oath of amnesty that the President prescribed; any citizens in the proscribed classes who desired to participate must also have been pardoned. These conventions were to alter or amend the states' constitutions and were otherwise clothed with all the powers necessary and proper to enable the loyal people of these states to be restored to their constitutional relations to the federal government. In letters of instruction to these provisional governors, President Johnson explained that at least fifty per cent of the voters must vote and that the conventions must repeal the ordinances of secession, repudiate the states' war debts, and abolish slavery by amending the constitutions of the states. The newly chosen legislatures must ratify the Thirteenth Amendment.

All this was done in the absence of Congress, and a number of the more radical of the lawmakers protested, as they had in Lincoln's day, against presidential usurpation. However, until December, 1865, there was little they could do. In the meantime the provisional governors performed their functions, and conventions and thereafter legislatures were chosen. The conventions followed Johnson's program and destroyed the results of the states' intransigence. But other actions of the reconstituted states gave the radicals in Congress fuel for the fire of their resentment against the President. A number of those whom the newly authorized voters chose for office were ex-Confederates and Democrats. As the ratification of the Thirteenth Amendment, proclaimed in December, 1865, abolished slavery, it also abolished the "other persons, not taxed," designated in the original Constitution. Therefore all Negroes, as well as whites, were now counted in the basis of representation, instead of merely three-fifths of the slaves as before. This would increase southern representation, and the elections indicated that this representation would be Democratic, thus threatening Republican supremacy. Few Negroes were permitted to vote, so there could be no chance of recruiting them as the bulk of the hoped-for southern Republican Party.

Further, the new southern legislators found themselves with a race problem on their hands. The former slaves were prone to wander, they tended to congregate in cities in a fashion dangerous to public health and civil order, and upon numerous occasions they showed a lack of a sense of social responsibility that gave much cause for concern. There were serious race riots in Memphis and New Orleans. Such manifestations of the racial problem confronted the reconstituted state legislatures as they undertook to function anew in the southern state capitols. Since some sort of legislation was necessary, they either revised the old slave codes, regulating the conduct of the freedmen in such matters as keeping them off the roads and forbidding them alcoholic beverages and weapons, or they borrowed some laws from the British West Indies passed at the time of emancipation there. Since this legislation did curtail the freedom of action of former slaves, it enabled such friends of the Negro as Charles Sumner to denounce Johnson's reconstruction policy as returning the Negro to slavery.

When Congress assembled in December, 1865, its leaders discovered that the seceded states had chosen in these recent elections the recent Vice-President of the Confederacy, four of its generals, five colonels, six cabinet officers and fifty-eight of the members of the Confederate Congress. The race riots and the Black Codes were equally disquieting. Widespread apprehension developed that the good results of the war were in process of destruction. The Negro was being driven back into bondage. The recent rebels were being restored to power. If the army were to be withdrawn from the South, the Union men and the Negroes would be at the mercy of the militant and unrepentant Confederates. These would be back in Congress stronger than ever and, joining with northern Democrats, might before long control Leviathan again, with Andrew Johnson, ex-Democrat, at their head. And the Union dead were hardly cold in their graves.

The radical congressional leadership persuaded a majority of the federal lawmakers to refuse admission to the congressional delegations from the eleven Confederate states until a joint committee of Congress should study the problem and report. What might then have happened had Johnson been able to organize a sufficient number of the uncommitted to his support can never be known. He failed; in fact, at first he did not seem to be trying to build up a party. Rather, he further antagonized Congress in a fashion that destroyed whatever support he might have secured from moderates. The result was that the joint committee on reconstruction took over the drafting of blueprints and in the end revised Leviathan under compulsion of certain determinants of the new era.

The chief work of the joint committee was a fourteenth amendment to the Constitution. This measure was designed ostensibly to insure civil rights to the Negro by making him a citizen and placing his rights under the protection of the federal courts. It also sought to insure him the vote by indirection. It provided that the representation in Congress of any state that did not permit him to vote might be reduced in the proportion of those deprived of the vote. This amendment, submitted on June 16, 1866, was proclaimed as ratified on July 28, 1868, and thereby a new dimension was added to the Federal Leviathan.

Finally a fifteenth amendment was presented to complete the work of the Fourteenth as it related to the Negro. The effort projected by the Fourteenth to give the Negro the privilege of voting had failed. Therefore another was designed to secure it to him. The privilege of voting hereafter could not be denied to anyone because of race, color or previous condition of servitude. Thus by amendment, slavery had been abolished, and racial discrimination in the matter of citizenship, civil rights and voting privileges were presumed to have been elminated. It was assumed that a homogeneous society as far as political equality was concerned had been assured. Thus, when Secretary Fish signed the proclamation announcing the ratification of the Fifteenth Amendment on March 30, 1870, the American Leviathan was complete.

The Thirteenth, Fourteenth, and Fifteenth Amendments placed a final touch on Leviathan's design by seeking to redefine the social and political status of about a sixth of the American population—the Negroes. Prior to the Thirteenth Amendment, most of them had been bondmen held to forced labor by their owners. As such they had been bought and sold, and each had a cash value. However, they had certain badly defined rights to life; killing them under certain circumstances might be punished, and most of them were protected very inadequately by law against grosser types of cruelty. Now by the three amendments they were emancipated, made citizens and declared eligible to vote.

The enabling legislation necessary to put these amendments into operation was neither well-considered nor effective. Despite the Fourteenth Amendment, the status of the freedmen was largely subject to state legislation and local opinion. The Negro did not enter society as the equal of the white man. Instead, though no longer a slave, he assumed a different type of cash value as a wage worker, share cropper or tenant, usually still in a position obviously inferior. His so-called political rights were shortly to become largely mythical, and his political participation was practically prohibited. The Negro, no longer a slave, a salable chattel, became often a dubious second-class citizen, sometimes in a situation resembling serfdom and peonage. The war did not solve the race problem; rather, it complicated it because the Negro's status was redefined in terms that were false. As a slave he knew what he was, as a freeman he was shortly to find it impossible to find himself. The blueprints assigned him a function in Leviathan that he was not permitted to perform. It was to be left to draftsmen of the next century to attempt a real adjustment.

The Fourteenth Amendment had a significance greater than its immediate objective of providing civil guarantees to the freedman. It also looked back more than a century to correct a defect that had been left by the authors of the Constitution. They had not attempted a definition of the republic; indeed, they had not even given the document a heading. Its preamble recited in curious phrase as a fact that a body described as "We the People of the United States . . . do ordain and establish this Constitution for the United States of America," and the document concluded with the statement that "the Ratification of the Conventions of nine states shall be sufficient for the Establishment of this Constitution between the States so ratifying the same." Furthermore, certain delegates from twelve states subscribed their names "In Witness" that the document had been adopted "by the Unanimous Consent of the States present" on the seventeenth day of September, 1787. From Article I, Section 2, it appeared that there were thirteen states somehow involved in creating the document, although one of them, Rhode Island, had completely ignored the effort. It is obvious that this document was in effect designing a new and more complex Leviathan, but there was no attempt to define the new polity in any terms known to political science. A series of independent political entities hitherto operating as a Confederation of states in "perpetual Union" declared they were undertaking to make this union "more perfect."

Since 1789 there had been no attempts at official definitions, save as they were undertaken by laws and judicial decisions that had other purposes. Chief Justice John Marshall of the Supreme Court of the United States had made certain incidental contributions, but the question of exact definition was still in dispute in 1861.

Mobilization, war, and victory, however, had wrought changes. In the minds of some who were influential in government there had developed the concepts of union, nationalism, central power and direction—in other words, they were thinking in terms of more efficient operation under unified control from a central source. The joint committee on the reconstruction of Leviathan now undertook to put into words in an amendment a new spirit but, like the authors of the original Constitution, they avoided any direct statement of precise definition. The Fourteenth Amendment contained this clause: "All persons born or naturalized in the United States, and subject to the Jurisdiction thereof, are citizens of the United States and of the State wherein they reside. No State shall make or enforce any law which shall abridge the privileges or immunities of citizens of the United States; nor shall any State deprive any person of life, liberty, or property without due process of law; nor deny to any person within its jurisdiction the equal protection of the laws."

This clause in effect served as a species of specification for the new Leviathan. There was now national citizenship, no longer trammeled by state-imposed limitations. Hereafter *all persons* born or naturalized within the bounds of the republic would be citizens and would be entitled to all the rights, privileges and immunities belonging to such. Even more significant, it would be the federal courts that would now have the jurisdiction in matters connected with disputes over these rights. On such basic questions federal law and federal legal jurisdiction were supreme, subject to final determination by the federal Supreme Court. A body blow had been dealt to local autonomy or state sovereignty.

Because of the use of the word "persons," this amendment could also be held to give federal courts jurisdiction over certain business developments. One of the objectives of the Fourteenth Amendment was to give aid and protection to national economic stability. In the first place, the federal war debt was guaranteed and the Confederate obligations repudiated. There was also a second, less obvious, device. Certain legislatures, both southern and northern, had shown a tendency to hamper the free enterprise of individuals and corporations by restrictive and even confiscatory legislation. Regulatory laws, heavy assessments and taxes, prohibition of business practice had been proposed in the South to control northern capitalists seeking to operate in that region; and in the North rural legislatures seemed unsympathetic, even hostile, to certain practices of those operating "big business" and their lobby efforts in state capitals.

Later, before the Supreme Court, Senator Roscoe Conkling produced the journal of the Committee of Fifteen as evidence that the authors of the Fourteenth Amendment had objectives beyond the protection of the civil rights of the Negro when they prohibited the states from depriving any person of his rights without due process of law or from denying to anyone the equal protection of the laws. This clause in the Fourteenth Amendment could be applied to white persons as well as to Negroes and to "artificial persons" such as corporations. Questions involving the impairing of such rights were therefore subject to the jurisdiction, not of state, but of federal courts. A new dimension was thereby added to federal power, a basic change in Leviathan had been designed to centralize the control of its mechanism.

These three amendments, although, like the Constitution, they did not profess in any set language to define a new Leviathan, did in effect create a new design. The old Leviathan, though built according to the specifications of a federal system, had operated as a partnership. Through the instrumentation of equality in the Senate, the North and the South had been more or less equal in power until 1850. But the direction of growth of the republic after 1850 and the war effort had together destroyed the equal partnership and reinstated the federal system that hereafter was going to operate in the form of an increasingly centralized government, or, to introduce another business concept, like a corporation run by representatives of the majority stockholders.

The autonomy of the states, the confederation of independent sovereignties, the recognized power of the South as a section with either positive control or a negative by veto—these elements of the republic were suppressed. Additional parts were introduced into the "engine" that were designed to arrest any tendency to disintegration. The most significant was the element of national citizenship, making all of American birth birthright members of a great common cause. The old sense of local rights, the privilege of independent state action, of community autonomy, had been superseded by a sense of superorganization and a concept of it as an instrument of power that demonstrated its superior capacity to bring pride and gratification. The question of the definition and protection of fundamental rights was in the hands of the federal courts, which thus became really supreme. The resistance of the South to the centralization, the nationalism, was for the time being broken, and those who thought in terms of the grand organization and central direction that had won the war were now free to develop their plans. On the basis of the Fourteenth Amendment they created their new Leviathan. New men would now think in terms of government for a great, unified society of enormous size and tremendous wealth. Human ingenuity would be encouraged and the inevitable greed accompanying the enterprise would be curbed in terms of nineteenth-century liberalism and the Progressive Era.

During the first ninety years of the life of the republic, amidst increasingly confusing situation, the draftsmen had been extremely busy with their designing. By March 30, 1870, twenty-four states had been added to the original thirteen. Of these, nineteen had passed through the territorial phase. Congress had also created ten territories not yet states. This process had not only required the writing of twenty-nine laws creating territories and of twenty-three acts of admission; but in thirteen instances, enabling acts were also passed granting the territorials permission to plan for statehood. Finally, twenty-four constitutions had been added to the original thirteen. In the preparation of these master documents there was a certain amount of copying. Those who took the lead in making new states generally had old statute books at hand, and it was often easier and more satisfying to copy something well-known and tried than to create some new formulation; further, the lawyers among them liked the idea of precedents. Of the thirty-seven states, a number had not been content with their original labors and had revised or superseded their basic charters. Before Reconstruction, sixty-five constitutions had been enacted, and a variety of others had been tried and either rejected or otherwise never completed. Through it all the Congress and the state and territorial legislatures had been endlessly drafting laws. The volumes of federal, state and territorial statutes were fast multiplying by a biennial output of thousands of pages.

Now, in the twentieth century, the United States is two world wars and a cold war away from the turn of the century and the Progressive Era. Is the republic in the throes of constructing, quite unconsciously perhaps, a new Leviathan, which no one has yet described? Is this a Leviathan of another sort, being designed by a people who are becoming preoccupied with such concepts as international insecurity, the welfare state, the new conservatism, social conformity, racial antagonism? In this period of mid-twentieth-century reconstruction it is well to remember that there are times in the history of men when they release force and accumulate energy that it seems beyond their intellectual power to control. Mankind today stands in all probability in such an age. Men have learned some of the secrets of genetic information, they have released the energy in the atom, they have created the atomic bomb and they are poised on the edge of space. It may well be questioned whether human intellectual power as at present developed is equal to the challenge. This does not mean that humanity does not have the intellectual potential; it does mean that if society is to survive, all concerned must work tirelessly to increase and mobilize it.

A century ago Americans stood in a somewhat similar position. They had a vast continent largely unpossessed but very rich in unrealized resources and opportunities. They had new sources of power, new population and a new treasure. They had a neat but old-fashioned system of control. They had a newly released set of emotions, driven wild by recently unbridled imaginations. This situation created a confusion almost certain to create conflict, which in Whitman's phrase was "significant of a grand upheaval of ideas and reconstruction of many things on new bases." [4] If people are truly to comprehend and account for the conflict of 1861-1865 and to apply their knowledge to the tasks of the twentieth century, they must do it in some such grand frame, summoning all they can of the available knowledge of why men behave as they do, as still a century later the process of adjusting Leviathan continues. Fifty-one legislatures are constantly at work studying the adaptations necessary to keep the design adequate to cope with constant change.

The question of the relative strength of the elements

of control in the great mechanism and the division of power continue to be subject to debate, in large part because this division of strength is not constant. Sometimes one element, sometimes another, seems dominant. Perhaps there is a basic equilibrium, the dynamics and measure of which no physicist-historian has ever been able to calculate. Perhaps none ever can, because he who rides the regulating pendulum can have no fixed point from which to observe its exact path and momentum. If he ever does come to rest, the stillness he finds will probably be the stillness of death.

The draftsmen who continue to work on the structure of the American Leviathan represent one of man's significant achievements. In seeking to solve such basic problems of human association as the prescription of government by the formulation of constitutions and statutes, they carry the ideal of rational thought to one of its highest culminations. By substituting writing for fighting, they have overcome one of the most destructive of human urges and have established the fact that the control of impulses dangerous to human welfare by scientific thought is possible. Such a capacity is one of the greatest achievements of the human race. May it always be cherished and perfected. One means to preserve it is to understand its intricacies and the temptations to conflict that threaten its fulfillment. All will do well to heed the words of Jefferson Davis and Abraham Lincoln, the opposing leaders of a century ago.

"And now that [secession] may not be again attempted, and that the Union may promote the general welfare, it is needful that the truth, the whole truth should be known, so that crimination and recrimination may forever cease; and then, on the basis of fraternity and faithful regard for the rights of the states—, there may be written on the arch of the Union, Esto perpetua.[5]

"The dogmas of the quiet past are inadequate to the

which I could conquer an empire. But the taking of such exceeded even my powers."

"Or mine," Pharaun said, "hard as that is to credit. So, lusting for what you couldn't have, you spied on the cities of the Underdark, didn't you, or one of them, anyway. You kept your eye on Menzoberranzan."

"Yes," Syrzan said, "I've watched your people for a long while. I discovered the cabal of renegade males some forty years ago. More recently, I observed the priestesses' debility; no mere dark elves could hide such an enormous change from an observer with my talents. I remembered the would-be rebels and arranged for them to make the same discovery, then I emerged from the shadows and offered them my services."

"Why?" Pharaun asked. "Your collaborators are drow, and you're, if you'll pardon my bluntness, a member of an inferior species. Jumped up vermin, really. You don't expect Houndaer and the boys to honor a pact with you once the prize is won? Dark elves don't even keep faith with one another."

"Fortunately, the prize won't be won for decades, and during those years, I'll be subtly working to impose my will on my associates. Long before they assume the rulership of the city, I'll be ruling them."

"I see. The fools have given you your opening, and now that which you could never conquer from the outside you'll subjugate from within, extending the web of compulsion farther and farther, one assumes, until all Menzoberranyr are mind-slaves marching to your drum."

"Obviously, you understand the fundamentals of illithid society," said Syrzan. "You probably also know that we prefer to dine on the brains of lesser sentients and that we share your own race's fondness for torture. Still, some of your folk will fare all right. I can't eat or flay *everyone*, can I?"

"Not unless you want to wind up a king of ghosts and silence. And where, may I ask, do these stone-burning fire bombs come from?"

"Menzoberranzan isn't the only drow city possessed of ambitious males," the illithilich said.

Pharaun was momentarily speechless. Another drow city—

"Now, it's your turn to satisfy my curiosity," Syrzan said, interrupting the drow's reverie.

"I live for the opportunity."

"When Houndaer and the others explained our scheme, did you sincerely consider joining us?"

Pharaun grinned and said, "For about a quarter of a second."

"Why did you reject the idea? You're no more faithful or less ambitious than any other drow."

"Or illithid, I'll hazard. Why then did I remain firm in my resolve to betray you to Gromph?" The slender dark elf spread his hands. "So many reasons. For one, I'm a notable wizard, if I do say so myself, and in Menzoberranzan we mages have our own tacit hierarchy. In recent years, I've channeled my aspirations into that. Should I rise to the top, it will make me a personage nearly as exalted as a high priestess."

Syrzan flipped its tentacles, a gesture that conveyed impatience, and a flake of skin fell off. Unlike the slimy hide of living mind flayers, the lich's flesh was cracked and dry.

"The renegades are trying to place themselves *above* the females," the undead creature said.

"I understand that, but I doubt it'll work out the way they plan, or even the way *you* plan."

"You believe the priestesses are too formidable, even divested of their spells?"

"Oh, they're powerful. They may well extinguish this little cabal. Yet for the moment, I'm more concerned about the undercreatures. Do you realize how many goblins there are, how fervently they hated us even before you maddened them, or how dangerous your stone-consuming fire is? It could be that after they riot, we won't have a Menzoberranzan left for anyone to rule."

"Nonsense. The orcs will have their hour, and your people will butcher them."

Pharaun sighed. "That's what folk keep telling me. I wish your consensus comforted me, but it doesn't. That's one of the drawbacks of knowing yourself shrewder than everybody else."

"I assure you, the orcs cannot prevail."

"At the very least, they'll destroy some of the lovely architecture the founders sculpted from the living rock, and they'll set a defiant example for future generations of thralls. Your scheme will harm not merely the priestesses but Menzoberranzan itself, and I disapprove of that. It's sloppy and inept. Only a fool mars the very treasure he's striving to acquire."

A sneer in its tone, Syrzan said, "I wouldn't have taken you for a patriot."

"Odd, isn't it? I'll tell you something even stranger. In my way, I'm also a devout child of Lolth. Oh, it's never kept me from pursuing my own ends—even past the point of murdering a priestess or two—but though I strive for personal preeminence, I would never seek to topple the entire social order she established. I certainly wouldn't conspire to place her chosen people and city under the rule of a lesser creature."

"Even gods die, drow. Perhaps Lolth is no more. If Menzoberranzan is indeed the mortal realm she loves best, why else would she abandon you?"

"A test? A punishment? A whim? Who can say? But I doubt the Spider Queen is dead. I saw her once, and I don't just mean the manifestation who visited Menzoberranzan during the Time of Troubles. I've gazed upon the Dark Mother in the full majesty of her divinity, and I can't imagine that anything could ever lay her low."

"You have looked upon the Spider Queen?"

"I thought you might be interested in that," said the mage. "It wasn't long after I graduated from Sorcere, returned home to serve my mother, and sided with my sister Sabal against her twin Greyanna. One night, a delegation of priestesses came to our stalactite castle. Triel Baenre herself led the expedition—she was Mistress of Arach-Tinilith in those days—and she'd brought along dignitaries from Houses Xorlarrin, Agrach Dyrr, Barrison Del'Armgo, and other families of note. It was a momentous occasion, especially for me, because all these great ladies had come to arrest me.

"I never did find out if Greyanna instigated the affair. It was the kind of thing she would have done, but it needn't have been her. You'll scarcely credit it, but in those days, I was considered an insolent, uppity scapegrace, a far cry from the meek and modest gentleman you see before you today. A good many clerics may have suspected me of irreverence."

"This is what happened to Tsabrak," Syrzan said. "The priestesses arrested him, turned him into a drider, and drove him forth."

"Sometimes they mete out punishments even fouler," Pharaun said, "but first they examine you to determine your true sentiments. I hoped my mother would intervene. She was one of the great Matrons of Menzoberranzan, and I'd scored a number of coups for House Mizzrym, but she never said a word. Perhaps she believed me a traitor in the making or was reluctant to disagree with the Baenre. Maybe she simply found my predicament amusing. Miz'ri's like that.

"Be that as it may, the priestesses threw me in a dungeon and put me to the question, employing whips and other toys. Somehow I managed to resist the urge to make a spurious confession merely to stop the pain. A fellow wizard cast a mind-reading spell, only to slap up against the defenses most mages erect to protect their thoughts. I imagine an illithid would have smashed right through, but he was unequal to the challenge."

"Then you passed the test?" Syrzan asked.

"Alas, no," Pharaun laughed. "The examiners deemed the results inconclusive and accordingly asked a higher power to make the determination. They laid me on an obsidian altar, performed a dancing, keening, self-mutilating ritual together, and the torture chamber faded away. You'd think I would have been glad of it, wouldn't you, but my new surroundings were no less ominous."

Pharaun's captors had ignored his silver ring, obviously thinking it mere jewelry, if they noticed it at all. As soon as he'd looked at Syrzan, he'd discovered its magic operated even within the confines

stormy present. The occasion is piled high with difficulty, and we must rise with the occasion. As our case is
new, so we must think anew, and act anew. We must
disenthrall ourselves, and then we shall save our country." [6]

NOTES

FOREWORD

1. Thomas Hobbes, *Leviathan*, Everyman's Library edition (London, 1914), 87.
2. *Ibid.*, 1.
3. Roy P. Basler, ed., *Collected Works of Lincoln* (New Brunswick, N.J., 1953), IV, 426.

CHAPTER I

The bibliographical notes for this and the other chapters are in no sense comprehensive, they are merely suggestive. In the main they represent books that may prove useful to the curious reader.

Many years ago, as a junior in college, I was introduced to the writings of three valiant American scholars whose work has passed through various editions and has stood the test of time: Edward P. Cheyney, *History of England from the Defeat of the Armada to the Death of Elizabeth,* 2 vols. (New York, 1914-1926); Albert B. White, *Constitutional History of England* (New York, 1908); George Burton Adams, *Constitutional History of England* (Revised by Robert L. Schuyler, New York, 1934); and George Burton Adams and H. Morse Stephens, eds., *Select Documents of English Constitutional History* (New York, 1911). Since then I have come to appreciate other works. Among them are: Frederick William Maitland, *Constitutional History of England* (Cambridge, 1911); Frederick Pollock and F. W. Maitland, *History of English Law* (Cambridge, 1911); W. S. Holdsworth, *History of English Law* (London, 1922-1926); M. M. Knappen, *Constitutional and Legal History of England* (New York, 1942); W. E. Lunt, *History of England* (New York, 1946); Carl Stephenson and F. G. Marcham, *Sources of English Constitutional History* (New York, 1937).

Studies of a more specialized nature are: J. E. A. Jolliffe, *Constitutional History of Medieval England* (New York, 1937); A. B. White, *Self-Government at the King's Command* (Minneapolis, 1933); R. F. Treharne, *Baronial Plan of Reform, 1258-1263* (Manchester, 1932); George L. Haskins,

Growth of English Representative Government (Philadelphia, 1948); S. B. Chrimes, *English Constitutional Ideas in the Fifteenth Century* (Cambridge, 1936); George Macaulay Trevelyan, *England in the Age of Wycliffe* (London, 1909); William E. Lingelbach, *Merchant Adventurers of England* (Philadelphia, 1902); William R. Scott, *Constitution and Finance of English, Scottish and Irish Joint Stock Companies to 1720* (Cambridge, 1910-1912); and Catherine Drinker Bowen, *The Lion and the Throne* (Boston, 1956).

CHAPTER II

1. The Cambridge-East Anglian story is drawn from J. B. Mullinger, *University of Cambridge from the Earliest Times* (Cambridge, 1873); Albert Peel, *Brownists in Norwich and Norfolk about 1580* (Cambridge, 1920); "History of Norfolk," v. XXIV, *Victoria Histories of the Counties of England* (London, 1900———); *Memoirs Illustrative of the History and Antiquities of Norfolk and the City of Norwich* (London, 1851); Augustus Jessop, *One Generation of a Norfolk House,* 3rd edition (London, 1913); Frederic William Russell, *Kett's Rebellion in Norfolk* (London, 1859); Roy F. Nichols, "English Origins of American Politics," *Pennsylvania Magazine of History and Biography,* LXXVI (1952), 5-29.

2. The literature of the English Reformation seems infinite in quantity. My guide was M. M. Knappen, *Tudor Puritanism* (Chicago, 1939). John Strype, *Annals of the Reformation* (Oxford, 1824) was a rich mine. John W. Allen, *History of Political Thought in the 16th Century* (London, 1928) shed light on the intellect, and Conyers Read, *The Tudors* (New York, 1936) and K. Pickthorn, *Early Tudor Government: Henry VIII* (Cambridge, 1934) on the statecraft and politics of the Tudors and their associates.

3. John Ponet, *A Short Treatise of Politike Power and of the True Obedience which Subjectes owe to Kynges and other Civil Governours, with an exhortation to all true naturall Englishe men* (London[?], 1556); Christopher Goodman, *How Superior Power oght to be obeyd* (Geneva, 1558); John Knox, *First Blast of the Trumpet against the monstrous Regiment of Women* (1558).

4. The Elizabethan story has many chapters, as Elizabeth's reign was as complex as she was; only a few titles are

cited: Christina H. Garrett, *Marian Exiles* (Cambridge, 1938); John E. Neale, *Elizabethan House of Commons* (London, 1949), *Elizabeth I and Her Parliaments* (London, 1953-1957), *Essays in Elizabethan History* (London, 1958); Albert Peel, *The First Congregational Churches* (Cambridge, 1920); Edna Bibby, "The Puritan Classical Movement of Elizabeth's Reign," Mss. Master's Essay, University of Manchester, 1929; Roland G. Usher, ed., *Presbyterian Movement in the Reign of Elizabeth as illustrated by the Minute Book of the Dedham Classes, 1582-1589* (London, 1905).

5. The seventeenth-century phase may be discovered in Basil Willey, *Seventeenth Century Background* (London, 1937); Frederick James Powicke, *Cambridge Platonists* (London, 1926); W. C. dePauley, *The Candle of the Lord* (London, 1937); J. F. Figgis, *Divine Right of Kings*, 2nd ed. (Cambridge, 1914); G. P. Gooch, *History of English Democratic Ideas in the Seventeenth Century*, 2nd ed. (Cambridge, 1927); G. M. Trevelyan, *Trinity College* (Cambridge, 1946). John Sherman, *A Greek in the Temple* (Cambridge, 1641) was one of a large collection of religio-political pamphlets that I used in Trinity College Library at Cambridge, with the help of A. H. Finkell, to whom I express my thanks.

CHAPTER III

1. The transit of the practices of self-government across the Atlantic was an arduous one, and it cost much in life and effort. Various phases of the experience are found in Charles M. Andrews, *Colonial Period of American History*, 4 vols. (New Haven, 1934-1938); Wesley Frank Craven, *The Southern Colonies in the Seventeenth Century, 1607-1689*, Vol. I, *The History of the South*, Wendell H. Stephenson and E. Merton Coulter, eds. (Baton Rouge, 1949); Alexander Brown, *The First Republic in America* (Boston, 1898); James Truslow Adams, *Founding of New England* (Boston, 1921); Samuel Eliot Morison, *Builders of the Bay Colony* (Boston, 1930); Curtis P. Nettels, *Roots of American Civilization* (New York, 1938); Lawrence H. Gipson, *The British Empire before the Revolution* (Caldwell, Idaho, and New York, 1936——); Charles S. Sydnor, *Gentlemen Freeholders* (Chapel Hill, 1952); George L. Haskins, *Law and Authority in Early Massachusetts* (New York, 1960); Daniel J. Boorstin, *The Americans: The Colonial Experience* (New York, 1958);

Carl Bridenbaugh, *Cities in the Wilderness*, 2nd ed. (New York, 1956); Roy F. Nichols, "Early Transatlantic Migration of Politics," *Cambridge Journal*, II (1949), 671-683, "Birth-pangs of American Democracy," *American Heritage*, New Series, I, 10-14.

2. The Revolutionary experience is the theme of John R. Alden, *American Revolution* (New York, 1954); John C. Miller, *Origins of the American Revolution* (Boston, 1943), *Triumph of Freedom* (Boston, 1948); Clinton Rossiter, *Seedtime of the Republic* (New York, 1953); Edward S. Morgan, *Birth of the Republic, 1763-1789* (Chicago, 1956); Curtis P. Nettels, *Washington and American Independence* (New York, 1951); Elisha P. Douglass, *Rebels and Democrats, the Struggle for Equal Political Rights and Majority Rule during the American Revolution* (Chapel Hill, 1952); Allan Nevins, *American States during and after the Revolution* (New York, 1924); Merrill Jensen, *Articles of Confederation* (Madison, 1948).

3. The Constitution comes into being. Charles A. Beard, *An Economic Interpretation of the Constitution* (Reprint, New York, 1936); Forrest McDonald, *We The People* (Chicago, 1958); Robert E. Brown, *Charles Beard and the Constitution* (Princeton, 1956); Lee Benson, *Turner and Beard* (Glencoe, Ill., 1960); Lord Macmillan, "Two Ways of Thinking," *Law and Other Things* (Cambridge, 1937).

4. The frontier begins to be organized. Thomas P. Abernethy, *From Frontier to Plantation in Tennessee* (Chapel Hill, 1932); Thomas D. Clark, *History of Kentucky* (New York, 1937); Beverly W. Bond, Jr., *The Foundations of Ohio* (Columbus, 1941); Thomas D. Clark, *Frontier America* (New York, 1959); Merrill Jensen, *The New Nation* (New York, 1950).

CHAPTER IV

1. The political and legal complications of the great expansion made inevitable by the Louisiana Purchase are discoverable in many scattered sources. The beginning should always be made in Henry Adams' massive work, *History of the United States during the Administrations of Jefferson and Madison*, 9 vols. (New York, 1889-1891), now to be compared with Irving Brant, *James Madison, Secretary of State, 1800-1809* (Indianapolis, 1953); *James Madison,*

President (Indianapolis, 1956); and *James Madison, Commander in Chief* (Indianapolis, 1961).

2. Adams, *op. cit.*, II, 118.

3. Brant, *James Madison, Secretary of State,* 134.

4. Adams, *op. cit.*, II, 107-108.

5. *Ibid.*, V, 325.

6. The process of territorial construction and state making can be followed in Max Farrand, *Legislation of Congress for the Government of the Organized Territories of the United States, 1789-1895* (Newark, N. J., 1896); Bayrd Still, "Statehood Process, 1800-1850," *Mississippi Valley Historical Review,* XXIII (1936), 189; Roy F. Nichols, "The Louisiana Purchase, Challenge and Stimulus to American Democracy," *Louisiana Historical Quarterly,* XXXVIII (1955), 1-25, "The Territories, Seedbeds of Democracy," *Nebraska History,* XXV (1954), 3-16; Clarence E. Carter, ed., *The Territorial Papers of the United States,* 26 vols. (Washington, 1934-1962). The early period has been covered by Frederick Jackson Turner, *Rise of the New West* (New York, 1906); and by George Dangerfield, *The Era of Good Feelings* (New York, 1952); Roscoe C. Buley, *The Old Northwest, 1815-1840* (Indianapolis, 1950); Glover Moore, *The Missouri Compromise, 1819-1821* (Lexington, Ky., 1953).

7. Later developments are detailed in Glyndon G. Van Deusen, *The Jacksonian Era, 1828-1848* (New York, 1959); Bernard De Voto, *The Year of Decision, 1846* (Boston, 1943); Norman A. Graebner, *Empire on the Pacific* (New York, 1955); James C. N. Paul, *Rift in the Democracy* (Philadelphia, 1951). Holman Hamilton has dealt with the Second Compromise, that of 1850, in *Zachary Taylor,* 2 vols. (Indianapolis, 1941-1951), and in "Texas Bonds and Northern Profits: A Study in Compromise, Investment and Lobby Influence," *Mississippi Valley Historical Review,* XLIII (1957), 579-594. He has a book on the Compromise that will soon be published. Reference should also be made to George D. Harman, "Douglas and the Compromise of 1850," *Journal of the Illinois State Historical Society,* XXI (1929), 453-499, and Robert R. Russel, "What was the Compromise of 1850," *Journal of Southern History,* 22 (1956), 292-309.

CHAPTER V

1. The technique of implementing the process inaugurated by the Northwest Ordinance after the passage of the Compromise of 1850 continued in a fashion that boded ill for the peace of the nation. The Kansas-Nebraska struggle precipitated a period of crisis that ended in bloodshed. The circumstances surrounding this legislative battle are detailed in Roy F. Nichols, "The Kansas-Nebraska Act: A Century of Historiography," *Mississippi Valley Historical Review,* XLIII (1956), 187-212, and *Franklin Pierce,* 2nd edition (Philadelphia, 1958).

Much ink has been spilled over the bill and Douglas' part in it, as can be discovered by examining P. Orman Ray, *The Repeal of the Missouri Compromise* (Cleveland, 1909), "The Genesis of the Kansas-Nebraska Act," American Historical Association, *Annual Report,* 1914, 2 vols. (Washington, 1916), I, 259-280; Frank H. Hodder, "The Genesis of the Kansas-Nebraska Act," State Historical Society of Wisconsin, *Proceedings,* 1912 (Madison), 69-86, and "Railroad Background of the Kansas-Nebraska Act," *Mississippi Valley Historical Review,* XII (1925), 3-22. These scholars indulged in a controversy that culminated in a state of complete misunderstanding. See also Albert J. Beveridge, *Abraham Lincoln, 1809-1858,* 4 vols. (Boston, 1928), III, 165-217; George Fort Milton, *Eve of Conflict* (New York, 1934), 114-54; Avery Craven, *The Coming of the Civil War* (New York, 1942), 328-332, *The Growth of Southern Nationalism, 1848-1861* (Baton Rouge, 1953), 172-205; Allan Nevins, *Ordeal of the Union,* 2 vols. (New York, 1947), II, 43-159; James C. Malin, *The Nebraska Question, 1852-1854* (Lawrence, Kansas, 1953); Gerald M. Capers, *Stephen A. Douglas, Defender of the Union* (Boston, 1959).

Anyone who wishes to follow the congressional maneuvering leading to the enactment of this measure, particularly the evolving text of the act, has an interesting but complicated task on his hands. He soon learns that lawmakers like nothing better than copying; there is nothing more comforting than cherishing a precedent. The process of securing a law authorizing the organization of Nebraska had been going on since the 28th Congress. When Douglas entered that body as a Representative, he introduced a Nebraska bill on December 11, 1844 (H.R. 444) as well as one to establish military posts in Nebraska and Oregon (H.R. 526). In the 29th Congress he became chairman of the House Committee on Territories and devoted himself to Oregon, moving forward bills to protect migration to Oregon and to organize territorial government there. However, nothing came of these efforts, and in 1847 Douglas went to the Senate. In the upper House he introduced bills to organize Oregon, Minnesota, Nebraska and New Mexico. He introduced S. 59 to set up the territory of Oregon and a duplicate H.R. 201 was presented to the House. This measure finally was passed in July, 1848.

Douglas was active in securing the organization of Minnesota in 1849 and of New Mexico and Utah in the Compromise of 1850, but for a while he took no further action on Nebraska. This project was taken up in the 30th Congress by Representative Willard P. Hall of Missouri. Since he wished to introduce a bill to organize what he called the Territory of the Platte, he took Douglas' House bill, H.R. 201 of the 30th Congress, 1st Session, for the organization of the territory of Oregon. Hall changed its phraseology from "Oregon" to "The Platte" and finally introduced it in the 2nd Session of the 32nd Congress (1852-1853) as H.R. 353. Richardson took this bill in the Committee on the Territories, changed "The Platte" to "Nebraska" and reported it out. The House passed it and Douglas tried unsuccessfully to get it through the Senate. This bill proposed to organize the region 36° 30' to 43° as the territory of Nebraska without reference to slavery. When the 33rd Congress convened, both Senator Dodge of Iowa and Congressman Miller of Missouri introduced this text in their respective Houses as S. 22 and H.R. 81. It was this bill that Senator Douglas had expected to put through until Senator Atchison told him differently. Douglas took this bill, then six years old, and moved his tortured version of January 4 as an amendment. The bill he reported on that date is the old bill in parenthesis and the new added as an amendment. In the House Richardson never used H.R. 87 when he came to report a bill on January 31 after his exasperating experience with Congressman English. He took Douglas' "amendment" and reported that as H.R. 236. For a few days S. 22 and H.R. 236 were identical, just as the original S. 22 and H.R. 87 had been alike from December 22, when Miller had introduced his, until January 31. These bills and their various amendments are in the curious manuscript version, often old prints altered by pen, which their proposers presented, now deposited in the files of the Senate and the House in the National Archives. Their printed versions used by the senators and representatives are in bound volumes in the Library of Congress. Otherwise the texts of the various versions must be sought in the newspapers; they are not recoverable in their entirety in the *Congressional Globe* of the 33rd Congress, 1st Session, or in the *Senate* (Ser. 689) or *House* (Ser. 709) *Journals* of that session. The Act itself is in *Cong. Globe, loc. cit.,* 2228-9 and in *U.S. Stat. L,* X, 277 ff. Douglas' and English's reports are #15 *33:1 Sen. Repts.* (Ser. 706) and #80 *33:1 H Repts.* (Ser. 742).

2. John A. Parker, "The Secret History of the Kansas-Nebraska Bill," *National Quarterly Review* (New York), XLI (July, 1880), 105-18, reprinted as a pamphlet under the title *The Missing Link . . . What Led to the War, or the Secret History of the Kansas-Nebraska Act,* with an introductory note by Waldorf H. Phillips (Washington, 1886); John A. Parker [clerk to the House Judiciary Committee in 1854] to Lyon G. Tyler, June 1, 1889, Tyler Papers (Library of Congress) ; Parker to James Buchanan, March 29, 1854, Buchanan Papers (Historical Society of Pennsylvania). See also *A Statement of Facts and a Few Suggestions in Review of Political Action in Missouri* (n. p., 1856); Ray, *Repeal of the Missouri Compromise,* 229-33; Blair to Van Buren, August 24, 1854, Van Buren Papers (Library of Congress); New York *Herald,* December 10, 1853; John A. Parker to J. F. H. Claiborne, December 23, 1853, Claiborne Papers (Library of Congress); *Cong. Globe,* 33 Cong., 1 Sess., Appendix, 44-45; Washington *Union,* December 8, 13, 17, 24, 1853; Everett Diary, December 12, 16, 1853 (Massachusetts Historical Society); Washington *Star,* December 13, 14, 17, 1853; St. Louis *Missouri Republican,* December 20, 1853; New York *Herald,* January 2, 4, 11, 25, 1854; Baltimore *Sun,* December 21, 1853, January 9, 1854; Philadelphia *Ledger,* January 9, 1854; Washington *National Intelligencer,* February 6, 1854; Washington *Union,* February 18, 1854; Everett Diary, December 10, 1853; New York *Herald,* December 10, 1853; Washington *Star,* March 4, 1854; Blair to William Allen, February 10, 1854, William Allen Papers (Library of Congress). See further Ray, *Repeal of the Missouri Compromise, passim,* particularly 274 *n.* and 276-288. Senator Andrew P. Butler declared on the floor of the Senate: "General Atchison . . . had perhaps more to do with

the bill than any other Senator." *Cong. Globe,* 34 Cong., 1 Sess., Appendix, 103. Senator James M. Mason also discussed the subject. *Cong. Globe,* 35 Cong., 2 Sess., 1248. *Private Letters of Parmenas Taylor Turnley* (London, 1863), 104-106. James Ford Rhodes, *History of the United States from the Compromise of 1850,* 7 vols. (New York, 1892-1906), I, 425 *n.,* says Douglas was the Committee on Territories, but this is questionable. Everett Diary, January 4, 1854.

3. *Cong. Globe,* 33 Cong., 1 Sess., 115; *Sen. Rept.* #15 (Ser. 742). When the bill was offered on January 4, it did not include this Twenty-first section and it was not in the first printed version in the press. By some inadvertence, Douglas later explained, the copyist had not included it in the fair copy that was handed in to the Senate. The omission was shortly discovered, and the provision is included in the printed bill distributed to the Senate. Examination of the Senate files shows that this section 21 in Douglas' handwriting is pasted on to the original. It had been torn in two between its first clause and the remainder and then fastened together again by a wafer. Any suggestion as to the reason for this situation other than Douglas' explanation is purely conjectural; to date there is no other evidence. In view of the fact that Section 21 merely restates the final paragraphs in Douglas' report almost verbatim, and that the provisions of the Compromise of 1850, which this section recapitulates, were already in the bill, one is tempted to accept Douglas' explanation, but the politics of this bill is almost unbelievably intricate and this omission may represent a stage.

There is other evidence of haste and carelessness in preparing the bill as illustrated in the boundary description. The original boundary description was nonsense, namely "west on 36° 30′ to 103 meridian, north to 38° thence west to summit of Rockies, thence north to western boundary of Minnesota [which is a description difficult to chart] thence southward on and with said boundary to the Missouri River, thence down the center of the main channel to State of Missouri." This was finally corrected, but not until the final draft of the statute, by including after the second mention of "north" the words "to the 49th Parallel, thence east." Minnesota as a territory was much larger than the present state, so Nebraska did not at first include much of what were to be North and South Dakota. J. Sterling Morton and Albert Watkins, *History of Nebraska* (3rd ed., 1911), 141; New York *Herald,* January 10, 11, 13, 1854; St. Louis *Missouri*

Republican, January 4, 6, 1854; Baltimore *Sun,* December 28, 1853.

4. William H. Seward to Thurlow Weed, January 7, 8, 1854, Thurlow Weed Papers (University of Rochester Library); Mrs. Archibald Dixon, *True History of the Missouri Compromise and Its Repeal* (Cincinnati, 1898), 457, 591; John G. Nicolay and John Hay, *Abraham Lincoln,* 10 vols., (New York, 1890), I, 345-50; Member of Western Bar [Henry M. Flint], *Life and Speeches of Douglas* (New York, 1860), 171-174; James T. Du Bois and S. Mathews, *Galusha A. Grow* (Boston, 1917), 144-45; Thomas L. Clingman, *Speeches and Writings* (Raleigh, 1877), 335.

5. The rumors of the difficulties of the draftsmen of this bill and the efforts that were being made to alter it gave the small group of Free-Soilers or independent Democrats an idea. Their number had been declining. Of the three senators who owed their places to antislavery coalitions, John P. Hale was gone, Salmon P. Chase had just been defeated and Charles Sumner and the congressmen who remained could take no comfort from their fate. They would capitalize this effort to repeal the Missouri Compromise. The Ohio men were particularly aggressive; Chase had been affronted only a few days before when Atchison had failed to appoint him to a select committee on the Pacific Railroad raised on Chase's motion. Malin, *Nebraska Question,* 300-302. They got together to plan strategy. Their first idea was to issue a manifesto to the people of Ohio to stir up enthusiasm against the Democrats in the October election. Chase and Giddings thereupon wrote the stirring "atrocious plot" plea. This was dated January 19 and was to be headed "To the People of the State of Ohio. Shall slavery be permitted in Nebraska?" It was expected that Senators Seward, Wade and Sumner and some Ohio congressmen including Lewis D. Campbell would sign this. In this form it was distributed through Associated Press without the consent of Seward, Wade and Campbell to this particular wording. Then it turned out that they would not sign it, at least in that form, and so it was decided to label it as coming from the Free-Soilers in Congress and address it to everyone. Its heading was therefore changed to "An Appeal of the Independent Democrats in Congress to the people of the United States" and it was to be signed by Chase and Sumner and four Free-Soil congressmen, two from Ohio and one each from New York and Massachusetts. The authors then tried to correct

it through Associated Press, with the result that it appeared in some papers, notably in the *National Era* and the *New York Times,* with the new heading bearing the date January 22 (Sunday) but without signatures, on January 24. In the New York *Post* and New York *Tribune* it appeared on January 25 bearing the date of January 23 (Monday), with the signatures. In this form it was printed in the *Congressional Globe* on January 24 but still dated January 19 although it had a postscript that showed evidence of having been written on January 23. Since those original copies dispatched to the Midwest could not be recalled, it appeared in the *Missouri Republican* of February 2 and other papers with the original address "To the People of Ohio," signed by Seward, Benjamin F. Wade, *et al.* This variety of headings, dates and signatures added no little to the emotional confusion that was fast accumulating. It gave Douglas in his turn an opportunity to charge its authors with a plot, hatched wickedly on Sunday, on the Lord's Day. *Cong. Globe* 33:1, 281-82, App. 939-40.

6. Henry Wilson, *Rise and Fall of the Slave Power,* 3 vols. (Boston, 1872-1877), II, 382-83; Jefferson Davis, *Rise and Fall of the Confederate Government,* 2 vols. (New York, 1881), I, 27-28; Varina H. Davis, *Jefferson Davis,* 2 vols. (New York, 1890), I, 669; Nicolay and Hay, *Abraham Lincoln,* I, 349-350; Charles E. Hamlin, *Hannibal Hamlin* (Cambridge, 1899), 270; Sidney Webster, "Responsibility for the War of Secession," *Political Science Quarterly,* VIII (June, 1893), 276; John Bach McMaster, *History of the People of the United States,* 8 vols. (New York, 1883-1913), VIII, 195-96 *n.;* Henry B. Learned, "Relation of Philip Phillips to the Repeal of the Missouri Compromise in 1854," *Mississippi Valley Historical Review,* VIII (March, 1922), 303-15; Notes of Philip Phillips, left for his children, Philip Phillips Papers (Library of Congress); John Wentworth, *Congressional Reminiscences* (Chicago, 1882), 54-55; John Moses, *Illinois, Historical and Statistical,* 2 vols. (Chicago, 1892), II, 588-89; George M. McConnell, "Recollections of Stephen A. Douglas," Illinois State Historical Society, *Transactions,* 1900 (Springfield), 48-49; Philadelphia *Ledger,* January 13, 14, 1854; George W. Jones to Howell Cobb, February 16, 1854, Robert P. Brooks, ed., "Howell Cobb Papers," *Georgia Historical Quarterly,* VI (June, 1922), 149; Everett Diary, January 23, 1854; Joseph Robinson to John H. George, January 24, 25, 1854, John H. George Papers (New

Hampshire Historical Society) ; Jefferson Davis to John A. Parker, June 13, 1888, Dunbar Rowland, ed., *Jefferson Davis, Constitutionalist,* 10 vols. (Jackson, Miss., 1923), IX, 459; John Bigelow, *Retrospections of an Active Life,* 5 vols. (New York, 1909-1913), I, 171; *Cong. Globe,* 33 Cong., 1 Sess., 221-222, 239-240.

7. New York *Herald,* February 3, 4, 8, 1854; Washington *Star,* February 6, 1854; Baltimore *Sun,* February 7, 1854; Philadelphia *Ledger,* February 8, 1854; Robert Toombs to W. W. Burwell, February 3, 1854, Ulrich B. Phillips, ed., *The Correspondence of Robert Toombs, Alexander H. Stephens, and Howell Cobb,* American Historical Association, *Annual Report,* 1911, 2 vols. (Washington, 1913), II, 342-43; Arthur C. Cole, *The Whig Party in the South* (Washington, 1913), 286; Craven, *Growth of Southern Nationalism,* 172-205; St. Louis *Missouri Republican,* February 23, 1854. One of the trial drafts of the crucial amendment in Douglas' handwriting was given by Senator Gwin of California to John S. Cunningham and is now in the Illinois State Historical Library. The final draft of the bill, written in a clerk's hand, is in the Senate Files (National Archives). That its wording received close attention up to the last minute is illustrated by the fact that in a sentence concerning "The principle of non-intervention by Congress with slavery in the States and Territories, as established by the legislation of 1850 . . ." the word "established" was crossed out and "recognized," written in another hand, substituted. *Cong. Globe,* 33 Cong., 1 Sess., 337-344.

8. *Ibid.,* 353.

9. *Ibid.,* 275, 279, 329, App. 133, 337, 421, 474, 520.

10. *Ibid.,* 532.

CHAPTER VI

1. The problems involved in passing the Nebraska bill through the House are difficult to analyze because so much of the maneuvering was veiled in secrecy. However, an understanding of Leviathan depends upon some comprehension of this complexity, and to supply such, this analysis has been literally quarried out of the almost solid rock of the *Congressional Globe* and the *House Journal* in a fashion not hitherto accomplished. *Cong. Globe,* 33 Cong., 1 Sess., 87, 294, 562, 700, 1051, 1128-1133, 1142, 1160-1183, 1189, 1240-

1255; *House Journal,* 33 Cong., 1 Sess. (Ser. 709), 15, 134, 296, 463, 542, 727, 728, 734-836, 845, 870-926. Some indications of the efforts made to secure votes are found in the *Globe, loc. cit.,* App. 31, 35, 47, 64. See also Sidney Webster to John H. George, June 5, 1854, John H. George Papers.

2. The debate on this bill was voluminous. It began in both houses in January, 1854, and continued intermittently through May. There were at least 128 speeches on the measure, 28 in the Senate and 100 in the House. They were almost equally divided for and against; in the Senate, 17 spoke for and 11 against, while in the House the proportion was reversed, 45 for and 55 against. In the House there were two giant sessions; that of May 11 lasted for 36 hours and fills 102 pages in the *Journal,* while that of May 22 lasted 11 hours and 25 minutes and took up 56 pages of that record.

3. The 119th Rule of the House, which Stephens used to stop the flow and enact the statute, had been adopted in 1822, but as early as 1852 a footnote in Joseph B. Burleigh's *Legislative Guide* (Philadelphia, 1852), p. 100, recorded that "of late years" it had fallen into disuse. Only a man of Stephens' ingenuity would have dug it up and attempted to employ it. Its terms were: "A motion to strike out the enacting words of a bill shall have precedence of a motion to amend; and if carried shall be considered equivalent to its rejection." It took ingenuity to think of using this in the Committee of the Whole, not to reject the bill but to insure its passage. Stephens had to push the managers into this tactic, or so he recorded on May 11. R. M. Johnston and W. H. Brown, *Alexander H. Stephens* (Philadelphia, 1878), 277.

4. At the last, eight southern Democrats and five northern Democrats did not vote; from their own statements and previous votes, the last five seem certainly to have been opposed to the measure. The eighteen who "obliged" just once were mostly from New England, Ohio and Indiana. They supplied the only substantial help the administration got from New England and Ohio in this struggle. *Cong. Globe,* 33 Cong., 1 Sess., 1241-54; *House Journal,* 33 Cong., 1 Sess., 870-926.

5. See Roy F. Nichols, "Kansas Historiography; The Technique of Cultural Analysis," *American Quarterly,* IX (1957), 85-91. This article deals with concepts developed in the following works of James C. Malin: *John Brown and the Legend of Fifty-Six* (Philadelphia, American Philosophical Society, 1942), *Winter Wheat in the Golden Belt of Kansas*

(Lawrence, 1944), *The Grassland of North America, Prolegomena to its History* (Lawrence, 1947), *Grassland Historical Studies, Natural Resources Utilization in a Background of Science and Technology,* Volume I, "Geology and Geography" (Lawrence, 1950), *The Nebraska Question, 1852-1854* (Lawrence, 1953), *On the Nature of History* (Lawrence, 1954), *The Contriving Brain and the Skillful Hand* (Lawrence, 1955).

CHAPTER VII

1. Merrill Jensen, ed., *Regionalism in America* (Madison, 1951); Frank L. Owsley, *Plain Folk of the Old South* (Baton Rouge, 1949); Stanley M. Elkins, *Slavery, A Problem in American Industrial Life* (Chicago, 1960); John Hope Franklin, *From Slavery to Freedom, A History of American Negroes,* 2nd edition (New York, 1956); *The Militant South, 1800-1861* (Cambridge, 1956); Kenneth M. Stampp, *The Peculiar Institution* (New York, 1956).

2. Charles M. Wiltse, *John C. Calhoun, Sectionalist, 1840-1850* (Indianapolis, 1951), 464.

3. John C. Calhoun, "A Disquisition on Government," *Works,* Richard K. Crallé, ed. (Charleston, 1851), I, 38.

4. Calhoun, "Discourse on the Constitution and Government of the United States," *loc. cit.,* 392.

5. Edward A. Pollard, *Lost Cause* (New York, 1867), 43.

6. Martin J. Crawford to Alexander H. Stephens, May 11, 1860. Stephens Mss. (Manhattanville College of the Sacred Heart).

7. Diary of Charles Francis Adams, January 1, 1861, Adams Mss. (Massachusetts Historical Society, microfilm, American Philosophical Society); Henry Adams, *The Great Secession Winter* (New York, 1958), 8.

8. Roy F. Nichols, *Disruption of American Democracy* (New York, 1948), *passim.*

9. *Sacramento Union,* August 4, 1860; *Charleston Mercury,* August, 1860, *passim,* Sept. 29, 1860; *Yorkville* (S.C.) *Enquirer,* October 18, 1860; *New York Times,* October 26, 27, 30, November 1, 5, 1860; New York *Herald,* October 31 (weekly edition), November 10, 1860; J. Henly Smith to A. H. Stephens, October 11, 18, 1860, Stephens Mss.; W. Porcher Miles, August 5, 1860, L. Keitt, September 10, 1860, G. D. Tillman to James H. Hammond, October 9, 1860,

Hammond Mss. (Library of Congress); Lamar Cobb to Mrs. Howell Cobb, November 14, 1860, Howell Cobb Mss. (University of Georgia); *Diary of Gideon Welles*, John T. Morse, ed. (Boston, 1911), I, 87, 128; William H. Trescott to Howell Cobb, Washington, December 14, 1860, "Correspondence of Robert Toombs, Alexander H. Stephens, and Howell Cobb," American Historical Association, *Annual Report*, 1911, 2 vols. (Washington, 1913), I, 522; Edward Mayes, *L.Q.C. Lamar* (Nashville, Tenn., 1896), 633-39.

10. New York *Herald* (weekly edition), November 17, 1860; Salomon de Rothschild, *Casual View of America*, Sigmund Diamond, ed. (Stanford, Calif., 1961), 82; Mercier to Thouvenel, Washington, November 16, 1860 (Archives du Ministère des Affaires étrangères, Paris, Correspondence politiques, États-Unis), 123:365-67, No. 10; Rudolph Schleiden to Bremen Senat, December 10, 1860, No. 74 (Staats Archiv., ad B. 13b 1a 2, Berichte des Minister Resident, Dr. Schleiden, Microfilm, Library of Congress).

11. M. J. Crawford to A. H. Stephens, December 8, 1860, Stephens Mss. (Manhattanville); Charles F. Adams Diary, November 12, 1860; New York *Herald,* November 12, 1860.

12. *New York Times,* December 4, 1860; New York *Herald,* December 3, 7, 18, 1860, January 3, 5, 6, 7, 1861; New York *Tribune,* December 19, 1860; Washington *Star,* December 29, 1860; Baltimore *Sun,* January 8, 1861; M. J. Crawford to A. H. Stephens, December 8, 1860, Stephens Mss. (Manhattanville); J. Henly Smith to A. H. Stephens, December 9, 1860, Stephens Mss. (Library of Congress).

13. Gideon Welles, *Civil War and Reconstruction,* Albert Mordell, Col. (New York, 1959), 264-268.

14. New York *Herald,* November 25, 1860; O. R. Singleton to W. T. Walthall, July 14, 1877, *Davis, Constitutionalist,* VII, 560-562; William E. Dodd, *Statesmen of the Old South* (New York, 1911), 220; Hudson Strode, *Jefferson Davis, American Patriot, 1808-1861* (New York, 1959), 364; Mary Boykin Chesnut, *A Diary from Dixie,* Ben Ames Williams, ed. (New York, 1949), 32.

15. F. Lauriston Bullard, ed., *The Diary of a Public Man* (New Brunswick, 1946), 35.

16. Edward A. Pollard, *Lost Cause,* 92.

17. Pollard, *Lee and His Lieutenants* (New York, 1867), 796-97; *Diary of a Public Man,* 56-57, 60.

18. John Bell to Nashville, December 10, 1860, John

Bell Mss. (Library of Congress).

19. To D. Gould, St. Augustine, Fla., February 2, 1861, enclosed in D. Gould to Thurlow Weed, New York City, February 22, 1861, Weed Mss. (University of Rochester).

20. Welles, *Diary,* II, 43, 229, 276-78, 312-13.

21. E. Merton Coulter, *The Confederate States of America,* vol. VII, *A History of the South* (Baton Rouge, 1950), 17; *Cong. Globe,* 36 Cong. 2 Sess., 328-332.

22. Lord Lyons to Lord Clarendon, December 10, 1860, Fo5, vol. 740, #311, British Foreign Office, photocopy (Library of Congress).

23. See note 11.

24. Crawford to Stephens, December 8, 1860, *loc. cit.;* New York *Herald,* February 4, 1861.

25. Mss. Diary of Gideon Welles, January 28, 1861 (Huntington Library).

26. Welles, *Diary,* I, 377, II, 276-78, 312-13.

27. See note 9. New York *Times,* December 1, 4, 10, 17, 20, 1860; New York *Herald,* December 3, 7, 8, 9, 10, 12, 13, 14, 19, 1860; Washington *Star,* December 10, 15, 1860.

28. Washington *Constitution,* December 15, 1860; James Ford Rhodes, *History of the United States since the Compromise of 1850,* III, 177 *n,* 178; C. C. Clay to Jefferson Davis, Oct. 30, 1875, *Davis, Constitutionalist,* VII, 459-62; James L. Pugh to W. T. Walthall, May 31, 1880, *ibid.,* VIII, 460-461.

29. Mercier to Thouvenel, December 17, 1860, #15.

30. See note 10. *Diary of a Union Lady, Maria Lydig Daly, 1861-1865,* Harold E. Hammond, ed. (New York, 1962), 162-163; Mss. Diary of John P. Kennedy, August 4, 1863 (Peabody Institute Library); *Diary of a Public Man,* 38-39; Rudolph Schleiden to Bremen Senat, January 7, 1861, #3; E. D. Keyes to John Sherman, December 26, 1860, John Sherman Mss. (Library of Congress); Winfield Scott to Abraham Lincoln, January 4, 1861, Robert T. Lincoln Mss. (Library of Congress); Benjamin F. Wade to Mrs. B. F. Wade, December 26, 1860, Wade Mss. (Library of Congress). The document 36 Cong., 2 Sess., *H. Rept. 79* (Ser. 1105) is the result of a hurried and imperceptive investigation. It failed to uncover or to comprehend to any realistic degree the danger of such confused and emotional behavior. One wonders today how the process of government avoided violence and overthrow. The answer is probably that there were too many plans, too many planners and no concentrated effort.

Washington was always the seat of a certain amount of futility.

31. Albert D. Kirwan, *John J. Crittenden* (Lexington, Ky., 1962), 368-421; James Buchanan, *Works* (Philadelphia, 1910), XI, 97; Chesnut, *Diary from Dixie*, 10, 23.

32. He probably was implying just that. Lord Lyons reported that Buchanan "trusted that by private arrangement with the South Carolinians" he could hold the forts during the remainder of his term of office. Lyons, December 31, 1860, #334, *loc. cit.*; J. P. Benjamin to S. L. M. Barlow, January 8, 1861, Barlow Mss. (Huntington Library).

33. Strode, *Jefferson Davis*, 370-372; Welles, *Diary*, II, 255.

34. *Ibid.*, 273; Benjamin P. Thomas and Harold M. Hyman, *Stanton* (New York, 1962), 94-118; Chesnut, *Diary from Dixie*, 61, 108; *Diary of a Public Man*, 42; William M. Browne to S. L. M. Barlow, January 14, 1861, Barlow Mss.

35. *The War of the Rebellion: A Compilation of the Official Records of the Union and Confederate Armies* (Washington, 1880-1925), 127 vols. and index, Series 1, vol. 53, III, 610, v. 52, pt. II, 3, v. 51, pt. II, 3; Kirwan, *John J. Crittenden*, 368-42.

36. George Eustis Mss. on Secession (Library of Congress); Ralph A. Wooster, *The Secession Conventions of the South* (Princeton, 1962), 23.

37. Bruce Catton, *The Coming Fury*, v. 1, *The Centennial History of the Civil War* (New York, 1961), 139, 189.

38. Lyons, January 15, 1861, #15, *loc. cit.*

39. Harold E. Hammond, *A Commoner's Judge, The Life and Times of Charles Patrick Daly* (Boston, 1954), 145.

40. Welles, *Diary*, I, 32, 34, 37, 171-2, 356, II, 388-89, III, 118, 134, 158, 163; Welles, *Lincoln's Administration*, Albert Mordell, Col. (New York, 1960), 58; *Diary of Gideon Welles*, Howard K. Beale, ed. (New York, 1960), III, 673, 726-727.

CHAPTER VIII

1. The comprehensive history of the Confederacy is E. Merton Coulter, *The Confederate States of America*. The basic documents adopted in the process of creating the Confederate Leviathan are found in James D. Richardson, ed.,

A Compilation of the Messages and Papers of the Confederacy, 1861-1865, 2 vols. (Nashville, 1906); "Journal of the Provisional Congress of the Confederate States of America," *58 Cong., 2 Sess., Senate Document #234* (Ser. 4610); James M. Matthews, ed., *The Statutes at Large of the Provisional Government of the Confederate States of America* (Richmond, 1864).

2. The workings of the Provisional Congress are illuminated by Wilfred Buck Yearns, *The Confederate Congress* (Athens, Ga., 1960); Chesnut, *Diary from Dixie,* 5, 9, 26, 27; "Correspondence of Thomas Reade Rootes Cobb," *Pubs. of the Southern History Assoc.,* XI, 147-185, 233-260; "Memoir of F. M. Gilmer," *Davis, Constitutionalist,* VIII, 461-463; William E. Dodd, *Statesmen of the Old South,* 220; Thomas B. Alexander, "Persistent Whiggery in the Confederate South, 1860-1877," *Journal of Southern History,* XXVII (1961), 305-329.

3. Davis Inaugural Address, "Journal of the Provisional Congress," 58 Cong. 2 Sess., *Sen. Doc. 234* (Ser. 4610), 65.

4. *Ibid.,* 66.

5. Robert G. Gunderson, *Old Gentlemen's Convention, The Washington Peace Conference* (New York, 1961).

6. See Ch. VII, note 40.

7. Nathaniel W. Stephenson, *Lincoln* (Indianapolis, 1922), 162-164, 443-447; Catton, *The Coming Fury,* 242-244, 298-300.

8. T. Harry Williams to author.

CHAPTER IX

1. This chapter draws on Roy F. Nichols, "American Democracy and the Civil War," *Proceedings American Philosophical Society,* XCI (1948), 143-149, "1461-1861: American Civil War in Perspective," *Journal of Southern History,* XVI (1950), 143-160, "The Operation of American Democracy, 1861-1865: Some Questions," *ibid.,* XXV (1959), 31-52, "The Problem of Civil War Historiography," *Proceedings American Philosophical Society,* CVI (1962), 36-40. Many suggestions are found in Stanley Elkins and Eric McKittrick, "A Meaning for Turner's Frontier," *Political Science Quarterly,* LXIX (1954), 321-53, 565-602; Charles S. Sydnor, *Gentlemen Freeholders: Political Practices in Washington's Virginia, The Development of Southern Section-*

alism, 1819-1848 (Baton Rouge, 1948); Avery O. Craven, *The Growth of Southern Nationalism, 1848-1861;* Allan Nevins, *Ordeal of the Union,* I, 412-545; Ulrich B. Phillips, *The Course of the South to Secession,* E. Merton Coulter, ed. (New York, 1939); Virginia Clay-Clopton, *A Belle of the Fifties* (New York, 1905), 20; Arthur C. Cole, *The Irrepressible Conflict* (New York, 1934), 34-79, *The Whig Party in the South;* Nathaniel W. Stephenson, "Southern Nationalism in South Carolina in 1851," *American Historical Review,* XXXVI (1931), 314; Dwight L. Dumond, *The Secession Movement, 1860-1861* (New York, 1931); Wooster, *The Secession Conventions of the South, passim.*

2. Catton, *The Coming Fury,* 339.

3. Concluding address of Howell Cobb, February 17, 1962, to the Provisional Congress, "Journal of the Provisional Congress," *loc. cit.,* 845.

CHAPTER X

1. There is a fascination to be found in reading extensively in the usually dull pages of the *Congressional Globe.* This has been indulged in for the five sessions of the 37th and 38th Congresses. The following throw much light on the complicated operations of those struggling to operate Leviathan in the midst of civil war: Andrew Wallace Crandall, *The Early History of the Republican Party, 1854-1856* (Boston, 1930); James A. Rawley, *Edwin D. Morgan* (New York, 1955); Nathaniel W. Stephenson, *Lincoln;* Benjamin P. Thomas, *Abraham Lincoln* (New York, 1952); Allan Nevins, *The Emergence of Lincoln,* 2 vols. (New York, 1950), and *The War for the Union,* v. 1 and 2 (New York, 1959, 1960); William E. Baringer, *A House Dividing* (Springfield, Ill., 1945); Reinhard H. Luthin, *The First Lincoln Campaign* (Cambridge, Mass., 1944); James G. Randall and Richard N. Current, *Lincoln, the President,* 4 vols. (New York, 1945-1955); David M. Potter, *Lincoln and His Party in the Secession Crisis* (New Haven, 1942); Burton J. Hendrick, *Lincoln's War Cabinet* (Boston, 1946); Kenneth M. Stampp, *And the War Came* (Baton Rouge, 1950); Harry J. Carman and Reinhard H. Luthin, *Lincoln and the Patronage* (New York, 1943); Edward Conrad Smith, *The Borderland in the Civil War* (New York, 1927); T. Harry Williams, *Lincoln and the Radicals* (Madison, Wis., 1941); William B. Hessel-

tine, *Lincoln and the War Governors* (New York, 1948);
Stewart Mitchell, *Horatio Seymour of New York* (Cambridge, Mass., 1938); William O. Stoddard, *Lincoln's Third Secretary*, William O. Stoddard, Jr., ed. (New York, 1955);
William F. Zornow, *Lincoln and the Party Divided* (Norman, Okla., 1954).

CHAPTER XI

1. The Permanent Constitution of the Confederacy enabled two Congresses to hold their sessions, and their Journals are found in *58 Cong. 2 Sess. Sen. Doc. #234,* vols. 26-31 (Sers. 4611-4616). No stenographic record was made of the debates but they were covered extensively by the Richmond press and the accounts that appeared in the Richmond papers have been compiled in "Proceedings of the Confederate Congress," *Southern Historical Soc. Papers,* vols. XLIV-LII, 1923-1959. Reading extensively in this material is even more intriguing than delving in the *Globe,* because it is more elusive and more tantalizing. These gentlemen spent so much time in unreported secret sessions—and for what?

The Congress provided for the publication of the *Statutes of the Confederacy* down through 2nd Congress, 1 Sess., closing June 14, 1864, edited by James M. Matthews (Richmond, 1862-1864). Then the late Professor Charles W. Ramsdell collected and published the remaining in *Laws and Joint Resolutions of the Last Session of the Confederate Congress* (November 7, 1864-March 18, 1865) *together with the Secret Acts of the Previous Congresses* (Durham, N.C., 1941).

The history of the Permanent Congress is found in Yearns, *op. cit.,* and something of the experience of continuing to perfect Leviathan can be followed in E. Merton Coulter, *The Confederate States of America, 1861-1865;* Clement Eaton, *History of the Southern Confederacy* (New York, 1954); Clifford Dowdey, *The Land They Fought For* (Garden City, 1955). An earlier summary is Nathaniel W. Stephenson, *The Day of the Confederacy* (New Haven, 1919). There is some analysis in Roy F. Nichols, *The Disruption of American Democracy* (New York, 1948), 460-73. Intimate glimpses of political operation can be found in Chesnut, *A Diary from Dixie;* John B. Jones, *A Rebel War*

Clerk's Diary, Howard Swiggett, ed. (New York, 1935); Bell
Irvin Wiley, ed., *Letters of Warren Akin, Confederate Congressman* (Athens, Ga., 1959); Robert G. H. Kean, *Inside the
Confederate Government,* Edward Younger, ed. (New York,
1957). See also Alexander H. Stephens, *A Constitutional
View of the Late War between the States,* 2 vols. (Philadel-
phia, 1868-1870); Frank L. Owsley, *State Rights in the Con-
federacy* (Chicago, 1925); Louise Biles Hill, *Joseph E.
Brown and the Confederacy* (Chapel Hill, 1939); Albert
Burton Moore, *Conscription and Conflict in the Confed-
eracy* (New York, 1924); Rudolph Von Abele, *Alexander H.
Stephens* (New York, 1946); Rembert W. Patrick, *Jefferson
Davis and His Cabinet* (Baton Rouge, 1944); Burton J.
Hendrick, *Statesmen of the Lost Cause* (Boston, 1939); John
Kenneth Galbraith, "The Moving Finger Sticks," *The Lib-
eral Hour* (Boston, 1960), 79-92; Thomas B. Alexander,
"Persistent Whiggery in the Confederate South," *loc. cit.*
See also Nichols, "The Problems of Civil War Historiog-
raphy," *loc. cit.* I am indebted to Kenneth M. Stampp, Eric
McKittrick and Bell Irvin Wiley for their comments on a
paper I read before the American Historical Association at
Washington in 1960 and to Stephen E. Ambrose for his comments on a paper I read before the American Studies Association of the Lower Mississippi at Louisiana State University, New Orleans, in 1961.

2. Anthony F. C. Wallace, "The Strategy of Threat and
Retaliation: Iroquois Warfare, 1755-1795," paper read be-
fore the Institute of Early American History and Culture,
Ann Arbor, Mich., May, 1961.

3. Abraham Lincoln, *Collected Works,* Roy P. Basler,
ed., 8 vols. (New Brunswick, N.J., 1953), VIII, 101.

4. Edward A. Pollard, *Lost Cause,* 750.

CHAPTER XII

1. The record of the making of the new Leviathan is
found interspersed haphazardly with that of the conduct of
the war in the pages of the *Congressional Globe* and of the
documents published by Senate and House during the 37th
and 38th Congresses. The new elements came into existence
sporadically and were added to the mechanism seemingly
without plan or attention to the working of the whole.

2. Basler, *Lincoln's Works,* V, 49.

3. *Ibid.*, IV, 438.
4. *Ibid.*, V, 51-53.
5. *Ibid.*, V, 537.

CHAPTER XIII

1. Basler, *Lincoln's Works,* Speech of April 11, 1865, VIII, 404.
2. *Ibid.*, Lincoln to Peirpoint, March 20, 1862, V, 166.
3. *Ibid.*, Speech of April 11, 1865, VIII, 403.
4. Walt Whitman, *I Sit and Look Out. Editorials from the Brooklyn Daily Times* (New York, 1932), 46.
5. Jefferson Davis, *A Short History of the Confederate States of America* (New York, 1890), 504-505.
6. Basler, *Lincoln's Works,* V, 537.

===

THE DOCUMENTARY
STRUCTURE OF LEVIATHAN

LEVIATHAN is an achievement of the intellect. At each stage of its construction new specifications have been thought out and reduced to writing. A succession of documents composed over some eight and more centuries in the Anglo-American community illustrate the evolution of this structure designed to permit men to live and, in an atmosphere of liberty, to engage in the "pursuit of happiness." During the English phase of this intellectual activity, which for illustrative purposes is dated from 1100 to 1689, the process was dictated in large part by expediency, and the emerging "unwritten" English constitution was a haphazard accumulation of precedents.

The second, American, phase was dominated by a different process. Its documentation was contrived in much greater part in advance of events, it was designed for a purpose, rationally conceived and implemented. Men decided what government they wanted, so that they might meet the needs of a society of ever-increasing complexity. Thereupon they thought out and reduced to writing the means they believed would enable them to achieve their purpose.

A. THE FEUDAL CONSENSUS

The English phase may be divided into two periods. The first, bounded loosely by the limits of the twelfth and thirteenth centuries, had its great impulse from the fortuitous circumstances arising out of the Norman Conquest. This clash of cultures required the contrivance of a consensus regarding operational procedures that had to be reached by a group of competing interests. These were the Norman king and his established military force of barons and retainers; the English society, with its traditional structure of leadership; and the Church, part English, part Norman and part in concept and allegiance Roman or supranational, characterized by a sense of superiority over the other elements. These various groups worked out a *modus operandi,* through a division of authority and responsibility designed hopefully to insure an orderly society, the nature of which was never conceived in advance. This consensus was a combination of feudal obligation and self-government at the king's command, recorded in a scattered, unorganized series of documents that is illustrative rather than comprehensive.

I. THE CONSTITUTION OR CORONATION
CHARTER OF LIBERTIES OF HENRY I 1100

The bases of government were recognized to be the good customs of the realm which were herein affirmed with a pledge henceforth to remove all the evil practices "by which the realm of England was unjustly oppressed." These good customs were a combination of English precedent and the feudal system of allegiance introduced by the Conqueror. By this instrument the government was purged of abuses perpetrated by his son, William II.

> George Burton Adams and H. Morse Stephens, *Select Documents of English Constitutional History* (cited as A. S.), 4-6

II. CONSTITUTIONS OF CLARENDON 1164

The church is commanded to accept the concept that English law is supreme and that prelates must be bound by it. The nature and content of this law is further defined. A. S., 11-14

III. ASSIZE OF CLARENDON 1166

This document describes a code of criminal law designed to protect the rights of the individual and defines the functions of the circuit justices sent out by the king to receive the presentments of local grand juries and to punish criminals. The function of the petty jury is suggested and the use of writs described.   A. S., 14-18

IV. THE DOMESDAY BOOK 1066-1087

An investigation designed to discover and record the good customs of local government in existence throughout the realm.

> Carl Stephenson and F. G. Marcham,

Sources of English Constitutional History
(cited as S. M.), 41-46

V. CHARTER OF LONDON post 1130

This definition describes the structure of local government in municipalities and boroughs.   S. M., 61-62

VI. MAGNA CHARTA 1215

This is a description of the consensus that has been achieved bringing together English custom and Norman authority in a feudal structure. The king accepts this definition and acknowledges himself to be subject to this charter or code of laws given by the Great Council or feudal Parliament of law givers.   A. S., 42-52

VII. PROVISIONS OF OXFORD 1258

The Great Council or Parliament of law givers produces a frame of government or an embryo constitution for the realm.   A. S., 56-62

VIII. CONFIRMATION OF CHARTERS AND A RECORD ENTITLED DE TALLAGIO NON CONCEDENDO 1297

In Magna Charta the King had acknowledged that he must live under the law, the common law of England, the unwritten constitution. Now he specifically acknowledges that he must gain the approval of Parliament for levying taxes. This completes the evolution of the lawmaking process. The king and Parliament will unite in this function, and under Edward I (1272-1307) a series of basic statutes are enacted. Parliament now begins to make law as well as give it.   A. S., 86-89

IX. STATUTE OF WESTMINISTER 1275

Elections to be free—"no man . . . shall disturb any to make free election."   A. S., 68-69

X. STATUTE OF WINCHESTER 1285

To prevent robbery, homicide and arson—penalties are prescribed for failure to testify, and provisions are made for better protection of citizens.   A. S., 75-76

XI. STATUTE OF MORTMAIN 1279

Land cannot be bought by Church or given to it without the consent of the overlord whom the alienation would deprive of medieval benefits.   A. S., 71-72

XII. STATUTE OF MERCHANTS   1283

Debts to merchants must be registered before mayor or a king's clerk, and if debt is not paid on date due, mayor or clerk will sell debtors' movables.   A. S., 72-74

XIII. STATUTE OF CIRCUMSPECTE AGATIS   1285

Gives a definition of the jurisdiction of the king's courts and the ecclesiastical courts.   A. S., 80-81

XIV. STATUTE OF QUIA EMPTORES   1290

The freeholder in selling land must do so on the understanding on the part of the purchaser that he owes the same services and customs to the overlord that the seller owed. A. S., 81-82

During the evolution of this feudal consensus, a rule of law of sorts had been established, at least to the extent of acknowledging certain obligations of contract. A series of constitutions, assizes, ordinances and statutes of the realm had been given existence by the king and parliament, and this law the Crown and the Church had accepted, though with uncertain and spasmodic sincerity. The rights of individuals had been recognized and somewhat vaguely defined. An administrative and judicial system, of self-government at the king's command, had been evolved in which all estates of the realm bore a responsibility. This common law had begun to function on two levels, recognizing the local communities and their liberties, and the central power and its authority. The king's courts and the High Court of Parliament were working to maintain a balance between the two authorities.

B.   THE MIDDLE-CLASS CONSENSUS

The second period of the English phase was conditioned by a basic change in the structure of the kingdom. A fundamental reordering of English society was being accomplished by the emergence of a middle class. It represented the rise in number and in importance of towns and cities and of those who dwell therein. These were men of enterprise with a capacity to make money who had neither titles nor estates such as were possessed by the nobility and country gentry. These men, backed by the power of their wealth, grew in influence in Parliament and were insistent upon limiting the power of the Crown for arbitrary action. They played their part also in reorganizing the Church as a national body. The English monarch became its head and appointed its bishops. Parliament assigned to the local parish vestries certain functions of a civil nature, and these local vestrymen assumed greater independence of episcopal orders. The English Church was on the way to greater independence; it was also approaching fragmentation. Certain of its members, stirred by ideas of the Reformation, wanted a more progressive clergy. They advocated a change in the Constitution of the Church of England, some wanting a Presbyterian or representative form of government while others sought congregational independence. The various phases of this change were worked out in legal form.

I. PARLIAMENT—REPRESENTATIVE AND SUPREME

a. Statute Concerning Justices and Sheriffs   1330
     Provides for annual parliaments.   A. S., 100
b. On Elections to Parliament   1445
     Method of voting for knights of the shire and members from the municipalities; the House of Commons to represent the people.   S. M., 277
c. Electors must be Forty-Shilling Freeholders   1429
     Provides a broad base for suffrage in the shires.
A. S., 190-191
d. King agrees not to alter the Petitions of the
     Commons   1414
     Parliament acknowledged to have the lawmaking responsibility.   A. S., 181-182
e. Deposition of Richard II and election of Henry
     IV   1399
     Parliament supreme over monarch.   A. S., 162-165
f. Articles of Impeachment against Suffolk   1386
     Power over the powerful.   A. S., 148-150
g. Unauthorized Charges and Taxes Abolished   1340
     Parliament to control taxation.   A. S., 104-105
h. Commons to Originate Money Bills   1407
     Tighter control over the purse.   A. S., 175-177
i. Persons Appointed to supervise Expenditures   1377
     Account of Expenditures required by Parliament.
A. S. 136-138   1378
j. Members excused for Matters spoken in
     Parliament   1401
     Freedom of debate.   A. S., 172-173

k. Privilege of Members from Arrest.
   A. S., 196-197   1460
l. Statute of Laborers   1351
   Prescribing employment and regulating wages.
A. S., 116-117
m. Ordinance of the Staples.   A. S., 124-126   1353
n. Early Navigation Acts   1382, 1485
   Regulating trade.   A. S., 144-145, 213-214

II.   LOCAL GOVERNMENT

a. An Act concerning the Justices of the Peace.   A. S.,
127-128   1361
b. Statute of Artificers   1563
   Functions of Justices of the Peace in shire government.
S. M., 348-349
c. Beggars Act.   S. M., 313-314   1536
d. Poor Relief Act   1598
   Functions of the parish in local government.
S. M. 356

III.   RELIGIOUS REFORMATION TRANSFORMS CHURCH

a. Act of Supremacy of Henry VIII   1534
   King becomes head of the Church.   A. S., 239-240
b. The Six Articles Act   1539
   New constitution for the Church.   A. S., 253-254
c. Act of Supremacy   1559
   Constitutional distinctions grow finer.   A. S., 296-
302
d. Act of Uniformity   1559
   Climax of the Elizabethan compromise.   A. S., 302-
306
e. Presbyterian faith and order
   An admonition to the Parliament   1572
   Contains the Puritans' reform platform.
                Walter H. Frere and Charles E. Douglas,
                Puritan Manifestoes, 8-19
   "Disciplina ecclesia"   1586
   A proposed constitution of a presbyterian order.
                Daniel Neal, *History of the Puritans,* II,
                440-445
f. Congregational independence   1568
   Covenant of Richard Fritz's Congregation in London.
                Albert Peel, *The First Congregational
                Churches,* 23

Covenant of Salem Church in New England   1629
Williston Walker, *Creeds and Platforms of
Congregationalism,* 116

IV. CONSTITUTIONAL REVISION BY REVOLUTION

a. Petition of Right   1628
   Classic statement of grievances.   A. S., 339-342
b. The Grand Remonstrance   1641
   A more elaborate catalogue.   A. S., 376-380
c. Solemn League and Covenant   1643
   The Rights of Englishmen.   A. S., 383-386
d. Agreement of the People   1649
   Promise of a more representative Parliament.
S. M., 511-516
e. Instrument of Government   1653
   An attempt at a constitution.   A. S., 407-416
f. Habeas Corpus Act   1679
   The great writ protecting the individual from arbitrary
arrest and imprisonment.   A. S., 440-448
g. Toleration Act   1689
   Freedom of religion on its way.   A. S., 459-462
h. Bill of Rights   1689
   The grand specifications.   A. S., 462-469

These acts completed the design for the British Leviathan. The English people had established a rule of law to
which all individuals and orders, from the king to the poor-
est subject, had to yield obedience. It was a system created
by the English people through their accepted and designated representatives, based upon the concept that the operating government recognizes and protects the well-defined
rights of all under the knowledge that the power to govern
is subject to possible review and change in conformity to the
popular will.

C. THE AMERICAN EXPERIENCE

The English had achieved the approximate solution of
their problems of government in the seventeenth century
just at the point where the American enterprise was beginning. During the English experience the emerging Leviathan
had been determined by the dictates of expediency, problems had been solved as they arose. But with the migration
to America, with the determination to create a new society

three thousand miles across the sea, a new element entered the picture—the element of planning. What hitherto had been done after the fact, under the pressure of events, hereafter would be done by design, in anticipation of social need. While England was regulated by an unwritten constitution, the Leviathan in America was to be created step by step in advance and developed according to written specifications.

I. THE COLONIAL DOCUMENTATION: A SELECTED LIST
(Texts are found in Thorpe's *Constitutions,* on pages indicated)

a. Charter of Sir Walter Raleigh   (Thorpe, 53)   1584
b. The First Charter of Virginia   (Thorpe, 3783)   1606
c. The Mayflower Agreement   (Thorpe, 1841)   1620
d. Ordinances for Virginia   (Thorpe, 3810)   1621
e. First Charter of Massachusetts   (Thorpe, 1846)   1629
f. Charter of Maryland   (Thorpe, 1669)   1632
g. Fundamental Orders of Connecticut (Thorpe, 519)   1639
h. Agreement of settlers at Exeter, New Hampshire (Thorpe, 2445)   1639
i. Plantation Agreement at Providence, Rhode Island (Thorpe, 3207)   1640
j. New England Confederation   (Thorpe, 77)   1643
k. Concession and Agreements, New Jersey (Thorpe, 2535)   1664
l. Fundamental Constitutions of Carolina (Thorpe, 2772)   1669
m. Charter of Fundamental Laws of West Jersey (Thorpe, 2548)   1676
n. Fundamental Constitutions of East Jersey (Thorpe, 2574)   1683
o. Frame of Government, Charter of Liberties, Pennsylvania   (Thorpe, 3064)   1683
p. Charter of Georgia   (Thorpe, 765)   1732
q. Albany Plan   (Thorpe, 83)   1754

II. ACHIEVING INDEPENDENCE
a. Resolutions of the Stamp Act
Congress   October 19, 1765
(Commager, *Documents of American History,* 57-58)

b. The Association   October 20, 1774
     Journals of the Continental Congress, I, 75
c. Declaration of Independence
   (Thorpe, 3)   July 4, 1776
d. The Articles of Confederation
   (Thorpe, 9)   November 15, 1777
e. Constitution of the United States
   (Thorpe, 19)   September 17, 1787-
                            June 21, 1788
f. The Bill of Rights   (Thorpe,
   29)   September 25, 1789-
                            December 15, 1791

III.   ADJUSTING THE CONSENSUS

a. The Missouri Compromise   1819-21
   (Commager, *Documents of American History*, 224-227)
b. Compromise of 1850   (*Ibid.*, 319-323)
c. Kansas-Nebraska Act   (*Ibid.*, 332)   1854
d. South Carolina Ordinance of Secession
   (*Ibid.*, 372)   1860
e. Constitution of the Confederate States of
   America   (*Ibid.*, 376)   1861-1862
f. The Homestead Act   May 20, 1862
               (*U. S. Statutes at Large*, XII, 392 ff)
g. Pacific Railway Act   (*Ibid.*, 489 ff)   July 1, 1862
h. Morrill Land Grant College Act
   (*Ibid.*, 503)   July 2, 1862
i. Emancipation Proclamation
   (*Ibid.*, 1268-9)   January 1, 1863
j. National Banking Acts   (*Ibid.*,
   XII, 665 and XIII, 99 ff)   February 25, 1863
                            and June 3, 1864
k. Act to Create a National Academy of
   Science   (*Ibid.*, XII, 806)   March 3, 1863
l. Contract Labor Law   (*Ibid.*, XIII, 386)   July 4, 1864
m. Amnesty and Reconstruction
   Proclamation   December 8, 1863
        (Richardson, *Messages and Papers*, VI, 213 ff)
n. Wade-Davis Bill and Lincoln's Proclamation thereon   (*Ibid.*, 222 ff)   July 8, 1864
o. President Johnson's Reconstruction
   Proclamations   May-June 1865

(Richardson, *Messages and Papers*, VI, 326
ff)

p. Thirteenth Amendment to U. S.
Constitution Abolishing Slavery
(Thorpe, *Constitutions*, 31)   December 18, 1865

q. Congressional Reconstruction Acts
        (*U. S. Statutes at Large*,
                    XIV, 428 ff March 2, 1867
                    XV,   2 ff March 23, 1867
                          14 ff July 19, 1867
                          41   March 11, 1868)

r. Fourteenth Amendment to the Constitution Establishing U. S. Citizenship
and including Negroes, and for other
purposes   (Thorpe, 31)   July 28, 1868

s. Fifteenth Amendment Designed to give
Negroes voting rights   March 30, 1870
        (Commager, *Documents*, 148)

D. DOCUMENTATION OF SYSTEMATIC
GROWTH

Since 1776 the American Leviathan has been operating,
if this is not carrying the metaphor too far, with two sets of
gears, one federal and the other state. While the Continental Congress and the Constitutional Convention of 1787
were writing up their specifications, each of the states was
working on an auxiliary mechanism that was to be geared
in with the major machine. Eleven states wrote new constitutions, while Connecticut and Rhode Island used their
colonial instruments with a change of heading. The legislatures continued meeting, generally annually or oftener,
and each session produced new chapters of laws. They also
in some instances began early revisions of the new constitutions.

Then, on the frontiers, at first independently, and then
under specification of the laws of 1789 and 1790, new states
began to emerge. After a haphazard independent action in
Vermont, Kentucky and Tennessee, a pattern began to
evolve that was followed in most of the states henceforth
to be created. Pioneers would go out into a new region
designated by Congress as a territory and follow the scheme

of political evolution described in the Northwest Act of 1789. Then, when the population in a certain region reached the number required, Congress would pass an enabling act authorizing the territory to adopt and submit a constitution. The usual procedure was completed by an act of admission passed by Congress. The achievement of statehood therefore generally required four documents—an act establishing the territory, an enabling act, a proposed constitution and an act of admission. Sometimes the procedure varied, as in Texas and California, which were never territories, and in a few other instances where circumstances complicated documentation by changing territorial boundaries. A new phase of drafting had begun on the local level in the territorial commissions and legislatures, and it was augmented by the new state lawmaking bodies.

I. Agreement of the Watauga Association
   (Tennessee) 1772
   A. V. Goodpasture, "The Watauga Association," *American Historical Magazine,* III, 103-110
II. Nine Laws of Transylvania (Kentucky) 1775
   Colonial Records of North Carolina, IX, 1278-9
III. First Constitution of Vermont (Thorpe, 3737) 1777
IV. Cumberland Compact (Tennessee) 1780
   A. W. Putnam, *History of Middle Tennessee,* 84-103
V. Resolution of Congress on Public Lands 1780
   Journals of Continental Congress, XVIII, 915
VI. Act of Cession by Virginia (Thorpe, 955) 1783
VII. Deed of Cession by Virginia (Thorpe, 957) 1784
VIII. Ordinance to Establish the Western Territory 1784
   Journals of the Continental Congress, XXVI, 275 ff
IX. Constitution for the State of Franklin (Tennessee) 1784
   State Records of North Carolina, XXII, 664-70

Of the seventeen states admitted between the conclusion of the above list (1816) and 1865, only four did not pass through the territorial phase—California, Maine, Texas and West Virginia. The creation of these seventeen states was accomplished by the adoption of sixty-six documents. Ten territories not admitted by 1865 were created by eleven documents. In the thirty-six states admitted prior to 1865, thirty constitutions were adopted besides the initial documents.

During the Reconstruction years, 1865-1877, it took twenty-seven more constitutions for the southern states to re-establish themselves. States in other sections adopted three more constitutions. Two territories became states through six documents, and one of them adopted a second constitution within this period.

BIBLIOGRAPHY

I. MANUSCRIPTS CITED

Charles Francis Adams MSS, Massachusetts Historical Society, Microfilm, American Philosophical Society.
William Allen MSS, Library of Congress.
S. L. M. Barlow MSS, Huntington Library.
John Bell MSS, Library of Congress.
James Buchanan MSS, Historical Society of Pennsylvania.
John F. H. Claiborne MSS, Library of Congress.
Howell Cobb MSS, University of Georgia.
George Eustis MSS, Library of Congress.
Edward Everett MSS Diary, Massachusetts Historical Society.
John H. George MSS, New Hampshire Historical Society.
James H. Hammond MSS, Library of Congress.
John P. Kennedy MSS Diary, Peabody Institute Library.
Robert Todd Lincoln MSS, Library of Congress.
Philip Phillips MSS, Library of Congress.
John Sherman MSS, Library of Congress.
Alexander H. Stephens MSS, Library of Congress.
Alexander H. Stephens MSS, Manhattanville College of the Sacred Heart, Purchase, New York.
John Tyler MSS, Library of Congress.
Martin Van Buren MSS, Library of Congress.
Benjamin F. Wade MSS, Library of Congress.
Thurlow Weed MSS, University of Rochester.
Gideon Welles MSS, Huntington Library.
Archives of Bremen, Archives of French Foreign Office, Archives of British Foreign Office, copies in Library of Congress.

II. OFFICIAL DOCUMENTS

Colonial Records of North Carolina, W. L. Saunders, ed., 10 vols., Raleigh, 1886-1890.
Commager, Henry, *Documents of American History,* New York, 1934.
Compilation of the Messages and Papers of the Confederacy, James D. Richardson, ed., 2 vols., Nashville, 1906.
Compilation of the Messages and Papers of the Presidents, 1789-1897, James Richardson, ed., Washington, 1907.
Frere, Walter H., and Douglas, Charles E., *Puritan Manifestoes,* London, 1907.
Henning, N. W., ed., *The Statutes-at-Large Being a Collection of*

all the Laws of Virginia 1619-1792, 13 vols., Philadelphia and New York, 1823.

Journal of Ninth Convention, Danville, Kentucky, Monday, July 26, 1790, MSS in Kentucky State Historical Society.

"Journal of the Provisional Congress of the Confederate States of America," *58 Cong. 2 Sess., Senate Document #234* (Ser. 4610).

"Journal of the Congress of the Confederate States of America, 1861-65," *58 Cong. 1 Sess., Sen. Doc. 234* (Sers. 4611-4616).

Journals of the Continental Congress, 1774-1789, W. C. Ford and John C. Fitzpatrick, eds., 34 vols., 1904-1937.

Laws and Joint Resolutions of the Last Session of the Confederate Congress . . . together with the Secret Acts of the Previous Congresses, Charles W. Ramsdell, ed., Durham, N. C., 1941.

Potter, Henry, Taylor, J. L., Yancey, Bart., *Laws of the State of North Carolina,* Raleigh, North Carolina, 1821.

"Proceedings of the Confederate Congress," *Southern Historical Society Papers,* XLIV-LII, 1923-1959.

Public Laws of the Confederate States of America, First Congress and Second Congress, 1st Session, James M. Matthews, ed., Richmond, 1862-1864.

Records of Congress, 1843-1865
  Congressional Globe, 32nd, 33rd, 37th and 38th Congresses.
  Senate Journals, 30th Cong., 1 Sess., Ser. 502, 2 Sess., Ser. 528.
    33rd Cong., 1 Sess., Ser. 689.

  House Journals, 28th Cong., 2 Sess., Ser. 462.
    29th Cong., 1 Sess., Ser. 479.
    32nd Cong., 1 Sess., Ser. 632, 2 Sess., Ser. 657.
    33rd Cong., 1 Sess., Ser. 709.

  Senate Reports, 3rd Cong., 1 Sess., Ser. 706.

  House Reports, 33rd Cong., 1 Sess., Ser. 742.
    36th Cong., 2 Sess., Ser. 1105.

Senate and House Bills, 28th-33rd Congs., Printed Copies, Library of Congress.

Senate and House Files, 28th-33rd Congs., National Archives.

State Records of North Carolina, Walter Clark, ed., 16 vols., Winston and Goldsboro, 1895-1905.

Statutes at Large of the Provisional Government of the Confederate States of America, James M. Matthews, ed., Richmond, 1864.

Statutes at Large of the United States of America, 1789-1873, 17 vols., Boston, 1850-1873.

The Territorial Papers of the United States, Clarence E. Carter, ed., 26 vols., Washington, 1934-1962.

Thorpe, Francis N., *The Federal and State Constitutions, Colonial Charters and other Organic Laws of the . . . United States*

of America, 7 vols., Washington, 1909.
Walker, Williston, *Creeds and Platforms of Congregationalism,* New York, 1893.
War of the Rebellion: A Compilation of the Official Records of the Union and Confederate Armies, 127 vols. and index, Washington, 1880-1925.

III. NEWSPAPERS

Baltimore *Sun*
Charleston *Mercury*
New York *Herald*
New York *Times*
New York *Tribune*
Philadelphia *Public Ledger*
Sacramento *Union*
St. Louis *Missouri Republican*
Washington *Constitution*
Washington *National Intelligencer*
Washington *Star*
Washington *Union*
Yorkville, S. C., *Enquirer*

IV. COLLECTED WORKS

Basler, Roy P., ed., *Collected Works of Abraham Lincoln,* New Brunswick, 1953.
Brooks, Robert P., ed., "Howell Cobb Papers," *Georgia Historical Quarterly,* VI (June, 1922), 149.
Clingman, Thomas L., *Speeches and Writings,* Raleigh, 1877.
"Correspondence of Thomas R. R. Cobb," *Pubs. of the Southern History Association,* XI, 147-185, 233-260.
Crallé, Richard K., ed., *Works of John C. Calhoun,* Charleston, 1851.
Moore, John Bassett, ed., *The Works of James Buchanan,* Philadelphia, 1910.
Phillips, Ulrich B., ed., "The Correspondence of Robert Toombs, Alexander H. Stephens and Howell Cobb," American Historical Association, *Annual Report, 1911,* 2 vols., Washington, 1913.

V. BRITISH PHASE

Adams, George Burton, *Constitutional History of England,* revised by Robert L. Schuyler, New York, 1934.

Adams, George Burton and Stephens, H. Morse, eds., *Select Documents of English Constitutional History*, New York, 1911.

Allen, John W., *History of Political Thought in the 16th Century*, London, 1928.

Bibby, Edna, "The Puritan Classical Movement of Elizabeth's Reign," MSS M.A. Thesis, University of Manchester, 1929.

Bowen, Catherine Drinker, *The Lion and the Throne*, Boston, 1956.

Cheyney, Edward P., *History of England from the Defeat of the Armada to the Death of Elizabeth*, 2 vols., New York, 1914-1926.

Chrimes, S. B., *English Constitutional Ideas in the Fifteenth Century*, Cambridge, 1936.

de Pauley, W. C., *The Candle of the Lord*, London, 1937.

Figgis, J. F., *Divine Right of Kings*, 2nd ed., Cambridge, 1914.

Garrett, Christina H., *Marian Exiles*, Cambridge, 1938.

Gooch, G. P., *History of English Democratic Ideas in the Seventeenth Century*, 2nd ed., Cambridge, 1927.

Goodman, Christopher, *How Superior Power oght to be obeyd*, Geneva, 1558.

Haskins, George L., *Growth of English Representative Government*, Philadelphia, 1948.

History of Norfolk, vol. XXIV, *Victoria Histories of the Counties of England*, London, 1900.

Hobbes, Thomas, *Leviathan*, Everyman's Library edition, London, 1914.

Holdsworth, W. S., *History of English Law*, London, 1922-1926.

Jessop, Augustus, *One Generation of a Norfolk House*, 3rd edition, London, 1913.

Jolliffe, J. E. A., *Constitutional History of Medieval England*, New York, 1937.

Knappen, M. M., *Constitutional and Legal History of England*, New York, 1942.

————, *Tudor Puritanism*, Chicago, 1939.

Knox, John, *First Blast of the Trumpet against the monstrous Regiment of Women*, n. p., 1558.

Lingelbach, William E., *Merchant Adventurers of England*, Philadelphia, 1902.

Lunt, W. E., *History of England*, New York, 1946.

Maitland, Frederick W., *Constitutional History of England*, Cambridge, 1911.

Memoirs Illustrative of the History and Antiquities of Norfolk and the City of Norwich, London, 1851.

Mullinger, J. B., *University of Cambridge from the Earliest Times*, Cambridge, 1873.

Neal, Daniel, *History of the Puritans*, New York, 1844.

Neale, John E., *Elizabethan House of Commons*, London, 1949.

————, *Elizabeth I and her Parliaments*, London, 1953-57.

————, *Essays in Elizabethan History,* London, 1958.
Peel, Albert, *Brownists in Norwich and Norfolk about 1580,* Cambridge, 1920.
————, *The First Congregational Churches,* Cambridge, 1920.
Pickthorn, K., *Early Tudor Government: Henry VIII,* Cambridge, 1934.
Pollock, Frederick and Maitland, F. W., *History of English Law,* Cambridge, 1911.
Ponet, John, *A Short Treatise of Politike Power and of the True obedience which Subjectes owe to Kynges and other Civil Governours, with an exhortation to all true naturale Englishe men,* London [?], 1556.
Powicke, Frederick J., *Cambridge Platonists,* London, 1926.
Read, Conyers, *The Tudors,* New York, 1936.
Russell, Frederic W., *Kett's Rebellion in Norfolk,* London, 1859.
Scott, William R., *Constitution and Finance of English, Scottish and Irish Joint Stock Companies to 1720,* Cambridge, 1910-1912.
Sherman, John, *A Greek in the Temple,* Cambridge, 1641.
Stephenson, Carl and Marcham, F. G., *Sources of English Constitutional History,* New York, 1937.
Strype, John, *Annals of the Reformation,* Oxford, 1824.
Treharne, R. F., *Baronial Plan of Reform, 1258-63,* Manchester, 1932.
Trevelyan, George Macaulay, *England in the Age of Wycliffe,* London, 1909.
————, *Trinity College,* Cambridge, 1946.
Usher, Roland G., ed., *Presbyterian Movement in the Reign of Elizabeth as illustrated by the Minute Book of the Dedham Classes, 1582-89,* London, 1905.
White, Albert B., *Constitutional History of England,* New York, 1908.
————, *Self-Government at the King's Command,* Minneapolis, 1933.
Willey, Basil, *Seventeenth Century Background,* London, 1937.

VI. AMERICAN PHASE

Abernethy, Thomas P., *From Frontier to Plantation in Tennessee,* Chapel Hill, 1932.
Adams, Henry, *The Great Secession Winter,* New York, 1958.
————, *History of the United States during the Administration of Jefferson and Madison,* 9 vols., New York, 1889-1891.
Adams, James Truslow, *Founding of New England,* Boston, 1921.
Alden, John R., *American Revolution,* New York, 1954.
Alexander, Thomas B., "Persistent Whiggery in the Confederate

South, 1860-1877," *Journal of Southern History,* XXVII (1961), 305-329.

Andrews, Charles M., *Colonial Period of American History,* 4 vols., New Haven, 1934-1938.

Annals of the War by Leading Participants North and South. Originally Published in the Philadelphia Weekly Times, Philadelphia, 1879.

Baringer, William E., *A House Dividing,* Springfield, Ill., 1945.

Beale, Howard K., ed., *Diary of Gideon Welles,* New York, 1960.

Beard, Charles A., *An Economic Interpretation of the Constitution,* Reprint, New York, 1936.

Benson, Lee, *Turner and Beard,* Glencoe, Ill., 1960.

Beveridge, Albert J., *Abraham Lincoln, 1809-1858,* 4 vols., Boston, 1928.

Bigelow, John, *Retrospections of an Active Life,* 5 vols., New York, 1909-1913.

Bond, Beverly W., Jr., *The Foundations of Ohio,* Columbus, 1941.

Boorstin, Daniel J., *The Americans: The Colonial Experience,* New York, 1958.

Brant, Irving, *James Madison, Secretary of State,* Indianapolis, 1953.

———, *James Madison, President,* Indianapolis, 1956.

———, *James Madison, Commander in Chief,* Indianapolis, 1961.

Bridenbaugh, Carl, *Cities in the Wilderness,* 2nd ed., New York, 1956.

Brown, Alexander, *The First Republic in America,* Boston, 1898.

Brown, Robert E., *Charles Beard and the Constitution,* Princeton, 1956.

Buley, Roscoe C., *The Old Northwest, 1815-1840,* Indianapolis, 1950.

Bullard, F. Lauriston, ed., *The Diary of a Public Man,* New Brunswick, 1946.

Burleigh, Joseph B., *Legislative Guide,* Philadelphia, 1852.

Capers, Gerald M., *Stephen A. Douglas, Defender of the Union,* Boston, 1959.

Carman, Harry J. and Luthin, Reinhard H., *Lincoln and the Patronage,* New York, 1943.

Catton, Bruce, *The Coming Fury,* vol. I, *The Centennial History of the Civil War,* New York, 1961.

Chesnut, Mary Boykin, *A Diary from Dixie,* Ben Ames Williams, ed., New York, 1949.

Clark, Thomas D., *Frontier America,* New York, 1959.

———, *History of Kentucky,* New York, 1937.

Clay-Clopton, Virginia, *A Belle of the Fifties,* New York, 1905.

Cole, Arthur C., *Irrepressible Conflict,* New York, 1934.

———, *The Whig Party in the South,* Washington, 1913.

Coulter, E. Merton, *The Confederate States of America,* Baton Rouge, 1950.

Crandall, Andrew W., *Early History of the Republican Party*, Boston, 1930.

Craven, Avery, *The Coming of the Civil War*, New York, 1942.

——, *The Growth of Southern Nationalism, 1848-61*, Baton Rouge, 1953.

Craven, Wesley Frank, *The Southern Colonies in the Seventeenth Century, 1607-1689*, vol. I, *The History of the South*, Wendell H. Stephenson and E. Merton Coulter, eds., Baton Rouge, 1949.

Dangerfield, George, *The Era of Good Feelings*, New York, 1952.

Davis, Jefferson, *Rise and Fall of the Confederate Government*, 2 vols., New York, 1881.

——, *A Short History of the Confederate States of America*, New York, 1890.

Davis, Varina H., *Jefferson Davis*, 2 vols., New York, 1890.

De Voto, Bernard, *The Year of Decision, 1846*, Boston, 1943.

Diamond, Sigmund, ed., *A Casual View of America. The Home Letters of Salomon de Rothschild, 1859-1861*, Stanford, Calif., 1961.

Dixon, Mrs. Archibald, *True History of the Missouri Compromise and Its Repeal*, Cincinnati, 1898.

Dodd, William E., *Statesmen of the Old South*, New York, 1911.

Douglass, Elisha P., *Rebels and Democrats, the Struggle for Equal Political Rights and Majority Rule during the American Revolution*, Chapel Hill, 1952.

Dowdey, Clifford, *The Land They Fought For*, Garden City, 1955.

Du Bois, James T. and Mathews, Gertrude S., *Galusha A. Grow*, Boston, 1917.

Dumond, Dwight L., *The Secession Movement, 1860-61*, New York, 1931.

——, *Antislavery: The Crusade for Freedom in America*, Ann Arbor, 1961.

Eaton, Clement, *History of the Southern Confederacy*, New York, 1954.

Elkins, Stanley M., *Slavery, A Problem in American Industrial Life*, Chicago, 1960.

Elkins, Stanley and McKitrick, Eric, "A Meaning for Turner's Frontier," *Political Science Quarterly*, LXIX (1954), 321-353, 365-602.

Farrand, Max, *Legislation of Congress for the Government of the Organized Territories of the United States, 1789-1895*, Newark, N. J., 1896.

Flint, Henry M., *Life and Speeches of Douglas*, New York, 1860.

Franklin, John Hope, *From Slavery to Freedom, A History of American Negroes*, 2nd ed., New York, 1956.

——, *The Militant South, 1800-1861*, Cambridge, 1956.

——, *Reconstruction: After the Civil War*, Chicago, 1961.

Galbraith, John Kenneth, "The Moving Finger Sticks," in *The*

Liberal Hour, Boston, 1960.

Gipson, Lawrence H., *The British Empire before the Revolution,* Caldwell, Idaho, and New York, 1936—.

Graebner, Norman A., *Empire on the Pacific,* New York, 1955.

Gunderson, Robert G., *Old Gentlemen's Convention, The Washington Peace Conference,* New York, 1961.

Hamilton, Holman, "Texas Bonds and Northern Profits: A Study in Compromise, Investment and Lobby Influence," *Mississippi Valley Historical Review,* XLIII (1957), 579-594.

————, *Zachary Taylor,* 2 vols., Indianapolis, 1941-1951.

Hamlin, Charles E., *Hannibal Hamlin,* Cambridge, 1899.

Hammond, Harold E., *A Commoner's Judge, The Life and Times of Charles Patrick Daly,* Boston, 1954.

Hammond, Harold E., ed., *Diary of a Union Lady, Maria Lydig Daly,* New York, 1962.

Harmon, George D., "Douglas and the Compromise of 1850," *Journal of the Illinois State Historical Society,* XXI (1929), 453-499.

Haskins, George L., *Law and Authority in Early Massachusetts,* New York, 1960.

Hendrick, Burton J., *Lincoln's War Cabinet,* Boston, 1946.

————, *Statesmen of the Lost Cause,* Boston, 1939.

Hesseltine, William B., *Lincoln and the War Governors,* New York, 1948.

Hill, Louise Biles, *Joseph E. Brown and the Confederacy,* Chapel Hill, N. C., 1939.

Hodder, Frank H., "The Genesis of the Kansas-Nebraska Act," State Historical Society of Wisconsin, *Proceedings,* 1912 (Madison), 69-86.

————, "Railroad Background of the Kansas-Nebraska Act," *Mississippi Valley Historical Review,* XII (1925), 3-22.

Jensen, Merrill, *Articles of Confederation,* Madison, 1948.

————, *The New Nation,* New York, 1950.

————, *Regionalism in America,* Madison, 1951.

Johnston, R. M. and Brown, W. H., *Alexander H. Stephens,* Philadelphia, 1878.

Jones, John B., *A Rebel War Clerk's Diary,* Howard Swiggett, ed., New York, 1935.

Kean, Robert G. H., *Inside the Confederate Government,* Edward Younger, ed., New York, 1957.

Kirwan, Albert D., *John J. Crittenden,* Lexington, Ky., 1962.

Learned, Henry B., "Relation of Philip Phillips to the Repeal of the Missouri Compromise in 1854," *Mississippi Valley Historical Review,* VIII (March, 1922), 303-315.

Luthin, Reinhard H., *The First Lincoln Campaign,* Cambridge, Mass., 1944.

Macmillan, Lord, "Two Ways of Thinking," in *Law and Other Things,* Cambridge, 1937.

Malin, James C., *Contriving Brain and Skillful Hand*, Lawrence, Kansas, 1955.

———, *Grassland Historical Studies*, vol. I, Lawrence, Kansas, 1950.

———, *Grassland of North America, Prolegomena*, Lawrence, Kansas, 1947.

———, *John Brown and the Legend of Fifty-Six*, Philadelphia, American Philosophical Society, 1942.

———, *The Nebraska Question, 1852-1854*, Lawrence, Kansas, 1953.

———, *On the Nature of History*, Lawrence, Kansas, 1954.

———, *Winter Wheat in the Golden Belt of Kansas*, Lawrence, Kansas, 1944.

Mayes, Edward, *L. Q. C. Lamar*, Nashville, Tenn., 1896.

McConnell, George M., "Recollections of Stephen A. Douglas," Illinois State Historical Society, *Transactions*, 1900, 48-49.

McDonald, Forrest, *We The People*, Chicago, 1958.

McMaster, John Bach, *History of the People of the United States*, 8 vols., New York, 1883-1913.

Miller, John C., *Origins of the American Revolution*, Boston, 1943.

———, *Triumph of Freedom*, Boston, 1948.

Milton, George Fort, *Eve of Conflict*, New York, 1934.

Mitchell, Stewart, *Horatio Seymour of New York*, Cambridge, Mass., 1938.

Moore, Albert B., *Conscription and Conflict in the Confederacy*, New York, 1924.

Moore, Glover, *The Missouri Compromise, 1819-21*, Lexington, Ky., 1953.

Morgan, Edward S., *Birth of the Republic, 1763-1789*, Chicago, 1956.

Morison, Samuel Eliot, *Builders of the Bay Colony*, Boston, 1930.

Morse, John T., ed., *Diary of Gideon Welles*, Boston, 1911.

Morton, J. Sterling and Watkins, Albert, *History of Nebraska*, 3rd edition, Lincoln, Nebraska, 1911.

Moses, John, *Illinois, Historical and Statistical*, 2 vols., Chicago, 1892.

Nettels, Curtis P., *Roots of American Civilization*, New York, 1938.

———, *Washington and American Independence*, New York, 1951.

Nevins, Allan, *American States During and After the Revolution*, New York, 1924.

———, *Ordeal of the Union*, 2 vols., New York, 1947.

———, *The War for the Union*, New York, 1959———.

Nichols, Roy F., "American Democracy and the Civil War," *Proceedings American Philosophical Society*, XCI (1948), 143-149.

———, "Birthpangs of American Democracy," *American Heritage*, New Series, I, 10-14.

——, *Disruption of American Democracy*, New York, 1948.

——, "Early Transatlantic Migration of Politics," *Cambridge Journal*, II (1949), 671-683.

——, "English Origins of American Politics," *Pennsylvania Magazine of History and Biography*, LXXVI (1952), 5-29.

——, "1461-1861: American Civil War in Perspective," *Journal of Southern History*, XVI (1950), 143-160.

——, *Franklin Pierce*, 2nd edition, Philadelphia, 1958.

——, "Kansas Historiography: The Technique of Cultural Analysis," *American Quarterly*, IX (1957), 85-91.

——, "The Kansas-Nebraska Act: A Century of Historiography," *Mississippi Valley Historical Review*, XLIII (1956), 187-212.

——, "The Louisiana Purchase, Challenge and Stimulus to American Democracy," *Louisiana Historical Quarterly*, XXXVIII (1955), 1-25.

——, "The Operation of American Democracy, 1861-1865: Some Questions," *Journal of Southern History*, XXV (1959), 31-52.

——, "The Problem of Civil War Historiography," *Proceedings American Philosophical Society*, CVI (1962), 36-40.

——, The Stakes of Power, New York, 1961.

——, "The Territories, Seedbeds of Democracy," *Nebraska History*, XXV (1954), 3-16.

Nicolay, John G. and Hay, John, *Abraham Lincoln*, 10 vols., New York, 1890.

Owsley, Frank L., *Plain Folk of the Old South*, Baton Rouge, 1949.

——, *State Rights in the Confederacy*, Chicago, 1925.

Parker, John A., "The Secret History of the Kansas-Nebraska Bill," *National Quarterly Review*, New York, XLI, July 1880, 105-118, reprinted in pamphlet form *The Missing Link . . . What led to the War, or the Secret History of the Kansas-Nebraska Act*, Washington, 1886.

Patrick, Rembert W., *Jefferson Davis and His Cabinet*, Baton Rouge, 1944.

Paul, James C. N., *Rift in the Democracy*, Philadelphia, 1951.

Phillips, Ulrich B., *Course of the South to Secession*, E. Merton Coulter, ed., New York, 1939.

Pollard, Edward A., *Lee and His Lieutenants*, New York, 1867.

——, *Lost Cause*, New York, 1867.

Potter, David M., *Lincoln and His Party in the Secession Crisis*, Yale Paperbound with new preface, New Haven, 1962.

Private Letters of Parmenas Taylor Turnley, London, 1863.

Putnam, Albincence W., *History of Middle Tennessee*, Nashville, Tenn., 1859.

Randall, James G., and Current, Richard N., *Lincoln the President*, 4 vols., New York, 1945-1955.

Rawley, James A., *Edwin D. Morgan*, New York, 1955.

Ray, P. Orman, *The Repeal of the Missouri Compromise*, Cleveland, 1909.

———, "The Genesis of the Kansas-Nebraska Act," *American Historical Association, Annual Report*, 1914, 2 vols., Washington, 1916, I, 259-280.

Rhodes, James Ford, *History of the United States from the Compromise of 1850*, 7 vols., New York, 1892-1906.

Rossiter, Clinton, *Seedtime of the Republic*, New York, 1953.

Rowland, Dunbar, ed., *Jefferson Davis, Constitutionalist*, 10 vols., Jackson, Miss., 1923.

Russel, Robert R., "What was the Compromise of 1850," *Journal of Southern History*, XXII (1956), 292-309.

Smith, Edward C., *The Borderland in the Civil War*, New York, 1927.

Stampp, Kenneth M., *And the War Came*, Baton Rouge, 1950.

———, *The Peculiar Institution*, New York, 1956.

A Statement of Facts and a Few Suggestions in Review of Political Action in Missouri, n. p., 1856.

Stephens, Alexander H., *A Constitutional View of the Late War Between the States*, 2 vols., Philadelphia, 1868-1870.

Stephenson, Nathaniel W., *The Day of the Confederacy*, New Haven, 1919.

———, *Lincoln*, Indianapolis, 1922.

———, "Southern Nationalism in South Carolina in 1851," *American Historical Review*, XXXVI (1931), 314.

Still, Bayrd, "Statehood Process, 1800-1850," *Mississippi Valley Historical Review*, XXIII (1936), 189.

Stoddard, William O., *Lincoln's Third Secretary*, William O. Stoddard, Jr., ed., New York, 1955.

Strode, Hudson, *Jefferson Davis, American Patriot*, New York, 1959.

Sydnor, Charles S., *Development of Southern Sectionalism, 1819-1848*, Baton Rouge, 1948.

———, *Gentlemen Freeholders*, Chapel Hill, 1952.

Thomas, Benjamin P., *Abraham Lincoln*, New York, 1952.

Thomas, Benjamin P. and Hyman, Harold M., *Stanton*, New York, 1962.

Turner, Frederick J., *Rise of the New West*, New York, 1906.

Van Deusen, Glydon G., *The Jacksonian Era, 1828-1848*, New York, 1959.

———, *Thurlow Weed*, Boston, 1947.

Von Abele, Rudolph, *Alexander H. Stephens*, New York, 1946.

Wallace, Anthony F. C., "The Strategy of Threat and Retaliation: Iroquois Warfare, 1755-1795," MSS kindly loaned by author.

Webster, Sidney, "Responsibility for the War of Secession," *Political Science Quarterly*, VIII (June, 1893), 276.

Welles, Gideon, *Civil War and Reconstruction*, collected by Albert Mordell, New York, 1959.

————, *Lincoln's Administration*, collected by Albert Mordell, New York, 1960.

Wentworth, John, *Congressional Reminiscences*, Chicago, 1882.

Whitman, Walt, *I Sit and Look Out. Editorials from the Brooklyn Daily Times*, New York, 1932.

Wiley, Bell Irvin, ed., *Letters of Warren Akin, Confederate Congressman*, Athens, 1959.

Williams, T. Harry, *Lincoln and the Radicals*, Madison, 1941.

Wilson, Henry, *Rise and Fall of the Slave Power*, 3 vols., Boston, 1872-1877.

Wiltse, Charles M., *John C. Calhoun, Sectionalist, 1840-1850*, Indianapolis, 1951.

Wooster, Ralph A., *The Secession Conventions of the South*, Princeton, 1962.

Yearns, Wilfred B., *The Confederate Congress*, Athens, 1960.

Zornow, William F., *Lincoln and the Party Divided*, Norman, Okla., 1954.

INDEX

ROY F. NICHOLS

Born in Newark, New Jersey, in 1896, Roy F. Nichols attended Rutgers and Columbia universities. He taught at Columbia for four years and then joined the University of Pennsylvania where he has been vice provost and dean of the graduate school of arts and sciences since 1953. From 1948 to 1949 he was Pitt Professor of American History at Cambridge University.

Mr. Nichols' books include *The Disruption of American Democracy*, 1948, which won him the 1949 Pulitzer Prize in History, *Advance Agents of American Destiny*, 1956, *Franklin Pierce*, 1958, *Religion and American Democracy*, 1959, and *The Stakes of Power, 1845-1877*, 1961.

Mr. Nichols has been awarded several honorary degrees: the Litt.D., Franklin and Marshall College, 1937; the L.H.D., Rutgers University, 1941; the LL.D., Moravian, 1953; the Litt.D., Muhlenberg, 1956; the LL.D., Lincoln University, 1959; the LL.D., Knox College, 1960, the S.Sc.D., Lebanon Valley College, 1961. In 1961 he received the John L. Haney Award of the Franklin Inn, Philadelphia, and in 1962, the Medal of the Athenaeum of Philadelphia for literary works.

He is one of the founders of the Pennsylvania Historical Association and has also served as its president. Mr. Nichols has been president of the Pennsylvania Federation of Historical Societies and the Middle States Council of the Social Studies, and is a member of the Philadelphia Historical Commission. He is a vice president of the American Philosophical Society, vice president of the Historical Society of Pennsylvania, a member of the Board of Governors of Rutgers University, and president of the Association of Graduate Schools.